ACT Purple Science

Version 2.0

ACT Purple Science
Table of Contents

sP1: ABOUT THE ACT SCIENCE SECTION

Directions: Read the explanation and examples below to learn about this lesson's topic.

TOPIC OVERVIEW

The ACT Science Test is different from most science tests you have taken in school. Instead of focusing on your knowledge of scientific facts and theories, the ACT Science Test assesses your ability to evaluate charts, graphs, scientific experiments, and conflicting viewpoints. You may be asked to interpret data, draw conclusions from scientific evidence, or analyze an argument between two members of the scientific community.

The ACT Science Test is broken into seven passages. Each passage has five to seven questions, for a total of forty questions. You will have thirty-five minutes to complete the section. Though the answer choices on the ACT alternate between A–B–C–D and F–G–H–J, the practice questions in these lessons will all use A–B–C–D.

There are three distinct types of passages in the ACT Science Test, each assessing a different type of reasoning or logical skill:

- *Data Representation* (three passages, five questions each): These passages contain graphs or charts.
- *Research Summaries* (three passages, six questions each): These passages describe scientific experiments and the results of those experiments.
- *Conflicting Viewpoints* (one passage, seven questions): These passages give you two or more conflicting arguments about some controversial scientific topic.

There are three basic types of questions in each passage:

- *Understanding*: These questions test your ability to identify facts from the passage and its charts or graphs.
- *Analysis*: These questions ask you to analyze trends and draw conclusions from the facts and data in the passage.

- *Generalization*: These questions ask you to extend the passage's trends and conclusions to events or experiments not mentioned in the passage.

Here are some tips to help you get the most out of the time and effort you spend on the ACT Science Test:

- **Don't read the passage in depth the first time through.** Scan the passage quickly, paying attention to the charts, graphs, and other data associated with the passage. You should be able to answer most of the questions based on just this information.
- **Limit your use of outside knowledge.** The questions reward you for your ability to analyze the information given, not your knowledge of the subject. Base your answers on the contents of the passage whenever possible.
- **If you see a scientific term or idea that you've never been exposed to, skip over it.** Most terms are defined in the passage, and many are not necessary to answer the questions. If a question requires an understanding of a difficult term, you can always reread the term's definition. The context in which a term is used can be very helpful, even if you cannot quite pin down the meaning of the word.
- **Skip the hard questions.** If you realize it's going to take more than 30 seconds to answer a question, skip it and come back to it after completing the rest of the test. If you run out of time, guess. Remember, there is no wrong-answer penalty on the ACT!
- **Don't calculate. Estimate.** Calculation takes too much time, and the answer values will almost always be far enough apart to make calculation unnecessary.

As a general rule, try to approach the ACT Science Test with these steps in mind:

1. Skim the passage.
2. Get a general idea about the charts and graphs.
3. Answer the questions.

sP1A

Directions: The following two passages are similar to real ACT test passages. Read each passage and answer the questions that follow. Use the methods and techniques that you learned in the instructions of this lesson.

PRACTICE PASSAGE 1 (TIME: 4 MINUTES)

Mate choice is a complex process, so an individual's mate preferences may not be realized, for reasons such as availability of potential mates, competition from rivals, and mutual selection. In humans, mate height is one commonly expressed preference. In this study from a European country, the heights of new parents (that is, those who had successfully mated) were recorded and categorized based on the difference between the paternal and maternal heights in each of 1,000 couples. Those data were then compared with predictions based on a random (i.e., no height preference) mate choice computer model. These data appear in Tables 1 and 2.

Table 1

Summary of Preferred Height Differences		
Qualitative Difference	Observed (# Couples)	Predicted (# Couples)
Male Shorter	41	65
Similar Height	34	36
Male Taller	925	899

Table 2

Summary of Observed vs. Predicted Height Differences		
Difference (cm)	Observed (# Couples)	Predicted (# Couples)
Less than −10	6	13
−10 to −6	15	26
−5 to 0	19	25
1 to 5	85	87
6 to 10	162	145
11 to 15	213	192
16 to 20	207	197
21 to 25	154	158
26 to 30	88	94
31 to 35	37	42
More than 35	14	21

1. For which parental height difference group did the random mating model most poorly predict the observed results?

   (A) Less than −10 cm
   (B) −10 to −6 cm
   (C) 6 to 10 cm
   (D) 11 to 15 cm

2. Which of the following factors most limits the ability to draw broader conclusions from this study?

   (A) The researchers only tested the observed data against one random mating model.
   (B) Only 1,000 couples participated in this study.
   (C) The data is taken only from couples of one European country.
   (D) Each parental height difference group spans too broad a range (5 cm).

3. Altogether, the data best supports which hypothesis about height preferences in human mating?

   (A) Humans prefer mates who are as similar in height as possible.
   (B) Humans prefer mates who are as dissimilar in height as possible.
   (C) Humans prefer the male to be taller in all cases.
   (D) Humans prefer the male to be taller, but within a certain range.

4. What were males more likely to do: choose a female who has a similar height or a female who is taller?

   (A) Males were more likely to choose a female who had a similar height.
   (B) Males were more likely to choose a female who was taller.
   (C) Both possibilities were just as likely.
   (D) It cannot be determined from the information given.

5. What would be a reasonable follow-up to this mate choice study?

   (A) Repeat the study in non-European countries and determine if the conclusions are applicable across cultures.
   (B) Repeat the study with couples who were married within the past month.
   (C) Compare the observed data with predictions from a different random mate choice model.
   (D) Compare the observed data with the heights of the couples' children once they reach adulthood.

PRACTICE PASSAGE 2 (TIME: 5 MINUTES)

Enzymes are biological molecules that speed up, or catalyze, chemical reactions by lowering their activation energies. Enzyme-catalyzed reactions consume reactants and produce products more quickly than uncatalyzed reactions. Enzyme efficiency is dependent on temperature, substrate (reactant) concentration, and pH.

In the following experiments, a student assesses the effects of temperature and substrate concentration on two different enzyme-catalyzed reactions.

Experiment 1

The student runs the following reaction in a closed container without the addition of an enzyme:

$$2H_2O_2(aq) \rightarrow 2H_2O(l) + O_2(g)$$

He records the temperature, H_2O_2 concentration, and pH within the container at regular 10-second intervals (Table 1). The initial temperature is 25°C, and the initial product concentrations are both zero. Assume all of the reactant (H_2O_2) is consumed by the end of the reaction.

Table 1

Time (s)	Temp. (°C)	H_2O_2 Concentration (mM)	pH
0	25	50	6.2
10	31	40	6.5
20	35	30	6.6
30	38	20	6.7
40	40	12	6.8
50	41	6	6.9
60	42	0	7.0

Experiment 2

The student then runs the same reaction, this time using a solution of 10mM Enzyme A to catalyze his reaction. He conducts two trials of the reaction, one without heating the container, and one with heating. Tables 2 (no heat added) and 3 (heat added) show his data.

Table 2

Time (s)	Temp. (°C)	H_2O_2 Concentration (mM)	pH
0	25	50	6.2
10	37	27	6.6
20	41	6	6.9
30	42	0	7.0

Table 3

Time (s)	Temp. (°C)	H_2O_2 Concentration (mM)	pH
0	60	50	6.2
10	73	18	6.8
20	77	0	7.0

Experiment 3

The student now uses Enzyme B to catalyze his reaction, and he doubles the initial reactant concentration. The data are shown in Table 4.

Table 4

Time (s)	Temp. (°C)	H_2O_2 Concentration (mM)	pH
0	25	100	6.2
10	35	71	6.5
20	42	49	6.6
30	49	27	6.7
40	54	12	6.8
50	57	6	6.9
60	59	0	7.0

6. Under which conditions is the greatest quantity of the reactant consumed within the first 10 seconds of the reaction?

(A) With Enzyme A, at an initial temperature of 25°C
(B) With Enzyme A, at an initial temperature of 60°C
(C) With Enzyme B, at an initial temperature of 25°C
(D) Without the addition of an enzyme, at an initial temperature of 25°C

7. Which of the following conclusions can be drawn about the effect of adding heat to the reaction?

(A) Adding heat but not adding Enzyme A causes the reaction to occur more quickly than adding Enzyme A but not adding heat.
(B) Adding Enzyme A but not adding heat causes the reaction to occur more quickly than adding heat but not adding Enzyme A.
(C) Adding both heat and Enzyme A causes the reaction to occur more quickly than adding Enzyme A but not adding heat.
(D) Adding both heat and Enzyme A causes the reaction to occur more slowly than adding Enzyme A but not adding heat.

8. If Experiment 1 were repeated with the same H_2O_2 concentration as that of Experiment 3, which of the following results would be most likely?

(A) It would take longer than 60 seconds for the reactant to be completely consumed, because there is more of it initially.
(B) It would take less than 60 seconds for the reactant to be completely consumed, because there is more of it initially.
(C) It would take longer than 60 seconds for the reactant to be completely consumed, because decreasing the concentration of an enzyme slows down the reaction.
(D) It would take less than 60 seconds for the reactant to be completely consumed, because increasing the concentration of an enzyme speeds up the reaction.

9. Assuming that the addition of heat has the same effect on the efficiency of Enzyme B as it does on the efficiency of Enzyme A, if Experiment 3 were repeated with an initial temperature of 60 C, after how many seconds would the pH in the container be 7.0?

(A) 0
(B) 20
(C) 40
(D) 60

10. In Experiment 3, which of the following is true about the relationship between the concentration of H_2O_2 and the rate of change of the concentration of H_2O_2?

(A) As the concentration of H_2O_2 decreases, its rate of change decreases.
(B) As the concentration of H_2O_2 decreases, its rate of change increases.
(C) As the concentration of H_2O_2 decreases, its rate of change stays constant.
(D) There is no relationship between the concentration of H_2O_2 and its rate of change.

11. Which of the following hypotheses could NOT have been tested in Experiment 1?

(A) As H_2O_2 concentration decreases, temperature and pH both decrease.
(B) Without the addition of an enzyme, H_2O_2 concentration decreases at a lower rate than with the addition of an enzyme.
(C) As time increases, temperature increases and H_2O_2 concentration decreases.
(D) As H_2O_2 concentration decreases, the rate of change of H_2O_2 concentration decreases.

sP1B

Directions: The following two passages are similar to real ACT test passages. Read each passage and answer the questions that follow. Use the methods and techniques that you learned in the instructions of this lesson.

HOMEWORK PASSAGE 1 (TIME: 6 MINUTES)

Malaria is an infectious disease that involves single-celled protozoan parasites (*Plasmodium*) that are only transmitted through mosquito bites. While human malaria is no longer present in the United States and other modern, urbanized countries, it remains a scourge worldwide, with only HIV rivaling it in total infections and deaths. Malaria has been known for centuries and intensely fought for nearly as long, but the complex life cycle of the parasite continues to pose problems for prevention and treatment. Below, two parasitologists debate possible avenues for treating malaria.

Parasitologist 1:

Vaccines have allowed us to nearly eradicate or significantly mitigate the health effects of once rampant infectious diseases (e.g., polio), so it seems imperative that we dedicate our efforts toward creating a vaccine for malaria. Such a vaccine would allow us to accomplish two tasks that have proved elusive thus far. First, a vaccine can act as a treatment for existing cases. The malaria parasite reproduces in humans and, by limiting or completely halting reproduction, a vaccine would speed up recovery and prevent fatalities. Second, a vaccine can act as a preventative tool for uninfected individuals. Vaccines would accomplish this by limiting transmission since there are fewer infected people for mosquitoes to spread the parasite from and by preventing infection when people are exposed to the parasite. While it is true that previous attempts at vaccines have failed largely because of how *Plasmodium* can hide from host immune systems, we have faced and overcome similar problems with other infections (such as influenza) that have successful vaccines.

Parasitologist 2:

Many of my colleagues are attracted by the novelty and promise of a malaria vaccine, but all this attention is at the expense of interventions that worked in the past—and still work today. Malaria is a complex disease with three components: humans, mosquitoes, and *Plasmodium* parasites. Addressing any one of those components is a valid way to treat the disease, but some components are easier to address than others. A vaccine has to work with the two most complicated components: humans and

parasites. Mosquitoes are the most ideal target because their biology is well-understood, they are arguably the "weakest link" in the transmission chain, and inexpensive yet effective interventions exist. That last point cannot be overstated: interventions (such as the use of spraying and waterway drainage) are far cheaper than vaccine development and delivery, and have a track record of success (such as the eradication of malaria in the United States). Finally, interventions targeting mosquitoes can be implemented almost immediately; any vaccine is at least years, possibly decades, away from implementation. Malaria can be eradicated if we simply refocus our energies and resources back on something that has worked incredibly effectively before, even if it is decidedly low-tech.

1. Which statement would appear to contradict information given in the introduction?

   (A) Medical records from Ancient Egypt describe disease symptoms and progressions similar to what is seen in malaria infections today.
   (B) London, England is prone to seasonal epidemics of malaria.
   (C) Malaria infection rates decrease as the populations of *Anopheles* mosquito decrease.
   (D) *Plasmodium* parasites cannot directly infect humans.

2. Which of the following statements best explains why Parasitologist 1 mentioned polio?

   (A) Polio is an example of a disease with a vaccine.
   (B) Polio is another disease that is spread by mosquito bites.
   (C) Polio is a disease that vaccine use has nearly eliminated.
   (D) Polio is a reason that malaria vaccines have failed in the past.

3. Parasitologist 2 feels that the most obvious point of attack for fighting malaria is the:

   (A) humans' well-understood anatomy.
   (B) vaccines' easily-produced nature .
   (C) *plasmodium's* susceptibility to vaccines.
   (D) mosquitoes' well-understood biology.

4. If a nationwide clinical trial found that the use of insecticide-treated bednets (nets that have mosquito repellent in the fibers and that are hung over beds while people sleep) decreased the number of new malaria infections by more than 50%, this finding would most likely support the viewpoint of:

(A) Parasitologist 1
(B) Parasitologist 2
(C) Both Parasitologist 1 and Parasitologist 2
(D) Neither Parasitologist 1 nor Parasitologist 2

5. How might Parasitologist 1 respond to Parasitologist 2's view on the use of non-vaccine interventions to stop malaria?

(A) While effective for malaria, these interventions will not help stop other diseases, like influenza.
(B) These interventions could be useful to buy time until a malaria vaccine is fully functional.
(C) These interventions will not help patients who are already infected with malaria.
(D) We should target the weakest link in the transmission chain first in order to tackle the malaria problem.

6. How might Parasitologist 2 suggest responding to an outbreak of a viral disease, like polio, that is spread when *pathogens*, or infectious agents, in fecal particles from one host are introduced into the mouth of another potential host?

(A) If a vaccine is not readily available, we should focus our efforts on making sure all water that is recycled from sewage is thoroughly disinfected before consumed by humans.
(B) If a vaccine is not readily available, we should focus our efforts on making nets to cover the mouths of humans that may ingest these pathogens.
(C) If a vaccine is not readily available, we should focus our efforts on eliminating the carriers of these pathogens.
(D) All of our efforts should be focused on researching and creating vaccines to stop further outbreaks of this disease.

7. When compared to Parasitologist 1, Parasitologist 2 seems to focus more on:

(A) technological advances.
(B) speed and efficiency.
(C) biological concerns.
(D) sound medical practices.

HOMEWORK PASSAGE 2 (TIME: 5 MINUTES)

Buoyancy is an upward force, exerted by a fluid on an object, which opposes the weight of the object. The *density* of an object or a substance is equivalent to its mass divided by its volume. In general, if an object is denser than the fluid it displaces, it will sink. If it is equally dense, it will float in position in the fluid, and if the object is less dense, it will rise until it is only partially submerged, and then float at the surface of the fluid.

In the following experiments, two students study the buoyant forces of different materials.

Experiment 1

The students place blocks of different masses one at a time into a pool of 100 L of water, making sure that the water contained the entire block and nothing else. Each previous block was removed before the next one was submerged. They record the final volume of the pool after each placement. Assume no water was absorbed by any of the blocks. The density of water is 1.0 kg/L. Table 1 shows their data.

Table 1

Block	Mass (kg)	Final Volume (L)
1	1.00	108
2	2.00	104
3	3.00	103
4	4.00	102

Experiment 2

The students repeat the procedure in Experiment 1, this time allowing the blocks to float or sink. If a block floated, they recorded the percentage of its volume submerged under water. Their data are shown in Table 2.

Table 2

Block	Sink or Float	% Volume Underwater
1	Float	12.5%
2	Float	50%
3	Float	100%
4	Sink	—

Experiment 3

The students repeat the procedures in Experiment 2 with identical blocks using two new liquids, Liquid A and Liquid B. Their results are shown in Tables 3 and 4, respectively.

Table 3

Block	Sink or Float	% Volume Underwater
1	Float	75%
2	Sink	—
3	Sink	—
4	Sink	—

Table 4

Block	Sink or Float	% Volume Underwater
1	Float	6.25%
2	Float	25%
3	Float	50%
4	Float	100%

8. To calculate the density of each block in Experiment 1, the student would need to:

    (A) subtract 100 L from the final volume and divide by the mass of the block.
    (B) subtract 100 L from the final volume and divide the mass of the block by that difference.
    (C) divide the final volume by the mass of the block.
    (D) divide the mass of the block by the final volume.

9. Based on the results of Experiments 1 and 2, which of the following conclusions can be drawn?

    (A) Blocks with density equal to or less than that of water floated, and the percentage of volume submerged was equal to the change in volume as a percentage.
    (B) Blocks with density less than that of water floated, and the percentage of volume submerged was equal to the change in density as a percentage.
    (C) Blocks with density equal to or less than that of water floated, and the percentage of volume submerged was equal to the density of the block as a percentage.
    (D) Blocks with density less than that of water floated, and the percentage of volume submerged was equal to the volume of water displaced as a percentage.

10. A fifth block is added to Experiment 2 that has a mass greater than that of Block 4 and a volume less than that of Block 3. Would it be expected to float or sink?

    (A) Float, because its density is lower than that of water.
    (B) Sink, because its density is higher than that of water.
    (C) Sink until its density decreases, and then float.
    (D) It cannot be determined from the given information, because we would need to know the percentage of its volume submerged.

11. Which of the following lists Liquid A, Liquid B, and water from greatest to least density?

    (A) Liquid B, Liquid A, water
    (B) Liquid A, water, Liquid B
    (C) Liquid B, water, Liquid A
    (D) water, Liquid B, Liquid A

12. A fifth block with greater mass and volume than Block 4 is placed in Liquid B. Will it sink or float?

    (A) It will sink.
    (B) It will float with less than 100% of its volume submerged.
    (C) It will float with 100% of its volume submerged.
    (D) It cannot be determined from the given information.

13. Which of the following predictions is NOT supported by the results of Experiments 1, 2, and 3?

    (A) If a block sinks in Liquid A, it will sink in water.
    (B) If a block floats in water, it will float in Liquid B.
    (C) If a block floats in Liquid A, it will float in water.
    (D) If a block sinks in Liquid B, it will sink in Liquid A.

sP2: Independent and Dependent Variables

Directions: Read the explanation and examples below to learn about this lesson's topic.

TOPIC OVERVIEW

Some science passages will focus on how one factor in an experiment influences or changes other factors. In these cases, it will serve you best to be able to determine the independent and dependent variables.

INDEPENDENT VARIABLE

The **independent variable** is the factor in an experiment that is manipulated or altered in some way. In simple terms, it can be viewed as the *input* portion of an equation.

DEPENDENT VARIABLE

The **dependent variable** is the measured and recorded factor or set of values in an experiment that is affected by the manipulation of the independent variable(s). In simple terms, it can be viewed as the *output* portion of an equation. The data is then measured and recorded.

SAMPLE PASSAGE

A botanist wanted to see how green beans would grow in different types of soil. She planted green beans in three different types of soil: silt, clay, and loam. To figure out which soil to use, she measured the number of inches that the green beans grew in each of the different soils. The graph below illustrates her results:

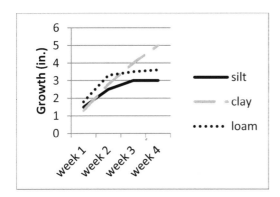

Explanation:

In this passage the type of soil is the **independent variable** and the amount of growth is the **dependent variable**. With this in mind, it is fairly easy to see the relationship between the type of soil and the growth of

green beans. By the fourth week, the clay has yielded five inches of growth and appears to be the best soil choice for growing green beans.

It's important to note that almost all of the data representation and research summary science passages on the ACT will in some way require you to analyze how the manipulation of the independent variable has affected the dependent variable. The more you can recognize the ways in which the dependent variable was altered and accurately analyze the measurements of the independent variable, the more prepared you will be when approaching these kinds of problems.

Example:

Let's examine how to answer a question that involves an analysis of the independent and dependent variables using the soil type graph from before.

1. A recent discovery shows that the results of the green bean experiment are also true for a number of other types of beans. If a gardener wanted to purchase the right kind of soil to plant her soy beans, which type of soil should she most likely buy?

    (A) A mixture of silt and clay.
    (B) Silt.
    (C) A mixture of loam and silt.
    (D) Clay.

Explanation:

The correct answer is **D**. If you analyze the independent variables (silt, clay, and loam) and analyze the dependent variable's data recorded on the graph (the number of inches), you will notice that clay clearly yields more growth than the other types of soil. Since the question states that this experiment is representative of most other beans, clay would provide similar results for the soy beans. Notice that an accurate understanding of the relationship between the independent and dependent variables made answering this question quite simple.

sP2A

Directions: The following two passages are similar to real ACT test passages. Read each passage and answer the questions that follow. Use the methods and techniques that you learned in the instructions of this lesson.

PRACTICE PASSAGE 1 (TIME: 4 MINUTES)

Aquatic animals require a wide range of nutrients and resources to thrive, so scientists investigated multiple sites in a river system to determine how different factors affect dissolved oxygen levels and the population of common shiner, a species of small fish. At noon each day for one week scientists measured the amount of shade, average temperature, speed of the water, amount of dissolved O_2, and estimated shiner population of nine different sites at three different rivers.

Table 1

Site #	River	Avg. Shade %	Average Temperature (°C)	Rapids	Dissolved O_2 (ppm)	Estimated Shiner Population
1	A	16	15	None	3	2
2	A	42	12	Weak	7	24
3	A	87	8	Weak	8	28
4	B	48	14	None	4	7
5	B	90	10	Weak	7	23
6	B	50	12	Strong	8	0
7	C	85	7	Strong	10	3
8	C	81	9	Weak	9	34
9	C	27	11	None	6	19

1. Based on the data in Table 1, what is the relationship between shade and dissolved oxygen?

   (A) There is a weak direct relationship between the amount of shade over a river and the amount of dissolved O_2 in that area of the river.
   (B) There is a strong direct relationship between the amount of shade over a river and the amount of dissolved O_2 in that area of the river.
   (C) There is no relationship between the amount of shade over a river and the amount of dissolved O_2 in that area of the river.
   (D) There is a strong inverse relationship between the amount of shade over a river and the amount of dissolved O_2 in that area of the river.

2. What is the relationship between the amount of water turbulence and dissolved oxygen?

   (A) The difference between the average oxygen levels of rivers with no rapids and rivers with weak rapids is much greater than the difference between rivers with weak rapids and rivers with strong rapids.
   (B) The difference between the average oxygen levels of rivers with no rapids and rivers with weak rapids is much less than the difference between rivers with weak rapids and rivers with strong rapids.
   (C) The three rivers are identical with respect to their water turbulence and oxygen levels.
   (D) The differences among rivers with all three amounts of water turbulence are negligible.

3. A new site several miles downstream from Site 7 on River C, Site 10, is analyzed and found to have 87% shade, strong rapids, and a temperature of 9°C. What would be the most probable amount of dissolved O_2 at Site 10?

   (A)   4
   (B)   9
   (C)   14
   (D)   19

4. An entrepreneur wants to build a facility for farming mosquitofish, a baitfish which thrives under similar conditions to, and is related to, the common shiner. Which of these aquatic habitats should he build to best promote mosquitofish growth?

	Avg. Shade %	Avg. Temp. (°C)	Rapids	Dissolved O_2 (ppm)
(A)	90	11	Strong	10
(B)	83	10	Weak	12
(C)	55	7	Weak	7
(D)	19	3	None	6

5. A scientist analyzed the results in Figure 1 and came to the conclusion that the amount of dissolved oxygen in a stream is the most important factor in determining shiner populations. Which of the following reasons and sites most obviously disproves the scientist's theory?

   (A) Site 2 has 42% shade, but relatively high levels of dissolved O_2 and a relatively high shiner population.
   (B) Site 4 has an average temperature of 14°C, but low levels of dissolved O_2 and a relatively low shiner population.
   (C) Site 6 has strong rapids, but high levels of dissolved O_2 and no shiners.
   (D) Site 9 has no rapids, but relatively high levels of dissolved O_2 and a relatively high shiner population.

PRACTICE PASSAGE 2 (TIME: 5 MINUTES)

Beer's Law describes the relationship between the absorption of light by a material and the property of that material. Every material has a distinct molar absorptivity constant that is directly proportional to its absorbance. The following experiments were conducted to study Beer's Law. Table 1 lists the colors of visible light and their corresponding wavelengths.

Table 1

Color	Wavelength (nm)
Red	620 – 750
Orange	590 – 620
Yellow	570 – 590
Green	495 – 570
Blue	450 – 495
Indigo	420 – 450
Violet	380 – 420

Experiment 1

A laser beam of 550 nm was shone through various solutions of cobalt (II) nitrate, a red colored solution, at different concentrations. A spectrophotometer was used to measure the absorbance of the solution on the opposite side of which the laser was located. Color intensity was marked from a scale of 0–8, 0 being the lightest shade and 8 the darkest. Table 2 lists the absorbances and colors of the various solutions. Figure 1 illustrates the setup.

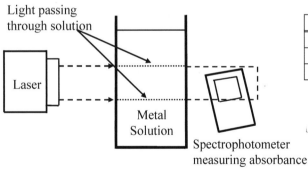

Figure 1

Table 2

Concentration (μM)	Absorbance	Color Intensity
50	0.24	1
100	0.47	2
150	0.71	3
200	0.94	4
250	1.18	5
300	1.42	6
350	1.65	7
400	1.89	8

Experiment 2

The absorbance of a cobalt (II) nitrate solution was measured as a function of light wavelength and solution concentration. Table 3 records the data.

Table 3

Wavelength (nm)	Concentration (μM)	Absorbance
550	100	0.47
600	200	0.25
650	300	0.10
700	400	0.09

Experiment 3

A laser of 650 nm was shone through three additional metal solutions, each at 200 μM concentrations. The absorbances and colors for each solution are shown in Table 4.

Table 4

Solution	Absorbance	Color
Potassium dichromate	0.02	Orange
Nickel (II) chloride	0.17	Green
Copper sulfate	0.22	Blue

6. Which of the following lists the solutions in order of decreasing absorbance at 650 nm and 200 μM?

(A) Potassium dichromate, cobalt (II) nitrate, nickel (II) chloride, copper sulfate
(B) Copper sulfate, nickel (II) chloride, cobalt (II) nitrate, potassium dichromate
(C) Cobalt (II) nitrate, copper sulfate, nickel (II) chloride, potassium dichromate
(D) Potassium dichromate, nickel (II) chloride, copper sulfate, cobalt (II) nitrate

7. Based on the results of Experiment 1 in the passage, which of the following could be the absorbance of a 500 μM solution of cobalt (II) nitrate exposed to a green-yellow laser beam?

    (A) 1.20
    (B) 1.56
    (C) 1.90
    (D) 2.35

8. Using a light wavelength of 550 nm, the absorbance of a 400 μM solution of copper sulfate will be:

    (A) Less than the absorbance of a 100 μM solution of cobalt (II) nitrate at 550 nm.
    (B) Greater than the absorbance of a 400 μM solution of cobalt (II) nitrate at 700 nm.
    (C) Less than the absorbance of a 200 μM solution of nickel (II) chloride at 650 nm.
    (D) Less than the absorbance of a 200 μM solution of potassium dichromate at 650 nm.

9. The absorbance of 400 μM cobalt (II) nitrate solution was found to be less than 1. Which of the following could NOT be the wavelength of the light that was shone through the solution?

    (A) 550 nm
    (B) 600 nm
    (C) 650 nm
    (D) 700 nm

10. Which of the following graphs correctly plots the color intensity, I, of a metal solution as a function of solution concentration, C?

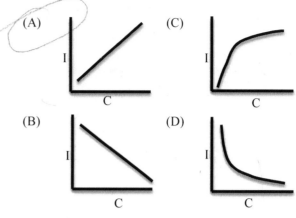

11. When light shines on an object, that object absorbs certain wavelengths of the light and emits others. The colors that we see are of those wavelengths that the object emits. Which of the following solutions emits orange light the MOST?

    (A) Cobalt (II) nitrate
    (B) Potassium dichromate
    (C) Nickel (II) chloride
    (D) It cannot be determined.

sP2B

HOMEWORK PASSAGE 1 (TIME: 4 MINUTES)

A geneticist caught *Drosophila* fruit flies from two different areas in the United States. He labeled fruit flies from one area as the "R" strain; he labeled the others as the "S" strain. *Drosophila* are known to colonize rotting fruits, which are teeming with bacteria and yeast that consume fruit sugar and produce alcohol as waste byproducts; the fruit flies, in turn, consume these microorganisms. The geneticist was particularly curious if the two fruit fly strains differed in their ability to resist exposure to the alcohol byproducts. The following graphs show the results of an experiment in which he mixed artificial food with two levels of alcohol seen in rotting fruit (4% and 8%, by volume), exposed fruit flies to the artificial food mixtures, and observed their survival over 24 hours. Figure 1 shows the survival rate of *Drosophilia* after being exposed to 4% alcohol, while Figure 2 shows the survival rate for 8% alcohol.

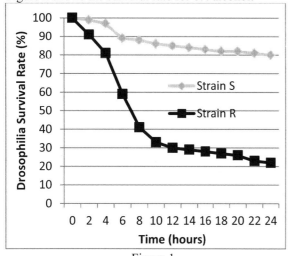

Figure 1

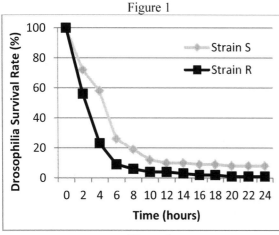

Figure 2

1. Based on Figure 2, what is a reasonable statement about what happened to Strain R flies?

   (A) Strain R flies were more resistant to alcohol than Strain S flies were.
   (B) Within four hours of exposure to 8% alcohol, about three out of every four flies were dead.
   (C) All of the flies had died after exposure to 8% alcohol for 18 hours.
   (D) Alcohol affects both strains to the same degree.

2. Wines often contain alcohol levels in excess of 10%. If a winery was suddenly overrun with fruit flies that kept trying to eat the yeast and bacteria in the barrels of fermenting wines, would either of these two strains be a likely culprit?

   (A) No; neither of the strains can survive even 8% alcohol for very long.
   (B) Yes; fermenting wines have plenty of the microorganisms that fruit flies feed on.
   (C) No; fruit flies would never seek food in wine barrels.
   (D) Yes; Strain S is very resistant to alcohol.

3. If an additional experiment had been done with the same two strains exposed to 10% alcohol, what might the geneticist expect to observe?

   (A) Strain R would have a higher survival rate than Strain S.
   (B) There would be more microorganisms producing alcohol in the food.
   (C) The majority of flies from both strains would die very rapidly.
   (D) The majority of flies from Strain S would be alive after 24 hours.

4. Bacteria and yeast are known to consume food and grow faster at higher temperatures. Based on this knowledge and the experimental results, which strain of flies likely was collected from a warmer, southern region of the United States? What is the best evidence for this?

    (A) Strain R; it was the less alcohol resistant strain of flies.
    (B) Strain R; it died at a faster rate so it was probably accustomed to consuming microorganisms that grow faster.
    (C) Strain S; it survived much better at 4% alcohol than at 8% alcohol.
    (D) Strain S; it was more alcohol resistant so it was probably accustomed to consuming microorganisms that produce alcohol very quickly.

5. In Figure 1, the two strains had very different survival rates; in Figure 2, the two strains had very similar survival rates, especially after 12 hours. What best explains this apparent contradiction in the results?

    (A) Strain R can only resist alcohol exposure for six hours or less.
    (B) Strain R does not consume bacteria and yeast as its primary food source.
    (C) Strain S is more resistant to alcohol than Strain R, but 8% alcohol is a toxic level for fruit flies.
    (D) Strain S can consume alcohol for energy at the 4% level, but not at the 8% level.

HOMEWORK PASSAGE 2 (TIME: 5 MINUTES)

Simple harmonic motion is a type of periodic motion in which the restoring force on a system is directly proportional to its displacement from its equilibrium position. It is typified by the motion of a mass attached to a spring or pendulum when it is subject to a restoring force.

A physics student conducts the following experiments to study simple harmonic motion using a pendulum.

Experiment 1

The student fastens a 1-meter rope onto a ceiling and ties a 1-kg block onto its free end. He then pulls up the block and releases it at a starting angle of 45 degrees from the normal. The student measures the length of one period (time needed to return to starting position) and repeats the trial with ropes of different length, releasing the block from different angles. Figure 1 shows the pendulum in its equilibrium position, and Figure 2 his data. Assume no energy is lost due to frictional forces.

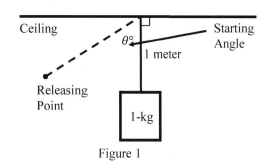

Figure 1

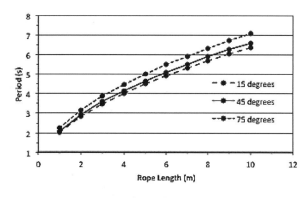

Figure 2

Experiment 2

The student then alters the mass of the block but finds that it has no effect on the period of the pendulum. He then decides to place his setup in a frictionless vacuum-sealed chamber and simulate the force of gravity of different planetary bodies to examine its effect on the pendulum's period. (The gravitational acceleration on Earth is 9.81 m/s².) He uses a 1-meter rope and 45 degree starting angle for each trial. His data are shown in Table 1.

Table 1

Planet	Gravitational acceleration	Period (*s*)
Moon	$1.62\ m/s^2$	5.13
Mars	$3.71\ m/s^2$	3.39
Jupiter	$24.79\ m/s^2$	1.31
Neptune	$11.15\ m/s^2$	1.96

Experiment 3

The student then tries to determine the relationship between the pendulum's initial position and its potential energy. He swings the pendulum at three different starting angles and plots the relative potential energies every three periods. He uses a 1-meter rope and a 1-kg mass. Consider normal gravity and friction forces. Figure 3 plots his data.

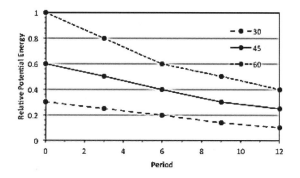

Figure 3

6. The period of a pendulum increases:

    (A) as initial angle increases, rope length increases, and gravitational acceleration increases
    (B) as initial angle increases, rope length increases, and gravitational acceleration decreases
    (C) as initial angle decreases, rope length increases, and gravitational acceleration increases
    (D) as initial angle decreases, rope length decreases, and gravitational acceleration decreases

7. The gravitational acceleration on Saturn is 10.44 m/s^2. The period on Saturn of a pendulum with double the mass of the block in Experiment 2 would be:

    (A) between 1.31 s and 1.96 s
    (B) between 1.96 s and 3.39 s
    (C) between 3.39 s and 5.13 s
    (D) greater than 5.13 s

8. On the moon, the period of a pendulum with half the mass of the block in Experiment 2, but twice the length of the rope, would be:

    (A) shorter than the period on Mars of the same pendulum used in Experiment 2
    (B) equal to the period on the Moon of the same pendulum used in Experiment 2
    (C) longer than the period on Earth of a 5-meter rope with an initial angle of 75 degrees
    (D) None of these

9. The relative potential energy of an object is directly proportional to its mass. The relative potential energy after 6 periods of a block with twice the mass of the block used in Experiment 3, released from a starting angle of 37 degrees, would be:

    (A) between 0.0 and 0.2
    (B) between 0.2 and 0.4
    (C) between 0.4 and 0.8
    (D) It cannot be determined from the given information.

10. Which of the following statements is true about Experiment 1?

    (A) The rope length and initial angle are held constant, the mass of the block is the independent variable, and the period is the dependent variable.
    (B) The mass of the block is held constant, the rope length is the independent variable, and the initial angle and period are dependent variables.
    (C) The mass of the block is held constant, the rope length and initial angle are dependent variables, and the period is the independent variable.
    (D) The mass of the block is held constant, the rope length and initial angle are independent variables, and the period is the dependent variable.

11. The student wants to plot the graph of the position of a 1-kg pendulum with a 1-meter-long rope, as a function of time. It would be most helpful for him to know:

    (A) the angle of the pendulum at different points in the period, and the gravitational acceleration on the pendulum
    (B) the angle of the pendulum at different initial positions, and the gravitational acceleration on the pendulum
    (C) the relative potential energy of different initial positions, and the length of the period
    (D) the angle of the pendulum at different points in the period, and the length of the period

sP3: UNDERSTANDING GRAPHS

Directions: Read the explanation and examples below to learn about this lesson's topic.

TOPIC OVERVIEW

While many of the graphs on the ACT are composed of traditional *x*- and *y*-axes and focus on linear, exponential, and other straightforward relationships, you may encounter graphs on the ACT which could be considered nontraditional. These graphs resort to visually representing data in unique ways because of their subject matter. Recognizing visual patterns and relationships in the graph is much more important than having a complete understanding of the subject matter. Look at the example below for an example of a nontraditional graph.

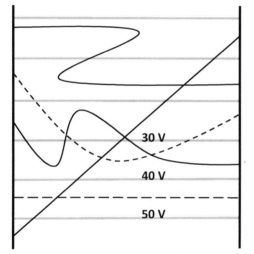

The above graph shows the movement of five *point charges* (charged particles which occupy a single minute point in space) across different voltages, and the initial and final voltages of each of those five point charges. Since we don't have all of the necessary information for this graph, we just need to analyze its contents and see what we can figure out.

- There seem to be two *y*-axes, one on each side of the graph, and each seems to tell us the voltage of our five different point charges.

- The different voltages seem to be evenly spaced throughout the graph, so we don't have to worry about any logarithmic or other type of scale.

- Nothing is labeled on the *x*-axis, but the paths the point charges make seem to move in a generally horizontal direction. More than likely, the lines represent potential paths the point charges take to get from their initial points to their final destinations in space.

Let's look at another similar graph and try a question.

SAMPLE PASSAGE

Metamorphic rocks form when temperature and/or pressure cause changes in preexisting rock. Figure 1 shows the temperature and pressure conditions at which certain *facies* (categories of metamorphic rocks) are formed.

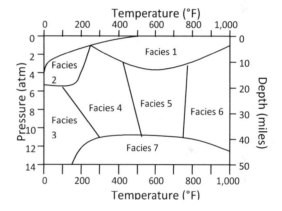

1. A certain type of iron ore is only found between 10 and 15 miles below the surface and at a temperature range of 500 to 600 °F. In which facies might this ore be found?

    (A) Facies 1 only
    (B) Facies 5 only
    (C) Facies 7 only
    (D) Facies 1 or 5

The answer is **D**. All we have to do is figure out where the 500-600°F range is located, and then follow that range down to a depth of 10 to 15 miles. Don't get confused by the left-hand *y*-axis and use pressure instead of depth!

sP3A

Directions: The following two passages are similar to real ACT test passages. Read each passage and answer the questions that follow. Use the methods and techniques that you learned in the instructions of this lesson.

PRACTICE PASSAGE 1 (TIME: 4 MINUTES)

The physical states of a compound are largely dependent upon the physical conditions surrounding it. A phase diagram can be used to determine the physical state of a compound at a given temperature and pressure. Different processes, such as *compression* (increasing pressure) and *expansion* (decreasing pressure) can be used to shift compounds from one state to another.

Figures 1 and 2 below show the phase diagrams for H_2O and CO_2.

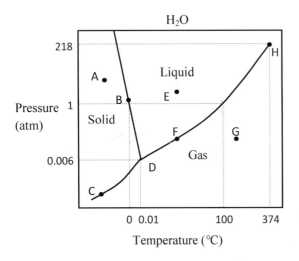

Figure 1

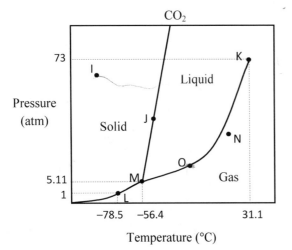

Figure 2

A mixture is composed of multiple pure compounds and can be classified as a solid, eutectic, or peritectic solution, among others. A *eutectic mixture* is one of two or more phases at a given composition that has a lower melting point than any other possible composition of the phases. In a eutectic system, a liquid can be frozen into multiple distinct solids (α, β, etc.) depending on the temperature and mixture composition. The temperature at which the eutectic mixture forms is called the *eutectic temperature*. The *eutectic point* is the intersection of the eutectic temperature and eutectic composition. Figure 2 shows a binary phase diagram for a generic eutectic system in which the eutectic point contains both solid forms and the liquid.

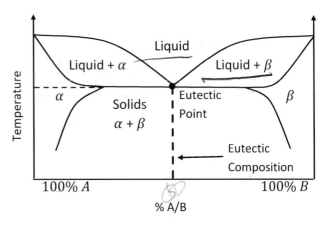

Figure 3

1. In the phase diagram of water, what process occurs as the temperature at Point E is increased by 100°C?

   (A) Melting
   (B) Vaporization
   (C) Sublimation
   (D) Deposition

2. Based on the phase diagrams in Figure 1, one can conclude that at 1 atm, the boiling point of water is:

   (A) less than the boiling point of carbon dioxide at 10 atm.
   (B) greater than the boiling point of carbon dioxide at 10 atm.
   (C) equal to the boiling point of carbon dioxide at 10 atm.
   (D) It cannot be determined.

3. Liquids 1 and 2 are mixed in a 1:1 ratio. Upon lowering the temperature to −20°C, a scientist finds that two distinct solids form. He then adds 10 mL of Liquid 1 while keeping the temperature constant. Which solids could possibly remain in the mixture?

   (A) Solid A and/or Solid B
   (B) Solid A only
   (C) Solid B only
   (D) Neither solid remains

4. In the phase diagram of carbon dioxide, what processes in order could be used to shift carbon dioxide from Point I to Point N?

   (A) Sublimation, heating, and boiling.
   (B) Melting and vaporization.
   (C) Melting and compression.
   (D) Condensation and freezing.

5. A liquid solution is made containing 30% A and 70% B. After the temperature is raised, which of the following could be present in the new solution?

   (A) Solid B and Liquid B only.
   (B) Solid B, Liquid B, and Liquid A.
   (C) Liquid A and Solid B only.
   (D) Solid A, Liquid B, and Solid B.

PRACTICE PASSAGE 2 (TIME: 4 MINUTES)

The *vapor pressure* of a liquid, a measure of the extent to which a liquid vaporizes, is inversely related to the strength of the liquid's intermolecular forces. Liquids with weak intermolecular forces vaporize more easily, which results in greater vapor pressure.

The pressure of a mixture of two ideal liquids in equilibrium with their vapors can be illustrated by Figure 1, in which P_T, the total pressure of the mixture, is the sum of P_A (the pressure contributed by liquid A) and P_B (the pressure contributed by liquid B). P_A° represents the vapor pressure of pure liquid A, and X_A the mole fraction of liquid A in the mixture. When $X_A = 1$, the mixture is pure liquid A, and when $X_A = 0$, the mixture contains no liquid A.

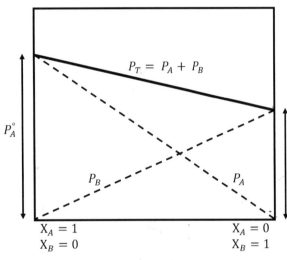

$$P_T = P_A + P_B$$

$X_A = 1$ $X_A = 0$
$X_B = 0$ $X_B = 1$

Figure 1

Table 1 shows the total pressures (atm) of mixtures formed from liquids A through F at 25°C. Assume a 1 mole quantity of each liquid. A mixture with two of the same liquids is a pure liquid.

Table 1

Liquid	A	B	C	D	E	F
A	8					
B	6	4				
C	5.5	3.5	3			
D	4.6	2.6	2.1	1.3		
E	4.2	2.2	1.7	0.9	0.5	
F	4.0	2.0	1.5	0.7	0.3	0.1

6. Which of the following sets of pure liquids is ranked from lowest to highest vapor pressure?

   (A) F, C, D, A
   (B) A, C, D, E
   (C) A, B, E, F
   (D) E, C, B, A

7. A new 2-mole mixture of liquids B and D is created that has 1.5 moles of liquid D. The vapor pressure of this mixture should be:

   (A) lower than 1.3 atm
   (B) between 1.3 and 2.6 atm
   (C) between 2.6 and 4 atm
   (D) higher than 4 atm

8. A seventh pure liquid, Z, has vapor pressure between that of A and B. Which of the following conclusions could be drawn?

   (A) Pure Z has the same vapor pressure as Mixture AB.
   (B) The vapor pressure of pure Z is equal to the average pressure between A and B.
   (C) Mixture ZE would have a higher vapor pressure than Mixture ZD.
   (D) Mixture ZB would have a higher vapor pressure than Mixture BC.

9. Which of the following sets of mixtures is ranked from weakest to strongest intermolecular forces?

   (A) EF, DE, CD, BC
   (B) DE, CD, BC, AB
   (C) BC, CD, BE, AF
   (D) AC, BC, DE, DF

10. If liquid A in Figure 1 represents liquid A from Table 1, and liquid B in Figure 1 represents liquid F from Table 1, which of the following conclusions CANNOT be drawn?

    (A) The intersection of the dotted lines represents the point at which the vapor pressure of Mixture AF is 4.0 atm.
    (B) There is some mixture between pure A and pure F whose vapor pressure is equal to that of Mixture CD.
    (C) P_T can never be lower than 0.1 atm.
    (D) There is some mixture between pure A and pure F in which the vapor pressure contributed by liquid A is equal to the vapor pressure contributed by liquid F.

sP3B

Directions: The following two passages are similar to real ACT test passages. Read each passage and answer the questions that follow. Use the methods and techniques that you learned in the instructions of this lesson.

HOMEWORK PASSAGE 1 (TIME: 4 MINUTES)

An astronomer observes five different planets of varying mass that each revolve around the same star. He tries to construct a to-scale schematic of the planets' orbits to depict their positions at the exact moment of his first observation.

He proposes three different models, shown in Figure 1. Each model illustrates a top-down view of the orbits. Assume the planets' orbits lie on approximately the same plane, but that the orbits are far enough apart that the possibility of collisions can be neglected.

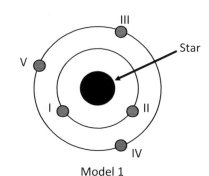

Model 1

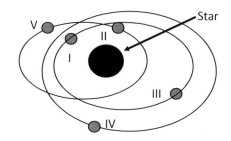

Model 2

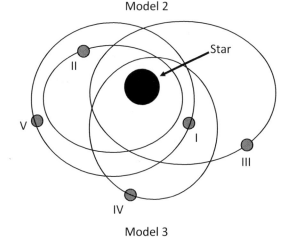

Model 3

For his models, the astronomer defines the length of a planet's year to be equal to the planet's orbital period—the amount of time it takes the planet to complete one revolution around the star. A planetary day is defined as the amount of time it takes the planet to make one complete rotation about its own axis.

All of the models take into account Kepler's Law, which states that planets in elliptical orbits move at their highest velocity (speed) when they are closest to the star they are orbiting, and at their lowest speed when they are farthest away.

All of the models contain the possibility of solar eclipses, which is when one planet comes in between the star and another planet, momentarily blocking the light from the star.

1. If all the planets in Model 1 have the same velocity, which remains constant throughout their orbits, which of the following must be true about their planetary years?

    (A) Planets I and II have a shorter year than Planets III, IV and V.
    (B) Planets I and II have a longer year than Planets III, IV and V.
    (C) All five planets have the same length year.
    (D) None of the planets have the same length year.

2. In Model 2, if Planets I and III have planetary years of equal length, what must be true about their velocities at their positions shown in the model?

    (A) Both planets have the same velocity.
    (B) Planet I is moving more slowly than Planet III.
    (C) Planet I is moving faster than Planet III.
    (D) Their velocities depend on the direction in which each planet is moving.

3. In Model 3, if Planets II and V take the same amount of time to make one revolution around the star (as measured in Earth time), but it takes less Earth time for Planet II to complete one rotation about its own axis than it takes Planet V to do so, which of the following is true?

    (A) Both planets have the same length day (in Earth time), but Planet II moves at a higher average velocity than Planet V.
    (B) Both planets have the same length day (in Earth time), but Planet V moves at a higher average velocity than Planet II.
    (C) Both planets have the same length year (in Earth time), but Planet V has more days in its year than Planet II.
    (D) Both planets have the same length year (in Earth time), but Planet II has more days in its year than Planet V.

4. Which of the following discoveries would weaken Model 1?

    (A) Planet I has a higher velocity than Planet II.
    (B) Planet IV and Planet V revolve in opposite directions.
    (C) Planet II has a longer year than Planet IV.
    (D) The velocity of Planet III varies throughout its year.

5. Which of the following discoveries would weaken Model 3?

    (A) It is possible, at different times, for each of the five planets to be moving faster than the other four.
    (B) It is possible, at different times, for each of the five planets to be farther from the star than the other four.
    (C) Planets II and V have the same orbital period, but Planet II has a higher average velocity than Planet V.
    (D) Planets I and V have different average velocities.

HOMEWORK PASSAGE 2 (TIME: 5 MINUTES)

In the following experiments, a physics student studies the motion of a spring-mass system. He uses an electric driver to power an oscillator, which oscillates left and right at constant amplitudes (distances). He attaches one end of a spring to the oscillator and the other end to a mass, as shown in Figure 1.

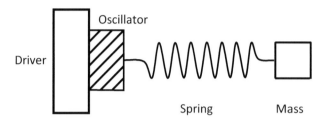

Figure 1

Experiment 1

With the electric driver powered off, the student pulls the mass out of its equilibrium position and releases it to set the spring in motion. As it oscillates, he measures the restoring force the spring exerts on the mass at different displacements (distances from the mass's equilibrium position). He repeats this experiment with two other springs, each with a different spring constant from the first. Table 1 lists his data. For displacement and restoring force, (+) and (−) indicate the direction relative to the equilibrium position: to the right or left, respectively.

Table 1

Spring Constant (N/m)	Displacement (m)	Restoring Force (N)
50	0.00	0.00
50	+0.10	−5.00
50	−0.20	+10.00
100	+0.05	−5.00
100	−0.10	+10.00
200	−0.10	+20.00

Experiment 2

The student sets the oscillator to a frequency of 1.00 Hz and amplitude of 1.00 cm. He first uses a 1-kg mass and measures the resonator frequency (how many times it oscillates per second) as a function of the spring constant k (Line 1, plotted along the bottom and left axes). He then repeats the procedure, this time using a 100-N/m spring constant and measuring the spring frequency as a function of mass m (Line 2, plotted

along the top and right axes). His results are plotted in Figure 2.

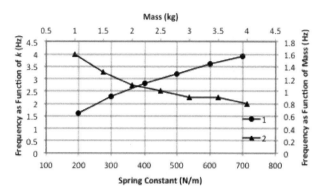

Figure 2

6. Which of the following conclusions can be drawn from the results of Experiment 1?

(A) A greater mass attached to the spring results in a greater restoring force.
(B) As distance from the equilibrium position increases, restoring force decreases.
(C) The restoring force always points in the direction that will move the mass away from its equilibrium position.
(D) The restoring force always points in the direction that will return the mass to its equilibrium position.

7. A spring with spring constant 200 N/m should be expected to have a restoring force of 30.00 N to the left when it is at a displacement of:

(A) 0.07 m to the right of equilibrium.
(B) 0.07 m to the left of equilibrium.
(C) 0.15 m to the right of equilibrium.
(D) 0.15 m to the left of equilibrium.

8. Based on the results of Experiment 2, the frequency of a spring-mass system:

(A) increases as spring constant increases, and increases as mass increases.
(B) increases as spring constant increases, and decreases as mass increases.
(C) decreases as spring constant increases, and increases as mass increases.
(D) decreases as spring constant increases, and decreases as mass increases.

9. The period of oscillation of a spring-mass system (the amount of time before the mass returns to its initial position and repeats the same motion) is inversely proportional to its frequency. Based on the results of Experiment 2, the period of a spring-mass system:

   (A) increases as spring constant increases, and increases as mass increases.
   (B) increases as spring constant increases, and decreases as mass increases.
   (C) decreases as spring constant increases, and increases as mass increases.
   (D) decreases as spring constant increases, and decreases as mass increases.

10. Based on the data in Figure 2, the frequency of a spring-mass system as a function of k with spring constant 800 N/m and mass 0.5 kg would most likely be:

   (A) lower than 4.0 Hz.
   (B) between 4.0 and 4.5 Hz.
   (C) higher than 4.5 Hz.
   (D) It cannot be determined from the given information.

11. Which of the following conclusions CANNOT be drawn from the data in Figure 2?

   (A) Increasing the spring constant by 300 N/m has a greater effect on the frequency than increasing the mass by 3 kg.
   (B) Decreasing spring constant and decreasing mass have opposite effects on frequency.
   (C) If a third line were added to Figure 2 to represent the frequency with a spring constant of 100 N/m and a mass of 2 kg, it would be parallel to Line 1 but lower on the graph.
   (D) At the point at which Line 1 and Line 2 intersect, the two springs have the same frequency.

sP4: ANALYZING TRENDS

Directions: Read the explanation and examples below to learn about this lesson's topic.

TOPIC OVERVIEW

Almost any time you come across a graph or table on the ACT, you will be required to engage in some degree of trend analysis. Trend analysis is a process in which you interpret the tendencies of data. This is usually accomplished on the ACT by *visually* observing the trend of the data on the graph. As was mentioned in the previous section on nontraditional graphs, do not spend too much time on the information in the passages; instead, study the general movements in the graphs. This should be enough to answer most of the questions related to analyzing trends.

Example:

In the 1900s, the census recorded the percentage of literate residents in a rural area over an 11-year span. The following graph shows the results found by the census. The black dots represent people under the age of 20; the gray dots represent people over the age of 20.

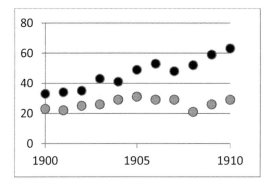

1. Which of the following statements is true?

(A) The percentage of literate residents in both age groups increased every year.
(B) Over the ten year span, the percentage of literate residents over the age of 20 increased at a slower rate than did the percentage of literate residents under the age of 20.
(C) Over the ten year span, the percentage of literate residents over the age of 20 increased at a faster rate than did the percentage of literate residents under the age of 20.
(D) Over the ten year span, the percentage of literate residents over the age of 20 increased at the same rate as the percentage of literate residents under the age of 20.

Explanation:

By noting the positions of both groups of dots on the graph, it is clear that as the years increase, both groups of dots increase. Since they both increase, try drawing a trend line and analyzing the slopes of those two lines.

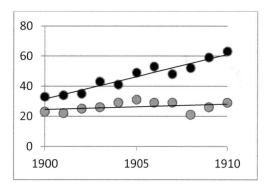

As you can see from the trend lines above, the trend line for the black dots is much steeper than the trend line for the gray dots. This makes **B** the best answer.

Extrapolation and Interpolation

A lot of the time, the questions will require you to make predictions about a specific data point that isn't represented. **Interpolation** occurs when a prediction is made about a data point that is not represented in the graph or table but is *within* the highest and lowest data points. **Extrapolation** occurs when a prediction is made beyond the highest or lowest data points in a graph or table.

Example:

A scientist took a sample of different radioactive isotopes. In an attempt to find a correlation between the atomic mass of an isotope and how quickly the isotope decays, she measured the decay times of isotopes of different weights. Below are her findings:

Time to decay completely	Atomic Mass of Sample
1011.22 sec	11
963.36 sec	22
757.39 sec	36
411.73 sec	100
266.33 sec	119
85.64 sec	218

1. After the experiment, the scientist found a sample whose atomic mass was 90. Which of the following would most likely be the time it took for the sample to decay?

    (A) 1101.26 seconds
    (B) 755.23 seconds
    (C) 430.22 seconds
    (D)   77.23 seconds

Explanation:

The correct answer is **C**.

This exercise is an example of **interpolation**: in order to find the correct answer, you had to make a prediction of a value *within* the highest and lowest data points in the table. Since the new atomic mass of 90 is between the given masses of 36 and 100, the time to decay would most likely be between 757.39 and 411.73. Both answers B and C are between these answers, but since 90 is much closer to 100 than it is to 36, our answer should probably be closer to 411.73 than to 757.39.

Example:

2. After the experiment, the scientist tested an isotope that took 1201.36 seconds to decay completely. Which of the following was probably the correct mass of the isotope?

    (A)   6
    (B)   27
    (C)   38
    (D) 309

Explanation:

The correct answer it **A.**

This exercise is an example of **extrapolation**: in order to find the correct answer, you had to make a prediction *beyond* the highest or lowest data points provided in the table. Since the atomic mass is less than 11, the time to decay is probably greater than 1011.22 All of the other choices are far too large to be reasonable answers.

sP4A

Directions: The following two passages are similar to real ACT test passages. Read each passage and answer the questions that follow. Use the methods and techniques that you learned in the instructions of this lesson.

PRACTICE PASSAGE 1 (TIME: 4 MINUTES)

A scientist collected soil samples from a forested area that local farmers then transformed into a field using *slash-and-burn*, a process in which large plants are cut down, allowed to dry, and then burned. Using these samples, the scientist measured key mineral and microbial growth factors to assess the viability of long-term slash-and-burn practices in an area.

The scientist used random sampling to take ten core samples of soil to a depth of 30 cm in a one hectare plot before farmers cleared the forest (phase A),

immediately after the vegetation was cut (phase B), three months later just before the burning event at the end of the dry season (C), immediately after the burning event (D), one week after the burn (E), two weeks after the burn (F), and after the first harvest (G). The scientist then measured the average amount of nitrogen, phosphorus, and potassium per centimeter of soil in each sample and averaged the ten samples' results. Later, the scientist returned to sample and analyze soil during the planting and harvest the following two years (phases H and I respectively). This information is presented in Table 1 below.

Average Nitrogen, Phosphorous, and Potassium Levels (ppm)

Phase	Soil Depth 0-10 cm			Soil Depth 11-20 cm			Soil Depth 21-30 cm		
	Average Nitrogen (ppm)	Average Phosp. (ppm)	Average Potass. (ppm)	Average Nitrogen (ppm)	Average Phosp. (ppm)	Average Potass. (ppm)	Average Nitrogen (ppm)	Average Phosp. (ppm)	Average Potass. (ppm)
A	73	39	182	50	36	212	47	38	150
B	73	39	183	51	36	210	46	38	150
C	78	39	198	53	37	211	46	38	150
D	78	40	255	53	37	220	45	38	150
E	72	38	242	51	37	219	45	37	149
F	45	28	201	50	34	223	50	35	155
G	22	14	143	31	23	200	45	33	148
H	9	7	110	11	14	166	37	22	140
I	3	1	82	5	4	116	14	8	131

Table 1

Phase	Number of bacteria (millions)
A	59
C	67
D	59
G	50
H	41
I	37

Table 2

Using a soil sample to estimate the population, the scientist measured the number of *actinomycetes* bacteria in the first 10 cm of soil following key slash-and-burn events: before the slash event (phase A), three months later just before burning (phase C), just after the burning event (D), and immediately after each of the first three harvests (G, H, and I). This information is found in Table 2 to the left.

1. Plant life must have access to nitrogen, phosphorous, and potassium in order to survive. Which of the following conclusions is best supported by the information presented in Table 1?

    (A) As the crops planted by the farmers use up more and more nitrogen, phosphorous, and potassium in the top levels of the soil, their roots must grow longer to try to reach the untapped nutrients below.
    (B) As the crops planted by the farmers use up more and more nitrogen, phosphorous, and potassium in the top levels of the soil, their stems must grow longer to obtain the untapped nutrients in the air.
    (C) The crops planted by the farmers need far less potassium to survive than either phosphorous or nitrogen.
    (D) As the crops became more used to the conditions of the soil they were planted in, they needed less and less nitrogen, phosphorous, and potassium to survive.

2. What effect did the fire have on *actinomycetes*?

    (A) The amount of *actinomycetes* present in the soil was nearly halved after the fire.
    (B) The amount of *actinomycetes* present in the soil decreased greatly after the fire.
    (C) The amount of *actinomycetes* present in the soil increased slightly after the fire.
    (D) The amount of *actinomycetes* present in the soil remained approximately the same after the fire.

3. *Actinomycetes* bacteria feed on decaying plant material and help rejuvenate the soil. Which of the following observations would help prove this fact?

    (A) After the burn, scientists noted a lack of uncharred plant material and heightened nutrient levels in the soil during Phase D.
    (B) After the burn, scientists noted a lack of plant material and lowered nutrient levels in the soil during Phase E.
    (C) After the burn, scientists noted that nutrient levels in the soil during Phase B remained approximately the same, accounting for the nutrients lost during the fire.
    (D) Before the burn, scientists noted that the number of *Actinomycetes* bacteria in the soil was much higher than the number after the burn.

4. Phase J occurred exactly 1 year after the end of Phase I. Which of the following is the most likely to occur?

    (A) The plants will continue to thrive, even though they do not have enough Nitrogen or Phosphorous to support them.
    (B) Because of a lack of Nitrogen and Phosphorous in the soil, the plants will have to use other nutrients, like Potassium, instead.
    (C) The plants will have to delve deeper into the soil to get the nutrients they need, or they will not survive.
    (D) The amount of *Actinomycetes* bacteria in the soil will increase to counteract the lack of Nitrogen and Phosphorous available in the soil.

5. Which of the following would best explain the higher amounts of nitrogen, phosphorous, and potassium found in deeper levels of the soil?

    (A) The nutrients in the upper levels of the soil are higher quality and will get used up first.
    (B) The nutrients in the upper levels of the soil are easier to obtain and will get used up first.
    (C) The nutrients in the upper levels of the soil are used by both the plants and the *Actinomycetes* bacteria and will get used up first.
    (D) Only the nutrients in the upper levels of the soil were affected by the fire.

PRACTICE PASSAGE 2 (TIME: 4 MINUTES)

Solubility describes the ability of solutes, such as salt, to dissolve in solvents, such as water. Each compound has a specific solubility in a given solvent. This solubility varies with factors such as temperature, concentration, and pressure. In water, *ionic compounds* break apart into their positively and negatively charged ions up to a given *saturation point*, after which no more solid can dissolve. Gas molecules, however, remain intact in solution and spread throughout the solvent.

Different amounts of the ionic solid sodium chloride, $NaCl$, were added into a beaker containing 100mL of water at 10°C and 1 atm of pressure. The concentrations of the resulting ions are recorded in Table 1. The procedure was repeated with another ionic compound, cesium sulfate, $Ce_2(SO_4)_3$. The data are shown in Table 2.

Table 1

[**$NaCl$**] added (g)	[**Na^+**] (g/mL)	[**Cl^-**] (g/mL)
20	20	20
30	30	30
40	34	34
50	34	34

Table 2

$Ce_2(SO_4)_3$ added (g)	[**Ce^{2+}**] (g/mL)	[**SO_4^{2-}**] (g/mL)
6	12	24
8	16	24
10	20	30
12	20	30

Changes in temperature can cause deviations in solubility, depending on the compound. Figure 1 shows the solubilities of $NaCl$ and $Ce_2(SO_4)_3$ in water at 1 atm of pressure as functions of water temperature.

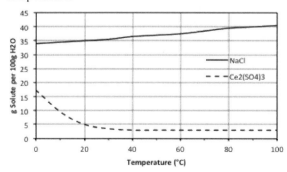

Figure 1

In contrast to ionic solids, gases often exhibit different behaviors when dissolved in liquids. One factor affecting gas solubility in water is *polarity*, or distribution of charge in the molecules. For instance, polar gases dissolve well in water, while nonpolar gases do not. Figure 2 shows the solubility curves for two gases, chlorine, Cl_2, and sulfur dioxide, SO_2, in water at 1 atm of pressure as functions of water temperature.

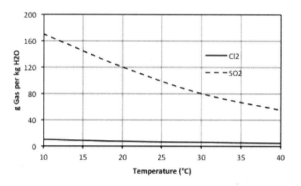

Figure 2

The effects of pressure on solubility in water depend on the nature of the solute. For instance, gases behave differently with respect to pressure than do solids. Figure 3 plots the solubility of chlorine gas relative to the solubility of solid sodium chloride as a function of pressure. Both solutes are in separate containers of 100 g of water held constant at 10°C.

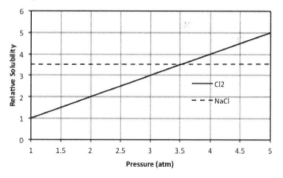

Figure 3

6. Twenty grams of $Ce_2(SO_4)_3$ are dissolved in 100 mL of water at 10°C and 1 atm. What is the total amount of dissolved ions in the solution?

(A) 40 grams
(B) 50 grams
(C) 60 grams
(D) 100 grams

7. Based on the plot in Figure 2 one can conclude that:

    (A) Chlorine is more polar than sulfur dioxide.
    (B) Sulfur dioxide is more polar than chlorine.
    (C) Chlorine is equally as polar as sulfur dioxide.
    (D) No relationship can be determined.

8. A common rule in chemistry regarding solubility is that "like dissolves like," that is, polar solutes are more soluble in polar solvents, and nonpolar solutes are more soluble in nonpolar solvents. Hexane, a nonpolar solvent, is mixed with 10 grams of chlorine and 10 grams of sulfur dioxide in separate containers at 25°C and 1 atm. Upon letting the solutions settle for several minutes, one would find that:

    (A) The sulfur dioxide–hexane solution has a greater ratio of dissolved solute to undissolved solute than does the chlorine–hexane solution.
    (B) The chlorine–hexane solution has a smaller ratio of dissolved solute to undissolved solute than does the sulfur dioxide–hexane solution.
    (C) The sulfur dioxide–hexane solution has a smaller ratio of dissolved solute to undissolved solute than does the chlorine–hexane solution.
    (D) Both hexane solutions have equal ratios of dissolved solute to undissolved solute.

9. Which of the following answer choices lists the compounds in order of increasing solubility in water at 20°C and 1 atm?

    (A) Sodium chloride, cesium sulfate, sulfur dioxide, chlorine
    (B) Sulfur dioxide, sodium chloride, chlorine, cesium sulfate
    (C) Cesium sulfate, chlorine, sodium chloride, sulfur dioxide
    (D) Chlorine, cesium sulfate, sulfur dioxide, sodium chloride

10. If one were to increase the pressure in Figure 1 to 5 atm, one would find that:

    (A) The line for the sodium chloride solution becomes exponential, and the curve for the cesium sulfate solution remains unchanged.
    (B) The curve for the cesium sulfate solution becomes linear, and the line for the sodium chloride solution remains unchanged.
    (C) The line for the sodium chloride solution becomes exponential, and the curve for the cesium sulfate solution becomes linear.
    (D) The curve for the cesium sulfate solution and the line for the sodium chloride solution remain unchanged.

sP4B

Directions: The following two passages are similar to real ACT test passages. Read each passage and answer the questions that follow. Use the methods and techniques that you learned in the instructions of this lesson.

HOMEWORK PASSAGE 1 (TIME: 4 MINUTES)

Proponents of global warming often use data relating various measures of Earth's environment to support their claims. Three of the claims supporters make include:

Claim 1: We know the Earth has been heating up because of increasing global temperatures over the past century.

Claim 2: The rising temperatures of the Earth are due to the increasing amounts of greenhouse gases like carbon dioxide trapped in our atmoshpere, caused by their release from significantly increased fuel emissions.

Claim 3: The increasing temperatures, in turn, have caused and will continue to cause significant changes to Earth's climate, such as more frequent extreme and catastrophic weather, receding ice glaciers, and shrinking ozone levels in the atmosphere.

Figure 1 shows the global glacier mass balance over the past 150 years. (*mm w.e.* = millimeters of water equivalents.)

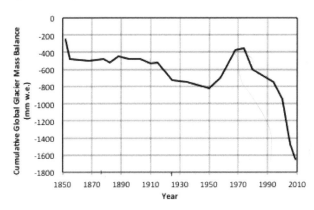

Figure 1

Figure 2 shows the changes in expected global, northern, and southern hemisphere temperatures from 1980 to 2000.

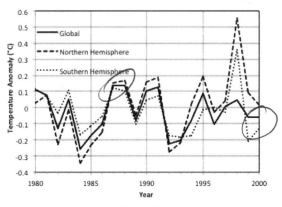

Figure 2

Figure 3 plots the global carbon dioxide emissions from 1970 to 2001.

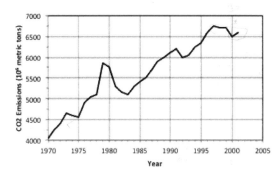

Figure 3

Figure 4 shows the annual number of deaths in the United States caused directly by tornadoes (direct death) from 1873 to 2009. An example of an indirect death would be falling while attempting to take shelter during a tornado.

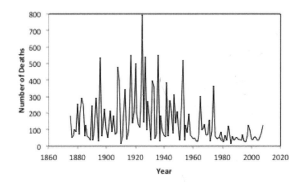

Figure 4

1. Which of the three claims for global warming are NOT supported by the data presented in the passage?

   (A) Claim 1
   (B) Claim 2
   (C) Claim 3
   (D) All of the above claims are supported by the data in the passage.

2. Which of the following points are NOT supported by the data presented in Figure 2?

   (A) The change in southern hemisphere, northern hemisphere, and global temperatures has relatively been the same for most of the period from 1980 to 2000.
   (B) Global temperatures significantly increased from 1997 to 1998.
   (C) From 1985 to 1995, the southern hemisphere went from having the greatest change in temperature to the lowest change in temperature of the three categories.
   (D) The change in global temperatures has remained constant at least twice from 1980 to 2000.

3. Which of the following conclusions can be drawn from the data presented in the passage?

   (A) Significant increases in northern and southern hemisphere temperatures from 1997 to 1998 may have caused the decline in global glacier levels during the same period.
   (B) The steady rise in direct deaths from tornadoes from 1880 to 1925 may have been due to the rise in global temperatures during the same period.
   (C) The gradual decline in global glacier levels from 1850 to 1950 may have been due to rising global temperatures during the same period.
   (D) The decline in global carbon dioxide emissions from 1980 to 1983 may be due to the decline in global temperatures during the same period.

4. Suppose some scientists found that levels of greenhouse gases in the atmosphere have actually been declining over the past ten years. How might this affect the strength of the claims and evidence presented in the passage?

   (A) It would weaken the evidence presented in Figure 3 by showing that greenhouse gas levels are actually declining, and not rising.
   (B) It would weaken the evidence presented in Figure 2 by showing that rising global temperatures have not actually been caused by rising carbon dioxide emissions.
   (C) It would weaken Claim 3 by showing that declining global glacier levels have not actually been caused by rising carbon dioxide emissions.
   (D) It would have no effect on the data presented in the passage.

5. Based on the data presented in the passage:

   (A) From 1995 to 1998, the Cumulative Global Glacier Mass Balance is positively correlated with northern and southern hemisphere temperatures.
   (B) From 1991 to 1992, global carbon dioxide emission is negatively correlated with global temperature changes.
   (C) From 1970 to 2000, the Cumulative Global Glacier Mass Balance is negatively correlated with global carbon dioxide emissions.
   (D) From 1880 to 1925, the Cumulative Global Glacier Mass Balance shows no correlation with number of direct deaths from tornadoes in the United States.

HOMEWORK PASSAGE 2 (TIME: 5 MINUTES)

Transcription is the process in which DNA is copied into RNA by the enzyme *RNA polymerase*. It is initiated by the binding of RNA polymerase to a region of DNA called a *promoter*, which is required for the production of one or more genes.

An *operon* is a sequence of DNA containing multiple genes controlled by a single regulatory mechanism. In an operon, the transcription of some genes, called the *structural genes*, occurs simultaneously in series from the upstream to downstream direction. The transcription of other genes, called *regulatory genes*, produces molecules that bind to the region in an operon called the *operator*, which regulates the expression of structural genes. Figure 1 shows a schematic of a generic operon.

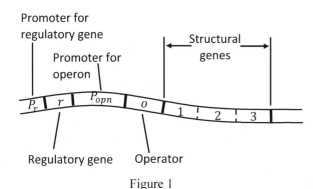

Figure 1

The *lac* operon is a set of genes used by the bacteria *Escherichia coli* to transport the sugar molecule lactose from the environment into the cell. It is also used to regulate its breakdown in the cell into galactose and glucose using structural proteins. The operon consists of two main structural genes—*lacY* and *lacZ* and one regulatory gene—*lacI*. In the following experiments, Genes 1, 2, and 3 are all part of the lac operon.

Experiment 1

A colony of *E. coli* containing a functional set of lac operon genes was streaked onto a petri dish containing a high quantity of lactose. Samples were taken of the bacteria and petri dish media every 30 minutes to determine the concentration of structural proteins produced and lactose in the media, respectively. The number of bacterial colonies in the dish was also recorded every 30 minutes. Table 1 shows the data.

Table 1

Time (min)	[Lactose] (M)	[Structural Proteins] (M)	Number of Colonies
0	2.0	0.0	0
30	1.2	0.5	3
60	0.6	0.3	4
90	0.2	0.1	5
120	0.0	0.0	5

Experiment 2

The genome of an *E. coli* bacterium was altered to remove Gene 1 and its promoter, after which the bacterium was streaked onto a new petri dish containing 2.0 M lactose. The concentrations of lactose in the petri dish and galactose and structural proteins inside the cells were measured every 30 minutes. The procedure was then repeated with new *E. coli* bacterium, each missing an additional gene and its promoter. The following tables show the data.

Table 2. Missing Gene 1

Time (min)	[Lactose] (M)	[Galactose] (M)	[Structural Proteins] (M)
0	2.0	0.0	0.0
30	1.2	0.4	0.5
60	0.4	0.8	1.0
90	0.1	0.9	1.5
120	0.0	1.0	2.0

Table 3. Missing Genes 1 + 2

Time (min)	[Lactose] (M)	[Galactose] (M)	[Structural Proteins] (M)
0	2.0	0.0	0.0
30	1.2	0.0	0.2
60	0.4	0.0	0.5
90	0.1	0.0	0.7
120	0.0	0.0	1.0

Table 4. Missing Genes 1 + 2 + 3

Time (min)	[Lactose] (M)	[Galactose] (M)	[Structural Proteins] (M)
0	2.0	0.0	0.0
30	2.0	0.0	0.0
60	2.0	0.0	0.0
90	2.0	0.0	0.0
120	2.0	0.0	0.0

6. One can conclude from the results in Experiment 1 that:

(A) Lactose was needed for the growth of bacteria only.
(B) Lactose was needed so that the bacteria could produce structural proteins only.
(C) Lactose was needed for both the growth of bacteria and the production of structural proteins.
(D) Lactose had no effect on either bacterial growth or the production of structural proteins.

7. Which of the following conclusions can one most likely make from the results of Experiment 2?

(A) Gene 2 is responsible for the absorption of galactose from the environment.
(B) Gene 2 is responsible for the breakdown of lactose.
(C) Gene 2 is responsible for the production of structural proteins.
(D) Gene 2 is responsible for the regulation of the production of structural proteins.

8. Which of the following would most likely be observed for the concentration of structural proteins at 150 minutes in Table 2?

(A) The concentration would increase.
(B) The concentration would decrease.
(C) The concentration would not change.
(D) It cannot be determined.

9. If three bacterial colonies were observed at 30 minutes for the trials in Table 2, which of the following could be the number of colonies observed at 60, 90, and 120 minutes, respectively?

(A) 4, 5, 5
(B) 3, 3, 4
(C) 3, 4, 3
(D) 4, 5, 4

10. Suppose that Gene 1 coded for the promoter for the regulatory gene of the lac operon. If, however, Gene 1 coded for the regulatory gene itself, how could the results seen in Table 1 change?

(A) The concentration of structural proteins produced would decrease.
(B) The concentration of galactose produced would decrease.
(C) The concentration of lactose in the petri dish would decrease.
(D) There would be no change in the results.

11. Which of the following could represent the galactose concentrations inside the cells in Experiment 1 at 0, 30, 60, and 90 minutes, respectively?

(A) 0 M, 0.9 M, 0.8 M, 0.4 M
(B) 0 M, 0.4 M, 0.4 M, 0.9 M
(C) 0 M, 0.4 M, 0.6 M, 0.7 M
(D) 0 M, 0.4 M, 0.6 M, 0.6 M

C2 education
be smarter

Unauthorized copying or reuse of any part of this page is illegal.

sP5: UNDERSTANDING QUESTIONS

Directions: Read the explanation and examples below to learn about this lesson's topic.

TOPIC OVERVIEW

One of the best parts about the ACT Science Reasoning Test is the fact that many of the questions—around half of them, in fact—are very straightforward. These questions, which we call "Understanding" questions, only require you to figure out what the passages, charts, and graphs are saying; you do not need to analyze the experiment or situation at all to answer these questions. You can answer these questions quickly and with confidence, allowing you to save most of your time and energy for the more difficult problems.

Since the questions on each ACT Science passage tend to be arranged in order of difficulty (from easiest to hardest), the first 2-3 questions on a given passage will often be Understanding questions. To further help you recognize these questions, here are some examples:

- In Table 1, what is the temperature of liquid mercury at a pressure of 7.8 atm?
- Based on Figure 1, what percent of spider monkeys reach 30 years of age?
- Which value of Q corresponds to the given m and T values?

Read the following sample passage and the questions that follow.

SAMPLE PASSAGE

A 45-year old man went to his annual doctor's visit and discovered that he was overweight for his age and that his diet was less than adequate. He was eating too many carbohydrates, not enough protein, and way too many calories. Unsure of how to lose weight, he sought help from a dietician. To determine what course of action needed to be taken in his diet, the dietician had the man record his regular eating habits for three weeks. After the third week, he and the dietician sat down and came up with rough averages for his weekly intake of calories and nutrients. The man told the dietician that some of his numbers would be higher on Fridays because of the large meal he ate with his coworkers after work. During this meal he always finished dinner with a large slice of pie. Below is a table showing his results:

	M	T	W	Th	F
Prot.(g)	40	33	45	41	35
Carb.(g)	500	488	505	515	580
Fat (g)	110	105	95	112	140
Cal. (kcal.)	3901	4103	4150	4080	4350

1. What was the man's average carbohydrate intake for Wednesday?

   (A) 488g
   (B) 505g
   (C) 95g
   (D) 45g

Explanation:

The correct answer is **B**. To answer this question, find the row for Carb.(g) and trace it to Wednesday. You'll see that the he consumes 505 g. Do not be confused by the term *average*. The numbers in the table are already averaged, so no math needs to be done.

2. It appears that there is a significant increase in the man's calorie and carbohydrate intake on Fridays. What explanation does the man provide for this increase?

   (A) The man eats large meals with his coworkers all week.
   (B) The man eats a large meal with a slice of pie after work on Fridays.
   (C) The man gave up on his diet.
   (D) The man changed his eating habits for three weeks.

Explanation:

For this passage we actually *do* need to look at the passage. If you scan the passage, you will see that the man explicitly says that he eats a large meal and a slice of pie every Friday after work. The answer is **B**.

Although most of the questions you see on the ACT Science Reasoning Test will be a little more "sciency" than this one, use the same strategy to tackle all of the Understand Questions you'll find.

sP5A

Directions: The following two passages are similar to real ACT test passages. Read each passage and answer the questions that follow. Use the methods and techniques that you learned in the instructions of this lesson.

PRACTICE PASSAGE 1 (TIME: 6 MINUTES)

Biotechnology is the use of technology to modify living organisms or processes in particular ways, such as the process known as genetic engineering. Genetic engineering in humans can be performed via germline gene therapy or somatic cell gene therapy. *Germline therapy* alters the genes in human sex cells, so the changes would be inherited. *Somatic cell therapy* would alter the genes of body cells, so changes would not be passed down to offspring. Below, two scientists discuss the use of genetic engineering in humans.

Scientist 1

Human genetic engineering can have remarkable and revolutionary impacts on mankind if utilized to its full potential. For one thing, it would make disease an enemy of the past. No longer would parents and grandparents forget their children and grandchildren from Alzheimer's. No longer would mothers and fathers have their lives cut short due to the brain-killing Huntington's disease. No longer would children have a significantly shortened lifespan due to Cystic Fibrosis. All of these conditions and more could be eliminated and prevented, allowing for individuals to live longer, more fulfilling lives.

What's more is that genetic engineering in humans can even prolong the lives of those who are already healthy, perhaps allowing them to live up to 150 years, thus, giving them the chance to further enjoy their lives and accomplish all their wishes and goals.

There are also financial benefits to human genetic engineering. Understanding and working with the nuances of biological mechanisms behind different diseases can lead scientists to develop drugs and therapies specific to an individual person's needs and body type to produce the best results with zero side-effects, a revolutionary breakthrough in the medical field. These new interventions would cost fractions of what the treatments of today cost, thus, ultimately saving millions of dollars spent in the healthcare industry, by both patients and providers.

Scientist 2

While the potential benefits of human genetic engineering do seem appealing, they cannot overshadow its significant harmful impacts, not only on the individual, but also on society. First, the manipulation, insertion, and deletion of human genes is done using viral genes, which have been known to fail and even result in the death of patients. Furthermore, we do not know the potential long-term ramifications of the gene-altering process. There have been no studies recording the health progress of patients over the long-term, such as 10 to 20 years after the genetic manipulation. Thus, human genetic engineering should not be widely utilized until its full scope of side-effects have been thoroughly studied and documented. Safety and health is a top priority and cannot be compromised for potential benefits.

In addition, over the long run, human genetic engineering may result in negative ramifications for society. Gene modification is a very expensive process in today's time that only those with sufficient funds would be able to utilize, either for themselves or their loved ones. These individuals may choose to eliminate or modify genes that confer advantages such as more attractive appearances, greater physical performance, or even greater intelligence. This would indubitably create undesirable social hierarchies that could result in unfair hiring practices, consumer insurance premiums, and school admissions, among others.

The impacts on society may not only be social, but also biological. Genetic engineering in the long-term may reduce genetic diversity and completely eliminate genes in humans that may unknowingly protect us from certain bacteria and viruses. Removal of these genes from the human species may leave us susceptible to such unknown threats which may result in our eventual extinction.

1. Scientist 1 believes that:

   (A) Genetic engineering in humans should be used with caution.
   (B) Humans can enjoy their lives to their full potential only through genetic engineering.
   (C) Human genetic engineering can completely eliminate disease on Earth.
   (D) All humans can live much longer, healthier lives with genetic engineering.

2. If germline gene therapy were found to be more safe than somatic cell gene therapy:

   (A) Scientist 1 would support it more than somatic cell gene therapy.
   (B) Scientist 2 would support it more than somatic cell gene therapy.
   (C) Scientist 1 would call for further studies of germline gene therapy.
   (D) Scientist 2 would call for further studies of germline gene therapy.

3. Which of the following is NOT a concern for Scientist 2?

   (A) Too much focus is being given to the advantages of human engineering, and not enough to the disadvantages.
   (B) We do not possess enough data about the long-term effects of human genetic engineering.
   (C) Individuals with money may choose to exploit the benefits of genetic engineering at the expense of other members of society.
   (D) Human genetic engineering may result in more deaths than lives saved.

4. Which of the following claims is NOT supported by Scientist 1?

   (A) Germline and somatic cell gene therapies can significantly improve the quality of life of individuals, as well as their longevities.
   (B) Human genetic engineering, though expensive, will save patients money in the long-run.
   (C) Treatments can eventually be produced that cause no negative side effects in humans.
   (D) All diseases worldwide can be eradicated.

5. Scientist 2 might respond to the claims made by Scientist 1 in the passage by:

   (A) Citing the number of deaths in genetic modification studies in primates.
   (B) Claiming that the long-term effects of genetic engineering on the human body are currently too dangerous.
   (C) Citing studies showing that the formation of social hierarchies in humans from innate individual differences.
   (D) Citing studies showing that social hierarchies lead to lower qualities of life for individuals given less social status.

6. Suppose Scientist 1 found a genetic modification study of one gene in five humans that lasted 12 months and resulted in no deaths. How might Scientist 2 respond to the finding?

   (A) By claiming that the study was not long enough.
   (B) By claiming that five people were too large a sample size.
   (C) By claiming that not enough genes were examined in the study.
   (D) By claiming that the study should be repeated with those five individuals.

7. Scientist 1 would most agree with Scientist 2 on which of the following?

   (A) Germline therapy studies should be given greater significance than somatic cell gene therapy studies.
   (B) The significant benefits of human genetic engineering should overshadow its current minor safety concerns.
   (C) Human genetic engineering will be much more commonplace in 10 to 20 years.
   (D) Human genetic engineering will have significant social impacts when used to its full potential.

PRACTICE PASSAGE 2 (TIME: 4 MINUTES)

Electronegativity measures the ability of an atom to attract electrons toward itself. Atoms with very large electronegativities tend to gain electrons during bond formation, while those with very small ones tend to lose them.

Differences in electronegativity between atoms as measured by the Pauling Scale determine the type of bond those atoms will usually form (Table 1). In an ionic bond, one atom fully transfers an electron to another. In a covalent bond, two atoms share electrons.

Table 1

Electronegativity difference	Type of bond formed
> 1.7	Ionic
0.4 − 1.7	Polar Covalent
< 0.4	Covalent

Figure 1 below plots the electronegativities on the Pauling Scale for the first nineteen elements. The electronegativities of the Noble Gases, which do not bond, are not shown.

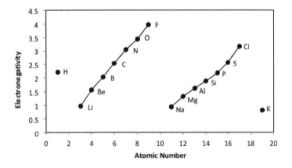

Figure 1

Atomic radius is a measure of the size of an atom, or the distance between an atom's nucleus and its outermost electron. Figure 2 plots the atomic radii of the first nineteen elements.

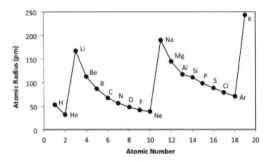

Figure 2

Ionization energy is the energy required to remove an outer electron from a neutral atom. The first ionization energy is the energy required to remove the outermost electron. Figure 3 plots the first ionization energies of the first nineteen elements.

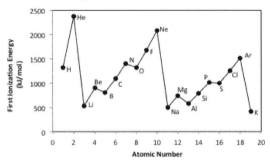

Figure 3

8. Based on the data in Table 1 and Figure 1, which type of bond would C most likely form with O?

(A) Ionic
(B) Polar covalent
(C) Covalent
(D) No bond

9. Based on the data in Table 1 and Figure 1, what would the Pauling Scale electronegativity of an atom have to be to form an ionic bond with Na?

(A) Less than 1.7
(B) Greater than 1.7
(C) Less than 2.7
(D) Greater than 2.7

10. The element with an atomic number of 20 would be expected to have:

(A) atomic radius less than 250 pm, and first ionization energy greater than 500 kJ/mol.
(B) atomic radius greater than 250 pm, and first ionization energy less than 500 kJ/mol.
(C) atomic radius less than 250 pm, and first ionization energy less than 500 kJ/mol.
(D) atomic radius greater than 250 pm, and first ionization energy greater than 500 kJ/mol.

11. Which of the following conclusions CANNOT be drawn from Figure 3?

(A) The element with an atomic number of 20 would be likely to have a first ionization energy greater than 500 kJ/mol.
(B) With a few exceptions, first ionization energy generally increases as atomic radius increases.
(C) Within a given period (a repeated portion of the graph), first ionization energy generally increases as atomic number increases.
(D) With a few exceptions, first ionization energy generally decreases as electronegativity decreases.

12. If Figure 2 were extended to include all currently known elements, and a student measured the atomic radius of an element to be approximately 200 pm, can the student assume that she would be able to identify the element?

(A) Yes, because each element has a unique electronegativity value.
(B) No, because in order to identify an element, you need the electronegativity as well as the atomic radius.
(C) Yes, because there is only one element with an atomic radius in that range.
(D) No, because there may be more than one element with an atomic radius in that range.

sP5B

Directions: The following two passages are similar to real ACT test passages. Read each passage and answer the questions that follow. Use the methods and techniques that you learned in the instructions of this lesson.

HOMEWORK PASSAGE 1 (TIME: 5 MINUTES)

The Doppler Effect is the change in frequency of a wave experienced by an observer moving relative to the source of the wave. The degree to which it affects the observed frequency depends on the *relative velocity*, or net difference in velocity, between the observer and the source of the wave. When two objects are moving in opposite directions, their relative velocity is the sum of their velocities, given that those velocities have opposite signs; when two objects are moving in the same direction, their relative velocity is the difference between their velocities. In the following experiments, two friends study the Doppler Effect through sound.

Experiment 1

Jamie drives a car at a constant speed of 20 m/s toward Ken, who stands at a fixed point. While driving, Jamie honks the car horn the entire time at a constant frequency. Ken records the horn frequency he observes as the car approaches him and as it moves away from him after it passes by. The two repeat several trials of the experiment using varying horn frequencies. Their data are shown in Table 1.

Table 1

Trial	Horn Frequency (Hz)	Observed Approaching Frequency (Hz)	Observed Passing Frequency (Hz)
1	400	425	378
2	425	450	402
3	450	478	425
4	475	504	449
5	500	531	472

Experiment 2

The two friends repeat the set of trials, this time using a constant horn frequency of 400 Hz and varying Jamie's speed in the car. Table 2 shows the results.

Table 2

Trial	Jamie's Speed (m/s)	Observed Approaching Frequency (Hz)	Observed Passing Frequency (Hz)
1	10	412	389
2	15	418	383
3	20	425	378
4	25	431	373
5	30	438	368

Experiment 3

Ken now decides to record the observed horn frequencies while driving his own car *away* from Jamie. For each trial Jamie drives at a constant speed of 20 m/s towards Ken and blows the horn at a constant 400 Hz. Ken, however, varies his speed each time. Table 3 lists the data. No passing frequencies were recorded for Trials 3 through 5, since Ken's speed was equal to or greater than Jamie's.

Table 3

Trial	Ken's Speed (m/s)	Observed Approaching Frequency (Hz)	Observed Passing Frequency (Hz)
1	10	412	389
2	15	406	394
3	20	400	–
4	25	394	–
5	30	388	–

Experiment 4

Ken now decides to record the observed frequencies while driving *toward* Jamie, who is also driving toward Ken at a constant speed of 20 m/s and honking the car horn at a constant frequency of 400 Hz. Ken varies his car speed each trial. Their results are shown in Table 4.

Table 4

Trial	Ken's Speed (m/s)	Observed Approaching Frequency (Hz)	Observed Passing Frequency (Hz)
1	20	450	356
2	25	456	350
3	30	462	345
4	35	468	339
5	40	474	334

1. Which of the following conclusions can be drawn from the results of Experiment 1?

    (A) When the source of a sound is moving toward the observer, the sound is observed at a lower frequency; when the source is moving away from the observer, the sound is observed at a higher frequency.
    (B) The difference between observed frequency and horn frequency is the same for each trial regardless of horn frequency.
    (C) When the source of a sound is moving toward the observer, the sound is observed at a higher frequency; when the source is moving away from the observer, the sound is observed at a lower frequency.
    (D) The degree to which relative motion between the source of a sound and its observer affects the observed frequency is dependent on the speed at which the source is moving.

2. Which of the following statements is true about Experiments 1 and 2?

    (A) In Experiment 1, the car's speed is varied and the horn frequency is held constant, while in Experiment 2, the horn frequency is varied and the car's speed is held constant.
    (B) In Experiment 1, horn frequency is the dependent variable and observed approaching and passing frequencies are the independent variables.
    (C) In Experiment 2, the car's speed and observed approaching frequency are the independent variables, and observed passing frequency is the dependent variable.
    (D) In Experiment 1, the car's speed is held constant and the horn frequency is varied, while in Experiment 2, the horn frequency is held constant and the car's speed is varied.

3. Which of the following statements about Experiments 1-4 is NOT true?

    (A) Experiments 1 and 2 use a variable that Experiments 3 and 4 hold constant.
    (B) Experiment 2 uses a variable that Experiments 1, 3 and 4 hold constant.
    (C) Experiments 1, 2, 3, and 4 use both variables and constants.
    (D) Experiment 1 uses a variable that Experiments 2, 3 and 4 hold constant.

4. Based on the data in Tables 1 and 2, if Jamie drives toward Ken (who is stationary) at 30 m/s and honks a horn with a frequency of 500 Hz:

    (A) the observed approaching frequency would be 531 Hz and the observed passing frequency would be 472 Hz.
    (B) the observed approaching frequency would be greater than 531 Hz and the observed passing frequency would be less than 472 Hz.
    (C) the observed approaching frequency would be 438 Hz and the observed passing frequency would be 368 Hz.
    (D) the observed approaching frequency would be less than 531 Hz and the observed passing frequency would be greater than 472 Hz.

5. Based on the results of Experiments 3 and 4, if Ken and Jamie are both driving cars, and Ken observes a frequency lower than the actual frequency of Jamie's horn, which of the following would be possible?

    (A) Jamie is driving toward Ken at a lower speed than Ken is driving away from Jamie.
    (B) Jamie is driving toward Ken at a higher speed than Ken is driving away from Jamie.
    (C) Ken's car is stopped, and Jamie is driving toward him.
    (D) Jamie's car is stopped, and Ken is driving toward her.

6. The Doppler Effect works the same way for light waves as it does for sound waves. The table below lists the frequencies of different colors of visible light.

Color	Frequency (Hz)
Red	400 – 484
Orange	484 – 508
Yellow	508 – 526
Green	526 – 606
Blue	606 – 668

Based on the results of Experiments 1-4, which of the following situations could cause Ken to observe Jamie's green light as being more blue?

(A) Jamie and Ken are driving away from each other.
(B) Jamie is driving away from Ken, whose car is stopped.
(C) Ken is driving toward Jamie at a lower speed than Jamie is driving away from Ken.
(D) Ken is driving away from Jamie at a lower speed than Jamie is driving toward Ken.

HOMEWORK PASSAGE 2 (TIME: 6 MINUTES)

The existence of global warming has been a much heated debate for most of the recent decades. Claims have been made that either fully support it or refute it. Some critics have even claimed false and inaccurate retrieval and interpretation of data by global warming proponents to negate any evidence-based claims made in support of the phenomenon. Below is a discussion about the possible causes and viability of global warming.

Scientist 1

The changes in Earth's temperatures over the past decades should be no cause for alarm. Earth's climate has not just been changing over the past several decades, but since its very creation. Humans were not present during the planet's early ages, yet the global climate changed during those times as well. While ice ages have been occurring in 100,000-year cycles for the past 700,000 years, there have also been periods that were warmer than recent years, despite the carbon dioxide levels being lower than they are today. In the Medieval Warm Period between 1000 and 1300 AD, temperatures in the Northern Hemisphere were higher than those during the Little Ice Age from 1400 to 1900 AD. This shows that the global climate has been following a set pattern throughout Earth's history and that humans have no role in significantly altering temperatures worldwide.

Additionally, over the past hundred years, the number of sunspots has been increasing, during the same time which the temperatures on Earth have been rising. Thus, the data seems to suggest that the sun has also been playing a significant role in the times global temperatures have increased, providing further evidence that humans are not responsible for the changing temperatures on Earth.

Proponents of global warming also point to the "reduction" in global glacier levels as evidence of Earth's warming climate. However, there have been reports from countries like Canada, New Zealand, Greenland, and Norway that for the first time in 250 years, glaciers there are actually growing. This could not be possible if human activity had actually caused the global temperatures to significantly increase like many scientists have purported.

As a result, there is no need to worry about the growing fuel emissions on this planet. There is no need to preserve forests and plant life other than the sole reason of admiring nature's beauty and advancing the field of natural and medicinal science.

The Earth's climate is just following its own natural course, and there is nothing mankind can do to change that.

Scientist 2

Earth's climate has been changing periodically since its very beginning. Those early changes, which occurred without the presence of human beings, were due to natural causes or external forces, such volcanic eruptions, solar variations, and anthropogenic changes in the composition of the Earth's atmosphere and land. However, human activities emitting greenhouse gases like carbon dioxide and methane have significantly accelerated the changes observed in Earth's climate. It is this increasingly rapid change that is alarming, since it has dire consequences for the future of Earth's habitability and mankind itself. Therefore, humans must make a concerted effort to control emissions of greenhouse gases from activities like mining and driving to help restore the ozone.

There has been a general increase in the number of sunspots over the past century, which do raise the temperature of the sun overall. However, there have also been periods, such as the past decade, when the temperature of the sun has actually decreased, while those on Earth have still increased. Thus, the sun's activity cannot provide a viable explanation for the warming global climate, which leaves the ozone-depleting activities of mankind as the significant contributing factor to Earth's warming climates.

The average changes in Earth's glacier sizes have also served as evidence for the detrimental effects of human activities like burning fossil fuels and cutting down forests and plant life. While some reported year-to-year changes do suggest growing glacier sizes in some areas in recent years, when considered over a period of several decades, the data indicate shrinking glacier sizes for ninety percent of Earth's glaciers. From 1970 to 2010, the Cumulative Global Glacier Mass Balance decreased by more than a factor of four. This is a significant change at an alarming late and one that cannot be explained by Earth's natural or other external forces alone.

7. What is the main point of conflict between Scientists 1 and 2?

(A) Earth's global temperatures are rising.
(B) Global warming does not exist.
(C) Humans need to make an effort to control their ozone-depleting activities.
(D) Glacier levels are decreasing worldwide.
(E) Sci 2 is a comme

8. Scientist 1 would most agree with Scientist 2 on which of the following?

(A) Earth's global temperatures are changing.
(B) Wild plant life should be preserved for the advancement of science.
(C) Earth's rising global fuel emissions are a cause for concern.
(D) There has been an increase in size for all of Earth's glaciers.

9. Which of the following does Scientist 2 NOT believe could help lower the rate of global warming?

(A) Reduce fossil fuel emissions.
(B) Preserve forests and plant life.
(C) Restore Earth's glacier masses.
(D) Control methane-releasing activities.

10. Scientist 1 believes that:

(A) Forests and plant life should be preserved.
(B) Earth's global temperatures are not rising.
(C) Global glacier levels are on the fall.
(D) Human activity can cause a change in Earth's climates.

11. Scientist 1 may refute the claim of Scientist 2 that the Cumulative Global Glacier Mass Balance has decreased by a factor or 4 by stating that:

(A) Global glacier levels have actually increased on average from 1970 to 2010.
(B) Individual countries like Canada and Norway have actually shown an increase in glacier size.
(C) The methods used to collect and analyze data in the report were flawed.
(D) The report was only for select year-to-year changes and does not reflect the conditions of glaciers in the long-term.

12. Scientist 2 would most likely respond to the claim of Scientist 1 that Earth's climate has been following a pattern since it's early history by claiming it is:

(A) False, because external forces like volcanic eruptions have been present since Earth's very beginning.
(B) False, because the ice ages have only been occurring in cycles for the past 700,000 years.
(C) True, but that human activity over the past decades have significantly accelerated the rate at which global warming is occurring.
(D) True, but that Earth's early climate has no importance for the climates of today.

13. Suppose a new study found that the volcanic eruptions and solar variations in Earth's early history actually raised carbon dioxide to levels greater than measured in Earth's atmosphere today. This finding would most likely:

(A) Weaken the claim of Scientist 2 because it shows that the Earth does not currently possess dangerous levels of carbon dioxide in its atmosphere.
(B) Strengthen the case of Scientist 1 because it shows that changes in Earth's carbon dioxide levels occur cyclically due to natural forces.
(C) Weaken the claim of Scientist 2 because it shows that human activity does not have any effect on the levels of carbon dioxide in Earth's atmosphere.
(D) Have no effect on the claims of either Scientist 1 or 2.

sP6: ANALYSIS QUESTIONS

Directions: Read the explanation and examples below to learn about this lesson's topic.

TOPIC OVERVIEW

You have already learned about *Understanding* questions, which test your ability to identify facts from data in the passage. In this lesson, you will work with *Analysis* questions, which require you to analyze trends and draw conclusions from facts and data in the passage. Since Analysis questions require more advanced comprehension, they are usually more difficult than Understanding questions.

Analysis questions require you to look at several pieces of information to get the right answer. You may be asked to figure out how pieces of information are related to each other, whether they are presented in a table, chart, or the passage itself.

The questions on each ACT Science passage tend to be arranged in order of difficulty from easiest to hardest. The first 2–3 questions on a given passage will often be Understanding questions, followed by 1–2 Analysis questions. To further help you recognize these questions, here are some examples:

- Based on the data presented in the passage, if the radius of the pipe is doubled, the flow rate will increase by:
- Based on the results of Experiments 2 and 3, which of the following could be the rate of the reaction at 10°C using a 20 μM substrate concentration?
- Which of the arguments made by Scientist 1 were NOT refuted by Scientist 2?

SAMPLE PASSAGE

The *transition state* of a chemical reaction is a high-energy configuration which the starting molecules of a reaction undergo while changing from reactants to products. The rate at which a reaction proceeds is determined by the energy of the transition state. Table 1 lists the times to completion for four reactions. Reaction 1 undergoes the highest energy transition state from the four reactions.

Table 1

Reaction	Time to completion (s)
1	43
2	13
3	25
4	30

Explanation:

By scanning this passage, we see that it defines the concept of a transition state. However, if we continue to read the passage, we realize that understanding this term is not even necessary to answer questions about it. This is because the passage clearly states that the rate of a reaction is dependent upon the energy of the transition state. So without even worrying about what a transition state is, we can automatically know to look for a relationship between energy of the transition state and rate of reaction. This is all the information you need to begin answering questions about the passage. The purpose of the ACT Science Reasoning Test is to assess your science reasoning ability, not your knowledge of the subject matter; so don't get held up on unfamiliar vocabulary or ideas.

You will, however, be expected to answer questions based on facts and data presented in the passage. To answer Analysis questions for this passage, you will be required to recognize trends, evaluate relationships, and draw conclusions based on the facts and data presented in the introduction and in Table 1.

1. Which of the following pairs of reactions has the largest difference in transition state energy?

(A) Reaction 1 and Reaction 2
(B) Reaction 1 and Reaction 3
(C) Reaction 2 and Reaction 3
(D) Reaction 2 and Reaction 4

Explanation:

The passage states that Reaction 1 possesses the highest energy transition state. Looking at Table 1, we can see that Reaction 1 also required the longest time to complete, meaning that it had the lowest rate. Thus, we can deduce that there is a negative correlation between transition state energy and rate of reaction. Since the question is asking for the largest difference in energy, we must now look for the reactions that have the largest and smallest rates, respectively; in other words, the shortest and longest times to completion. By simply subtracting the difference in completion times between each pair, we can see that 30 seconds between Reactions 1 and 2 is the biggest difference among the pairs in this question. Thus, the answer is (A).

sP6A

Directions: The following two passages are similar to real ACT test passages. Read each passage and answer the questions that follow. Use the methods and techniques that you learned in the instructions of this lesson.

PRACTICE PASSAGE 1 (TIME: 4 MINUTES)

About 5% of a person's weight may not be from his own cells. Humans have large numbers of bacteria living on their bodies, such as on their skin and in their intestines. While bacteria can be harmful, most of those living on our bodies either do no harm or, in some cases, provide important benefits such as producing vitamins from food consumed; these bacteria are often referred to as *commensals*. Interestingly, the bacteria that we possess as commensals are heavily dependent on our ethnicities and travels. Thus, people who share ethnicities or have lived in, or even visted, the same places can possess the same commensals. Microbiologists surveyed five individuals for the skin and intestinal commensal bacteria they possess. Table 1 below lists the bacteria that the microbiologists were able to isolate from the skin of five individuals, while Table 2 lists the bacteria that the microbiologists were able to isolate from the intestines of those same five individuals.

Table 1

Bacteria	Individual				
	A	B	C	D	E
Corynebacterium amycolatum	X	X	X	X	X
Micrococcus luteus	X	X		X	X
Propionibacterium acnes			X	X	X
Staphylococcus aureus			X	X	
Staphylococcus epidermidis	X	X	X		X

Table 2

Bacteria	Individual				
	A	B	C	D	E
Bacteriudes fragilis	X	X		X	X
Clostridium innocuum		X	X	X	X
Enterobacter aerogenes	X		X		
Enterococcus faecalis	X	X			X
Escherichia coli	X	X	X	X	X
Lactobacillus acidophilus	X	X	X	X	

1. Based on their skin commensal profiles, which two individuals most likely live in the same area of the world?

   (A) Individuals D and E
   (B) Individuals C and D
   (C) Individuals A and B
   (D) Individuals A and E

2. *Streptococcus pharyngitis* is a *pathogenic* (non-commensal) bacteria typically found in the throat of children worldwide. In children of European decent, there is a very small risk (1:100,000) of a patient acquiring rheumatic fever after an infection by *Streptococcus pharyngitis* bacteria, while in children of Maori decent, there is a larger risk (70:100,000). The table below shows the incidence of *Streptococcus pharyngitis* and Rheumatic Fever in five individuals.

Bacteria / Disease	Individual				
	A	B	C	D	E
Streptococcus pharyngitis		X	X	X	
Rheumatic Fever		X			X

   Which of the following conclusions can be made?

   (A) Individual B is of Maori descent.
   (B) Individuals C and D are not of Maori descent.
   (C) Individual B is more likely to be of Maori descent than Individuals C and D.
   (D) No conclusions can be made based on the data and information above.

3. A sixth individual, Individual F, tested positive for both *Enterobacter aerogenes* and *Propionibacterium acnes*. This individual is most likely from, or has visited, the same part of the world as:

   (A) Individual A
   (B) Individual B
   (C) Individual C
   (D) Individual D

4. A Wood's lamp is a tool used by dermatologists to detect the presence of certain bacterial strains. It is especially useful for detecting bacteria of the *Corynebacterium* and *Propionibacterium* genuses, as these bacteria glow green and orange, respectively, when exposed to the light of a Wood's lamp. Which of the following results is most expected as a result of shining a Wood's lamp on each of the following individual's skin?

(A) Individual A's skin would only glow orange.
(B) Individual C's skin would only glow green.
(C) Individual B's skin would glow both green and orange.
(D) Individual D's skin would glow both green and orange.

5. Individual G tested positive for the same skin and intestinal commensals as Individual D with the exception of *Lactobacillus acidophilus*, a bacteria involved in the fermenting of sugars into lactic acid. Which of the following most clearly explains these results?

(A) Individuals G and D live in different areas of the world, thus the commensal bacteria found in their bodies are very different.
(B) Individuals G and D live in the same area of the world. However, Individual G is lactose intolerant and does not regularly ingest foods like milk that contain lactic acid.
(C) Individual G and D are part of the same family, hence the nearly identical commensal bacteria found in their bodies.
(D) Individuals G and D are of different racial backgrounds who both consume dairy products regularly. This explains the differing commensal bacteria found in their bodies.

PRACTICE PASSAGE 2 (TIME: 5 MINUTES)

The atomic emission spectrum of an element or compound is the spectrum of frequencies of electromagnetic radiation emitted due to the change in energy from the movement of an atom's electron across different energy levels. When an electron in an atom is excited, such as through absorption of energy from a collision with another electron, it moves from its ground energy level to a higher energy level. The electron then descends to a lower energy level, which causes the release of a photon whose energy is equal to the difference in energy of the electron's excited and ground energy states. Since each element has a distinct set of possible energy levels, each possesses a distinct emission spectrum that can be used to identify it in different compounds. Table 1 lists the characteristics of different types of electromagnetic radiation, and Table 2 the colors and wavelengths of the visible spectrum.

Table 1

Name	Wavelength (nm)	Energy (eV)
Radio wave	> 1,000,000	$10^{-28} - 10^{-24}$
Microwave	$1000 - 1,000,000$	$10^{-23} - 10^{-22}$
Infrared	$750 - 1000$	$10^{-21} - 10^{-19}$
Visible light	$400 - 750$	10^{-18}
Ultraviolet	$10 - 400$	10^{-17}
X-ray	$0.01 - 10$	$10^{-16} - 10^{-14}$
Gamma ray	< 0.01	$10^{-13} - 10^{-10}$

Table 2

Color	Wavelength (nm)
Red	$621 - 750$
Orange	$591 - 620$
Yellow	$571 - 590$
Green	$496 - 570$
Blue	$451 - 495$
Indigo	$421 - 450$
Violet	$380 - 420$

The following experiments were conducted to study the atomic emission spectra of different elements.

Experiment 1

The positive and negative terminals of a 30 Volt battery were connected to opposing metal plates in an enclosed chamber filled with hydrogen gas to create an electric field. One of the metal plates was connected to a heater whose power was set to 20%. The battery was turned on for 60 seconds, and the wavelengths of the resulting emission spectrum were recorded. The procedure was repeated using Mercury and Sodium. Table 3 lists the results.

Table 3

Gas	Wavelengths (nm)
Hydrogen	410, 435, 485, 655
Mercury	365, 405, 440, 545, 575
Sodium	330, 590, 620

Experiment 2

The procedure from Experiment 1 was repeated, this time setting the heater to 0% power. No emission spectra were observed for any of the elements.

6. Which of the following elements produced an emission spectrum with the MOST amount of energy?

    (A) Hydrogen
    (B) Mercury
    (C) Sodium
    (D) It cannot be determined.

7. Which of the following types of electromagnetic radiation were NOT recorded in the emission spectrum of Hydrogen?

    (A) Radio waves
    (B) Microwaves
    (C) Infrared waves
    (D) All of the above.

8. Based on the data presented in the passage, which of the following lists the colors in order of increasing energy?

    (A) Red, orange, green, indigo
    (B) Indigo, blue, yellow, red
    (C) Red, yellow, indigo, blue
    (D) Orange, green, violet, indigo

9. Based on the data presented in the passage, the difference in energy between the excited and ground states for the 410 nm wavelength emitted by Hydrogen is:

   (A) Less than the difference in energy between the excited and ground states for the 485 nm wavelength emitted by Hydrogen.
   (B) Greater than the difference in energy between the excited and ground states for the 330 nm wavelength emitted by Sodium.
   (C) Less than the difference in energy between the excited and ground states for the 365 nm wavelength emitted by Mercury.
   (D) Greater than the difference in energy between the excited and ground states for the 405 nm wavelength emitted by Mercury.

10. Based on the information presented in the passage, as the wavelength of a photon increases, its energy:

    (A) Increases directly.
    (B) Decreases directly.
    (C) Increases exponentially.
    (D) Decreases exponentially.

11. Which of the following could be the energy of one of the photons emitted from Mercury in Experiment 1?

    (A) 6×10^{-23} eV
    (B) 5×10^{-21} eV
    (C) 4×10^{-19} eV
    (D) 3×10^{-17} eV

sP6B

Directions: The following two passages are similar to real ACT test passages. Read each passage and answer the questions that follow. Use the methods and techniques that you learned in the instructions of this lesson.

HOMEWORK PASSAGE 1 (TIME: 5 MINUTES)

Young's Modulus, E, is a measure of a material's stiffness and represents the ratio of stress (pressure applied to an object) to strain (degree to which the object is deformed while under stress) on an object of a given material. Strain is also defined as the ratio of the change in length of an object under stress (ΔL) to the object's original length (L).

Materials with a large E constant can undergo greater stress without experiencing the same degree of strain than can materials with a small E constant. If the stress on an object surpasses its yield point, the object can no longer regain its original shape after the stress is removed. If stress is increased beyond the object's yield point, the object will remain intact, but deformed, up to its fracture point. Beyond the fracture point, additional stress placed on an object will cause it to break.

In the following experiments, a physics student compares the Young's Moduli of several different materials.

Experiment 1

The student places each of six cubes, made from six different materials, under a stress machine one at a time to exert pressure and records the cube's change in length (ΔL). The stress machine exerts a constant pressure of $100\ kN/mm^2$. He finds that after all the trials, one of the cubes broke, two deformed but did not break, and three did not change shape at all. Table 1 shows his data.

Table 1

Material	Length of Cube (*mm*)	ΔL (*mm*)
Rubber	10	10.00
Nylon	10	2.50
Oak Wood	10	1.00
Concrete	10	0.33
Steel	10	0.05
Graphene	10	0.01

Experiment 2

The student then uses the stress machine to apply different pressures to seven new cubes of different sizes and materials. He applies pressure to each cube until it breaks and records its yield and fracture points. Figure 1

plots the stress applied to each cube as a function of its strain. Table 2 lists the yield and fracture points of each material.

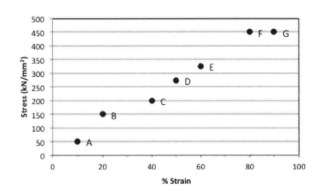

Figure 1

Table 2

Material	Yield Point (*kN*)	Fracture Point (*kN*)
A	600	750
B	800	900
C	550	650
D	700	850
E	700	775
F	650	750
G	650	800

1. If both fracture point and yield point are directly proportional to Young's Modulus, which of the following is possible as a result of Experiment 1?

    (A) The rubber cube broke, the nylon and oak wood cubes deformed, and the concrete, steel, and graphene cubes did not change shape.
    (B) The graphene cube broke, the steel and concrete cubes deformed, and the oak wood, nylon, and rubber cubes did not change shape.
    (C) The rubber cube broke, the graphene and steel cubes deformed, and the nylon, oak wood, and concrete cubes did not change shape.
    (D) The rubber, nylon, and oak cubes broke, the concrete and steel cubes were deformed, and the graphene cube did not change shape.

2. Based on information from the passage and on the data in Figure 1, which two materials have Young's Moduli closest to that of G?

   (A) B and C
   (B) A and C
   (C) B and F
   (D) F and E

3. Each of the seven materials in Experiment 2 is placed under a stress machine, which increases the pressure applied at a constant rate. Which three materials will take the longest time to go from yield point to fracture point?

   (A) A, B, C
   (B) A, D, G
   (C) E, F, G
   (D) B, D, G

4. Would the data for materials F and G in Figure 1 and Table 2 support the hypothesis that the fracture point of a material is directly proportional to its Young's Modulus?

   (A) No, because F has a higher Young's Modulus and a lower fracture point than G.
   (B) No, because F has a lower Young's Modulus and a higher fracture point than G.
   (C) Yes, because F has a higher Young's Modulus and a higher fracture point than G.
   (D) Yes, because F has a lower Young's Modulus and a lower fracture point than G.

5. The data in Table 1 and Figure 1 support the prediction that, for a given degree of strain experienced:

   (A) Material G could undergo greater stress than Material F.
   (B) Material F could undergo greater stress than Material C.
   (C) Material C could undergo greater stress than Material B.
   (D) Material G could undergo greater stress than Material B.

6. The student determines that an eighth unknown material, H, experiences twice as much strain as Material A, under the same degree of stress. Which of the following predictions is supported by the data?

   (A) Material H would have a yield point and fracture point higher than those of Material A.
   (B) Material H would be plotted directly above A in Figure 1, and would have a Young's Modulus higher than that of nylon.
   (C) Material H would have a yield point and fracture point lower than those of Material A.
   (D) Material H would be plotted directly to the right of A in Figure 1, and would have a Young's Modulus lower than that of nylon.

HOMEWORK PASSAGE 2 (TIME: 6 MINUTES)

Evolutionary game theory is an adaptation of classical game theory to biological models to describe organismal competition. A *game* is a simulation of the interactions of these strategies, the result of which can show how effective each species' strategy is.

One type of game, known as the Hawk-Dove game, models a contest between two organisms over a shareable resource such as food. The participants in the game are classified either as Hawk or Dove, not to indicate separate species, but different strategies played by two individuals of the same species. When it encounters a competitor for the resource, the Hawk contestant displays aggression and escalates into fights until it either wins or becomes injured. A Hawk will win half of its fights with other Hawks (winning the full resource), and lose half of them (winning nothing). The Dove initially also displays aggression, but if threatened into a fight by a Hawk, the Dove will flee for safety and obtain nothing, while the Hawk gets the full resource to itself. If a Dove meets another Dove, the two will share the resource equally.

Below is a discussion of two strategies for the Hawk-Dove game by two scientists.

Scientist 1

Because a Hawk will always attempt to fight for a resource, it always maintains a chance of getting injured. An injured Hawk would not be in optimal shape for its next encounter, which reduces its chances of survival. Doves, on the other hand, never incur any costs to their health. Even though they may not obtain a resource in one encounter, they will always maintain optimal health to acquire resources in other encounters, as well as to produce progeny. Thus, it seems logical to always employ the Dove strategy over the Hawk.

Scientist 2

It is not wise to always employ the Dove strategy. Even though a Dove will never incur costs to its health through encounters, it cannot survive for long without the resources it needs to survive and reproduce. Constantly avoiding aggressive encounters reduces a Dove's opportunities to acquire resources, which reduces its chances of survival over time. In addition, if it were always more beneficial to utilize the Dove strategy, then a greater number of organisms would use it. But this would dramatically lower the chances of Hawk-Hawk encounters and increase the chances of Hawk-Dove encounters, which favors the Hawk strategy. The strategy an organism should employ,

therefore, depends on the prevalence of that strategy in the population at any given time.

7. Both Scientists 1 and 2 would agree that:

   (A) Doves can never be injured.
   (B) Avoiding aggressive encounters is more beneficial than engaging in them.
   (C) Avoiding aggressive encounters is less beneficial than engaging in them.
   (D) If there are equal numbers of Hawks and Doves, a Hawk is expected to obtain the full resource in three-fourths of its total encounters.

8. In a population with more Hawks than Doves, which strategy would Scientist 1 recommend?

   (A) Hawk, because an organism should choose the strategy that is dominant at any given time.
   (B) Dove, because Doves have a lower chance of injury from encounters.
   (C) Hawk, because more competition results in more resources for each Hawk.
   (D) Dove, because Doves will obtain part of the resource in a majority of their encounters.

9. A certain group of individuals in a population has a mutation that boosts their aggression when injured, increasing their ability to win fights. Which scientist's argument would be weakened for this group?

   (A) Scientist 1, because Scientist 1's argument is based on the assumption that injury reduces an organism's ability to win fights.
   (B) Scientist 1, because Scientist 1 believes that the strategy an organism should employ does not depend on the prevalence of that strategy.
   (C) Scientist 2, because Scientist 1's argument is based on the assumption that injury reduces an organism's ability to win fights.
   (D) Scientist 2, because Scientist 2 believes that the strategy an organism should employ depends on the prevalence of that strategy.

10. Scientist 1 would most strongly *disagree* with which of the following?

    (A) Avoiding aggressive encounters does not reduce an organism's chance of survival over time.
    (B) The time interval between encounters with organisms using the same strategy is a factor in deciding which strategy is more advantageous in a given environment.
    (C) A Dove that meets only Doves and a Hawk that meets only Hawks would need to have the same number of encounters to end up with the same amount of resources.
    (D) In a Hawk-Dove encounter, the Hawk always has the advantage.

11. A researcher runs a simulation of the Hawk-Dove game, programming it to run according to certain parameters. Which of the following parameters would favor Scientist 1's suggested strategy?

    (A) The population starts out with half of the organisms using the Dove strategy and half using the Hawk strategy.
    (B) The probability that a Dove will encounter a Hawk is higher than the probability that a Dove will encounter a Dove.
    (C) Hawks win more than half of their encounters, but they gain fewer resources each time they win.
    (D) The recovery time for injured Hawks is increased.

12. A researcher runs a simulation of the Hawk-Dove game and finds that the numbers of Hawks (solid line) and the numbers of Doves (dashed line) fluctuate over time, as shown by the graph below. Which of the following is the most likely explanation of the graph?

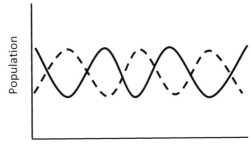

    (A) The researcher programmed half of the organisms to always use the Hawk strategy and half to always use the Dove strategy.
    (B) The researcher programmed each organism to use its starting strategy for a given period of time, and then switch to the other strategy, and then repeat.
    (C) The researcher programmed each organism to be more likely to switch strategies if its own strategy was the more common one.
    (D) The researcher programmed each organism to be more likely to switch strategies if its own strategy was the less common one.

13. A simulation is run in which the full resource in every encounter is worth 2 points. A Hawk encounters 10 Doves and 30 Hawks. What is the ratio of encounters in which it won 2 points, to encounters in which it won 1 point, to encounters in which it won nothing?

    (A) 10:30:0
    (B) 15:15:10
    (C) 30:10:0
    (D) 25:0:15

sP7: BEYOND THE GIVEN INFORMATION

Directions: Read the explanation and examples below to learn about this lesson's topic.

TOPIC OVERVIEW

The hardest questions on the ACT Science Reasoning Test are the ones that require you to go beyond the information and experimental results you're given and look at the bigger picture. You might be asked how events described in the passage may relate to situations not described in the passage or to predict the results of an experiment performed under different conditions. You could even be asked to assess the impact a finding might have on the real world.

The most important strategy for figuring out generalization questions is to discover a pattern that holds true for all the information in the passage. Once you've discovered the pattern, you can apply this to situations that aren't already included in the passage. Look at the passage below and the sample questions that follow.

SAMPLE PASSAGE

In biology, a *heterotroph* is an animal that cannot convert inorganic carbon to organic carbon for sustenance. Therefore, it must ingest, or consume, organic carbon from the environment, which its digestive system can then break down to use for energy. Foxes are heterotrophs that prey on other heterotrophs, such as rabbits, which feed only on plants. In an isolated area of the wilderness containing only rabbits and wolves, the population of each species was counted during different times of the year. Figure 1 plots the data.

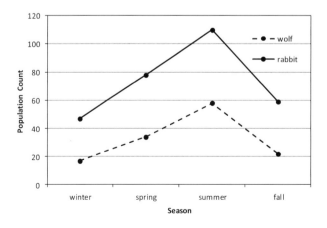

Figure 1

SAMPLE PROBLEMS

1. Autotrophs are organisms that convert inorganic carbon obtained from the environment into organic carbon for energy. The only autotroph present throughout the year in the passage is grass. During which season was the grass least abundant?

   (A) Winter
   (B) Spring
   (C) Summer
   (D) Fall

Explanation:
Looking at the plots in Figure 1, we can see that a pattern exists—the wolf count follows that of the rabbit. We can conclude from this that wolves are surviving on the rabbits. So as the rabbit population increases, so does the wolf. The opposite is also true. The passage also states that rabbits feed only on plants. Since the question stated that grass was the only autotroph present throughout the year, we can conclude that rabbits survived on grass during the year. So, where grass is less abundant, rabbit count will be lower. Since the question is asking for the season in which grass was least abundant, we can reason that it would be winter, which had the lowest rabbit count. So, **(A)** is correct.

2. If a bear were introduced into the wilderness, which ate only wolves, which of the following would occur?

   (A) The population of wolves would rise.
   (B) The population of rabbits would decline.
   (C) Plants would become more abundant.
   (D) Plants would become less abundant.

Explanation:
If a bear were introduced into the wilderness, the wolf population would decline, which would cause the rabbit population to consequently rise. Since rabbits feed on plants, plants would then become less abundant; thus the answer is **(D)**. Note that the other choices are based on identical reasoning. If the number of wolves rose, then the rabbit count would decrease, which would then allow the grass to become more abundant. So, none of them can be correct. You can apply this same strategy to many questions in which multiple answer choices are obtained from the same reasoning or say the same thing.

sP7A

Directions: The following two passages are similar to real ACT test passages. Read each passage and answer the questions that follow. Use the methods and techniques that you learned in the instructions of this lesson.

PRACTICE PASSAGE 1 (TIME: 5 MINUTES)

In sexual reproduction in animals, a process known as chromosomal crossover occurs, in which maternal and paternal DNA are exchanged in *homologous chromosomes*--chromosomes that contain the same genes (e.g., eye color) but may have different traits for the same gene (e.g., blue vs. brown). The exchange produces new recombinant DNA in the offspring, so that it is possible for offspring to have combinations of alleles that were not found in the parents.

If two genes on the same chromosome are far apart, there is a greater chance that crossover will occur at some point on the chromosome in between the two genes, separating them as if they were on different chromosomes. The closer two genes are on a chromosome, the less chance there is that crossover will occur between them, which means their traits have a higher chance of occurring together in the offspring. Traits that occur together significantly more than should be expected if they were on different chromosomes are said to be *genetically linked*.

The *recombination frequency* — the probability that a given pair of genes in a DNA fragment will be separated as a result of chromosomal crossover — is directly proportional to the distance between those genes, measured in map units. One map unit represents a 1% chance of recombination, up to 50%, which is the recombination frequency for genes found on different chromosomes, and for genes found at opposite ends of the same chromosome. For example, two genetic *loci*, or locations of specific genes, that are 20 map units apart have a 20% chance of recombination.

In the following experiments, a student mates fruit flies to determine the relationships between various genes.

Experiment 1

The student mates a generation of fruit flies that have black bodies and scarlet-colored eyes. He compares the distribution of the different phenotypes of the offspring to the expected distribution, based on the parents' genotypes, if the genes were on separate chromosomes.

Table 1

Phenotype	Expected	Observed
Black body, scarlet eyes	360	354
Black body, cardinal eyes	120	125
Specked body, scarlet eyes	120	119
Specked body, cardinal eyes	40	43

Experiment 2

The student mates a generation of fruit flies that have black bodies and vestigial wings, and compares the distribution of the different phenotypes of the offspring to the expected distribution, based on the parents' genotypes, if the genes were on separate chromosomes.

Table 2

Phenotype	Expected	Observed
Black body, vestigial wings	90	116
Black body, curly wings	30	10
Specked body, vestigial wings	30	7
Specked body, curly wings	10	27

Experiment 3

The student mates fruit flies that have scarlet-colored eyes and vestigial wings. Table 3 shows the distribution of traits among the 800 offspring, in order of decreasing expected frequency, as in Tables 1 and 2. The ratios of the expected frequencies of the phenotypes are also the same as in Experiments 1 and 2.

Table 3

Phenotype	Observed
Scarlet eyes, vestigial wings	322
Scarlet eyes, curly wings	224
Cardinal eyes, vestigial wings	235
Cardinal eyes, curly wings	19

 1. The distance between Gene A and Gene B is 20 map units. The distance between Gene B and Gene C is 13 map units. What is the recombination frequency for Genes A and C?

(A) 33%
(B) 7%
(C) 16.5%
(D) It cannot be determined from the given information.

2. Which of the following conclusions can be drawn from the results of Experiment 1?

    (A) Black body and scarlet eyes are genetically linked.
    (B) Specked body and scarlet eyes are genetically linked.
    (C) Specked body and cardinal eyes are genetically linked.
    (D) None of the above

3. Before conducting the experiments, the student hypothesizes that no genetic linkage occurs between any of the fruit fly traits studied. How would the three experiments affect his hypothesis?

    (A) Experiment 1 supports it, but Experiments 2 and 3 weaken it.
    (B) Experiment 1 weakens it, but Experiments 2 and 3 support it.
    (C) Experiments 1 and 2 support it, but Experiment 3 weakens it.
    (D) Experiments 1, 2, and 3 support it.

4. Which of the following hypotheses could NOT have been tested in Experiment 2?

    (A) Black body and vestigial wings are not genetically linked.
    (B) The recombination frequency for black body and curly wings is less than 50%.
    (C) Black body and scarlet eyes are not genetically linked.
    (D) Specked body and curly wings are genetically linked.

5. Compared with the results that would be expected in the absence of genetic linkage, a fruit fly with a specked body would be:

    (A) more likely to have cardinal eyes and less likely to have curly wings.
    (B) equally as likely to have curly wings, and more likely to have cardinal eyes.
    (C) more likely to have curly wings, and equally as likely to have cardinal eyes.
    (D) more likely to have curly wings and less likely to have cardinal eyes.

6. A chromosome is shown below, with different genes at loci Q, R, S, and T.

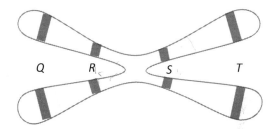

    Based on the results of the three experiments, which of the following sets of genes and their loci is the most plausible?

    (A) R: specked body, S: cardinal eyes, T: curly wings
    (B) Q: black body, R: scarlet eyes, T: vestigial wings
    (C) R: specked body, S: curly wings, T: cardinal eyes
    (D) Q: black body, S: cardinal eyes, T: vestigial wings

C2 education
be smarter

PRACTICE PASSAGE 2 (TIME: 6 MINUTES)

A mental illness or disorder is a psychological abnormality, often reflected in behavior, which causes distress or disability and is not a normal part of development in a person's culture. Currently, no exact explanation has been provided for the cause of mental illness, and many different hypotheses exist. Some believe that the emergence of a mental disorder is not due to a single categorical factor, but to a combination of them. The hypotheses below discuss possible causes of mental illnesses.

Hypothesis 1

The brain is made up of cells called neurons, which are activated or inhibited by molecules called neurotransmitters. An imbalance of these molecules can result in the abnormal activation or inhibition of certain neurons, phenomena that manifest behaviorally as various mental conditions.

Clinical depression, for instance, a condition of prolonged sadness, low self-esteem, and loss of pleasure, is caused by an underactivity of chemicals in the brain called monoamines, such as dopamine, serotonin, and norepinephrine. Therefore, treatment of depression involves medications called monoamine oxidase inhibitors (MAOIs), which prevent the breakdown of monoamines to raise their activity levels.

Schizophrenia, a mental disorder characterized by abnormal thought processes and deficits of normal emotional responses, may be due to the hyperactivation of dopamine in the brain. Drugs called phenothiazines block dopamine function and can, consequently, help reduce the psychotic symptoms of schizophrenia.

Hypothesis 2

The development of mental illness may be due to factors surrounding birth and pregnancy. Maternal exposure to serious infections or famine, along with birth complications and fetal exposure to alcohol and other drugs, can significantly affect specific areas of the fetal brain during gestation. Abnormal brain development can, in turn, lead to the emergence of various mental disorders.

Birth weight also maintains a significant influence on a child's survival and overall health and is affected by demographic and socioeconomic factors, prenatal behavioral and environmental factors, as well as medical factors that may or may not be related to pregnancy. In some cases, babies are born prematurely, which has been associated with nearly half of all neurological birth defects reported.

Hypothesis 3

Social and environmental influences, including neglect, abuse, bullying, or other significant adverse life experiences can lead to the development of mental illness. Other factors like relationship issues, problems with communities and cultures, poverty, unemployment, and lack of social support can also lead to the development of mental disorders.

These negative life events have been implicated in the development of mood and anxiety disorders. While it is usually the accumulation of multiple such experiences over time that lead to mental illness, single major traumatic experiences can also result in mental disorders like posttraumatic stress disorder (PTSD), a severe anxiety disorder.

A person's resilience to these social and environmental events can vary, not only from one event to another, but also from one person to another. Any individual's resilience can be influenced by numerous factors, such as cognitive set and coping patterns, genetic vulnerability, temperamental characteristics, as well as other experiences.

7. Hypothesis 1 states that:

   (A) A disequilibrium of certain molecules in the brain leads to the development of mental disorders.
   (B) Depression is due to the hyperactivity of monoamines in the brain.
   (C) Schizophrenia is mainly due to the hyperactivation of dopamine in the brain.
   (D) Low self-esteem and loss of pleasure is due to an underactivity of monoamines in the brain.

8. Hypothesis 3 does NOT state that:

   (A) Prolonged and multiple episodes of bullying, neglect, and abuse can lead to the development of mental illness.
   (B) A person may be resistant to some forms of negative life experiences but susceptible to other forms.
   (C) Even a single major life event can lead to the development of PTSD.
   (D) Problems with significant others and members in a community will most likely result in the development of a mood or anxiety disorder.

9. Based on the information in the passage, one can conclude that:

    (A) Clinical depression is best diagnosed using a biochemical approach.
    (B) The development of the human brain can be significantly affected during gestation, but not immediately after birth.
    (C) Demographic and socioeconomic factors play some of the largest roles in the development of most mental disorders.
    (D) Environmental factors may contribute to the development of mental illness just as much as biological factors.

10. The main point of difference between Hypothesis 2 and Hypothesis 3 is that:

    (A) Hypothesis 2 mentions demographic and socioeconomic factors in the development of mental disorders, while Hypothesis 3 does not.
    (B) Hypothesis 2 deals largely with the social and environmental influences on mental health, while Hypothesis 3 deals largely with the factors surrounding birth and pregnancy.
    (C) Hypothesis 3 deals largely with the social and environmental influences on mental health, while Hypothesis 2 deals largely with the factors surrounding birth and pregnancy.
    (D) Hypothesis 3 provides examples of single major traumatic experiences, while Hypothesis 2 does not.

11. From the period of 5 months after birth to 15 months, the human brain starts to develop the ability to register and store visual stimuli. According to the information presented in the passage, which of the following will most likely be true if a pregnant mother consumes excessive amounts of alcohol during her pregnancy?

    (A) The child has a greater chance of developing visual defects or disorders as an adult.
    (B) The child may have a greater chance of developing schizophrenia as an adult.
    (C) The child has a greater chance of developing PTSD or other anxiety disorders as an adult.
    (D) The child may be at a greater risk of consuming alcohol as an adult.

12. Before experiencing serious relationship issues with his significant other, a 30-year old male was on a regimen of MAOIs for four weeks. Which of the following MUST be true of the individual at the end of the four weeks immediately before the relationship issues started?

    (A) He was suffering from depression.
    (B) He was experiencing a significant adverse life event.
    (C) He had underactivity of monoamines in his brain.
    (D) None of the above.

13. Suppose a female developed a mental disorder at the age of 40. Upon undergoing a full brain scan, she was found to possess a fully developed brain with normal activity levels of monoamines. Which of the hypotheses in the passage could help explain the cause(s) of her disorder?

    (A) Hypotheses 1 and 2.
    (B) Hypotheses 2 and 3.
    (C) Hypothesis 1 and 3.
    (D) Hypothesis 3 only.

sP7B

Directions: The following two passages are similar to real ACT test passages. Read each passage and answer the questions that follow. Use the methods and techniques that you learned in the instructions of this lesson.

HOMEWORK PASSAGE 1 (TIME: 5 MINUTES)

Escherichia coli is a bacteria that thrives in the intestines of warm-blooded animals. A biofilm is a group of microorganisms, like *E. coli*, that stick to each other on a surface. Biofilms are considered to be highly resistant to antibiotics for several reasons, including restricted penetration of antibiotics into biofilms, slow growth due to nutrient limitation, production of proteins in response to the antibiotics, and emergence of biofilm-specific phenotypes by the bacteria. A representation of a biofilm in a petri dish is shown below.

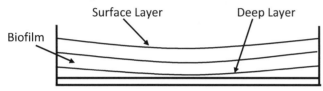

In a series of experiments, a scientist investigates the antibiotic susceptibility of *E. coli* cells in biofilms and determines which genes cause antibiotic resistance.

Experiment 1

The scientist applies three different antibiotics to *E. coli* cells in the *planktonic*, or free-floating, state and then allows the cells to incubate in two different media. She then collects the remaining cells at different times after the incubation. Tables 1 shows the percentage of cells recovered in glucose-deficient media, while Table 2 shows this for glucose-enriched media.

Table 1

Antibiotic	Early Stationary (12 hours)	Late Stationary (24 hours)	Late Stationary (72 hours)
Ampicillin	0.0%	0.06%	0.2%
Kanamycin	0.0%	0.08%	0.4%
Ofloxacin	0.0%	0.03%	0.8%

Table 2

Antibiotic	Early Stationary (12 hours)	Late Stationary (24 hours)	Late Stationary (72 hours)
Ampicillin	7%	98%	200%
Kanamycin	0.8%	83%	150%
Ofloxacin	0.8%	72%	140%

Experiment 2

The scientist then repeats the procedure from *Experiment 1*, except this time using an *E. coli* biofilm. She removes the surface layers of the film and administers the antibiotics in the deep layer. She then records whether cells were recovered at the Late Stationary Phase.

Table 3

Antibiotic	Growth Observed at Late Stationary Phase (72 hours)
Ampicillin	Yes
Kanamycin	No
Ofloxacin	No

Experiment 3

The scientist applies ampicillin to the *E. coli* cells at three stages of biofilm formation: attachment, colony formation, and maturation. She marks whether growth was observed during the Late Stationary Stage.

Table 4

Stage	Growth Observed at Late Stationary Phase (72 hours)
Attachment	No
Colony Formation	No
Maturation	Yes

Experiment 4

Next, the scientist administers ampicillin to a young *E. coli* biofilm and finds that 74.4% ± 7.8% of the cells were killed 24 hours post administration. She then repeats the procedure with mature *E. coli* biofilms using ampicillin, kanamycin, and ofloxacin and again records the percentage of cells killed 24 hours post application of the antibiotic (Table 5).

Table 5

Antibiotic	% Cells Killed
Ampicillin	44.3 ± 8.2
Kanamycin	93.7 ± 4.7
Ofloxacin	91.5 ± 3.3

1. Which of the following hypotheses was most likely being tested in Experiment 1?

   (A) Antibiotics are more effective in the absence of a biofilm than with a biofilm present.
   (B) Antibiotics are more effective when applied to the deep layer of a biofilm than when applied to the surface layer.
   (C) The percentage of cells recovered affects the formation of a biofilm.
   (D) The availability of nutrients affects the ability of antibiotics to kill E. coli.

2. If the results in Table 1 were presented in the same format as Table 3, would the table show that growth was seen with ampicillin after 72 hours?

   (A) No, because the rate of growth was less than 1%.
   (B) Yes, because the rate of growth increased by 0.2%.
   (C) No, because fewer cells were recovered than were initially present.
   (D) Yes, because more cells were recovered than were initially present.

3. Experiment 1 is repeated with the addition of a fourth antibiotic that, in glucose-enriched conditions, undergoes a delay before it begins to work, and then is extremely effective for a period of time, but wears off sooner than the other three antibiotics. Table 1 results for the new antibiotic would most likely read:
   (A)

Antibiotic	Early Stationary (12 hours)	Late Stationary (24 hours)	Late Stationary (72 hours)
Antibiotic X	0.0%	0.4%	0.9%

   (B)

Antibiotic	Early Stationary (12 hours)	Late Stationary (24 hours)	Late Stationary (72 hours)
Antibiotic X	90%	42%	6%

   (C)

Antibiotic	Early Stationary (12 hours)	Late Stationary (24 hours)	Late Stationary (72 hours)
Antibiotic X	0.0%	130%	2%

   (D)

Antibiotic	Early Stationary (12 hours)	Late Stationary (24 hours)	Late Stationary (72 hours)
Antibiotic X	220%	0.02%	160%

4. Based on the results of the experiments, what is the most likely reason that in Experiment 2, growth of E. coli was observed 72 hours after ampicillin was administered?

   (A) Not enough glucose was present when ampicillin was administered.
   (B) Ampicillin was administered too late in the biofilm's formation.
   (C) An insufficient dose of ampicillin was administered.
   (D) Ampicillin was not applied deep enough in the biofilm.

5. Experiment 3 is repeated with ampicillin replaced by a different antibiotic that is only effective when applied to a biofilm no later than the attachment stage. What results would be shown in Table 4 for the attachment stage, the colony formation stage, and the maturation stage, respectively?

   (A) "No, No, No," because the antibiotic prevents biofilm formation from reaching the later stages.
   (B) "Yes, No, Yes," because the antibiotic works when administered at the attachment stage, but not the colony formation stage.
   (C) "No, Yes, Yes," because the antibiotic stops E. coli growth only if administered at the attachment stage.
   (D) "No, No, Yes," because the fourth antibiotic functions similarly to ampicillin.

6. Experiment 1 is repeated with the addition of a fourth antibiotic that is effective even with limited nutrients available. How would its Table 1 results compare to its Table 2 results?

   (A) Its Table 1 results would contain percentages that increase over time, while its Table 2 results would contain percentages that decrease over time.
   (B) Its Table 2 results would have higher percentages overall than its Table 1 results.
   (C) Its Table 1 results would have higher percentages overall than its Table 2 results.
   (D) Its Table 1 results would be similar to its Table 2 results.

HOMEWORK PASSAGE 2 (TIME: 7 MINUTES)

Nuclear fission is a reaction in which the nucleus of an atom splits into smaller nuclei to release vast amounts of energy. The process is currently being used by thirty-one countries in 437 operational nuclear power reactors to generate electricity. Below, two scientists discuss the advantages and disadvantages of nuclear power.

Scientist 1

The world is headed in a positive direction by utilizing the capabilities of nuclear power. With the current growth rate of the world's population and its advanced technologies, natural and even renewable resources will become depleted, thus, rendering them an unviable long-term solution to the global energy and climate crises. Nuclear fuel, however, is virtually limitless due to the vast amounts of uranium available in the Earth's oceans. Additionally, advanced technologies of the future, like fast nuclear reactors, would further expand the available resource base through efficient use of fertile materials as nuclear fuel, such as uranium-238 and thorium. These reactors can also produce more fuel than they consume, allowing the recovered fuel to be recycled for even more energy. Some scientists have estimated that with these advanced technologies, Earth's total recovered nuclear supply can generate electricity for over 35,000 years.

Advanced fast breeder reactors and thorium-based fuel cycles can be beneficial not only for energy production, but also waste reduction. Both technologies output less waste than do current ones. So over time, the Earth can see a reduction in nuclear waste, helping to prevent further threats of radioactivity on the health of living species. Even more, these technologies would not directly produce greenhouse gases or other pollutants like sulfur dioxide and mercury, all of which are associated with the combustion of fossil fuels and negatively impact Earth and its inhabitants.

Scientist 2

Certainly many of Earth's precious resources currently being used for energy production will run out in the next several hundred years. Concerted efforts must be made to develop and efficiently harness the power of new renewable energy sources. While nuclear fuel may be an optimal, environmentally friendly resource for the future, perhaps a hundred or so years from now, it cannot be utilized efficiently in present times to halt the growing impacts of global climate change. Advanced nuclear technologies will require several decades for research, development, and optimization, by which time greenhouse gases will have significantly accumulated in

the Earth's atmosphere and perhaps caused considerable global weather changes.

One must also consider the exorbitant costs for the research and development of advanced nuclear technologies, and even for the continuation of current ones. Construction of a single power plant costs billions of dollars, money that can be invested in other promising technologies that can yield faster results, such as solar energy and cellulosic ethanol. Unfortunately, in countries like the United States, this is not the case. Rather, greater funds are being allocated toward nuclear research and development than to such renewable energy resources.

Finally, with the immense power of nuclear energy comes an even greater threat of nuclear war. Nations worldwide may engage in a nuclear arms race, one that increases the risk of nuclear attacks and threatens the safety of mankind itself. With the already increasing frequency of violent attacks on innocent people worldwide, one can only imagine what devastation evil forces may wreak if they acquire nuclear weapons.

7. Scientist 1 believes that:

(A) Nuclear fuel is the best resource for generating the world's electricity in the future.
(B) Nuclear fuel can be used to generate electricity for thousands of years due to its unlimited supply.
(C) It may take several decades of nuclear research and development to obtain efficient methods to harness nuclear energy.
(D) Uranium-238 and thorium are fertile materials than can be used as nuclear fuel.

8. Scientist 1 would disagree with Scientist 2 on all of the following EXCEPT:

(A) More money must be invested into renewable resources like solar and wind energy rather than nuclear energy.
(B) A global energy crises exists that will eventually result in the complete exhaustion of many of Earth's natural resources.
(C) Nuclear fuel is an optimal energy source for the production of electricity in current times.
(D) None of the above.

9. Scientist 2 does NOT believe that:

   (A) Several of Earth's natural resources used for energy production will run out in the coming centuries.
   (B) Positive environmental impacts from current nuclear technologies are not able to match the rate of current global climate change.
   (C) Nuclear fuel may be one of the best resource options for generating electricity in the future.
   (D) The threat of a global nuclear war increases with increased developments of advanced nuclear technologies.

10. Scientist 1 would most disagree with Scientist 2 on which of the following?

   (A) The development of advanced nuclear technologies will cause violent attacks on innocent people worldwide.
   (B) The accumulation of significant amounts of greenhouse gases and other pollutants may cause drastic shifts in Earth's weather patterns in the future.
   (C) More money must be invested into renewable resources like solar and wind energy rather than nuclear energy.
   (D) Solar energy and cellulosic ethanol may be favorable substitutes for nuclear energy in the short-term.

11. For some countries, nuclear power affords energy independence from foreign nations. Countries currently responsible for more than 30% of the world's uranium production include Kazakhstan, Namibia, Niger, and Uzbekistan, all of which are politically unstable and extremely volatile. This fact would:

   (A) Support the claims of Scientist 1 but have no effect on the claims of Scientist 2.
   (B) Support the claims of Scientist 2 but have no effect on the claims of Scientist 1.
   (C) Weaken the claims of Scientist 2 but have no effect on the claims of Scientist 1.
   (D) Have no effect on the claims of either Scientist 1 or 2.

12. The capacity factor of a power plant is the total amount of energy produced during a period of time divided by the amount of energy the plant would have produced at full capacity during the same period of time. According to the United States Energy Information Administration (EIA), the 2009 capacity factor for nuclear energy was 90.3%. This finding would:

   (A) Support the claims of Scientist 1 but have no effect on the claims of Scientist 2.
   (B) Weaken the claims of Scientist 1 but have no effect on the claims of Scientist 2.
   (C) Weaken the claims of Scientist 1 and support the claims of Scientist 1.
   (D) Have no effect on the claims of either Scientist 1 or 2.

13. According to a 2011 projection by the International Energy Agency, solar power generators may produce most of the world's electricity within 50 years, with wind power, hydroelectricity, and biomass plants supplying most of the remaining electricity. Scientist 1 would most likely respond to this projection by:

   (A) Claiming that projection is very unlikely since most funding for energy research and development is allocated toward nuclear energy and not other renewable energy sources.
   (B) Agreeing that wind power, hydroelectricity, and biomass plants are some of the best options for the generation of electricity in the future.
   (C) Claiming that Earth's rapidly growing human population will ultimately require greater electricity output than what is provided by these renewable energy sources.
   (D) Claiming that the usage of these energy sources to generate the world's electricity should slowly be phased out after the next 50 years.

sP8: DATA REPRESENTATION

Directions: Read the explanation and examples below to learn about this lesson's topic.

TOPIC OVERVIEW

The data representation section of the ACT Science Reasoning Test is the most straightforward of the three sections. It consists of a short introduction followed by one or more graphs, charts, tables, or diagrams. There are three data representation passages on the ACT, and each has five questions.

Understanding the information contained in the charts and graphs is much more important than reading the introduction in detail. You can always read the introduction more closely later if you need the information to answer a question.

As you read these passages, remember the C2 strategy for attacking ACT Science Reasoning passages: skim the passage, use charts and graphs for the main information, and then answer the questions.

Look at the passage below and read the explanation to see the techniques in action.

SAMPLE PASSAGE

Mixtures are material systems made up of two or more different substances mixed in a given ratio, or mole fraction, but not combined chemically. A mole fraction of 1 indicates a compound containing 100% of that substance.

A binary boiling point diagram shows the mole fractions of vapor and liquid concentrations of two substances in a compound when boiling at different temperatures. At any given temperature where boiling is present, the vapor phase of a component exists at a certain mole fraction in equilibrium with the liquid phase of that component at a particular mole fraction, often different from the vapor one. These mole fractions are both on a line of constant temperature, called an isotherm. The dew point curve represents the vapor mole fractions of two components in a mixture at different temperatures, and the bubble point curve represents the boiling liquid mole fractions of the components at different temperatures.

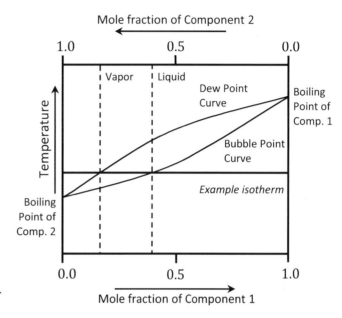

SAMPLE PROBLEM

1. 0.5 moles of Component 1, with a boiling point of 70°C, were mixed with 0.5 moles of Component 2, with a boiling point of 40°C. As the temperature of the mixture is raised from 50°C to 60°C, which of the following will NOT occur?

   (A) The liquid mole fraction of Component 1 will increase.
   (B) The liquid mole fraction of Component 2 will decrease.
   (C) The vapor mole fraction of Component 1 will increase.
   (D) All of the above will occur.

Explanation:

This passage and its figure may seem complicated at first, but upon further inspection we will see it is fairly understandable. First, the mole fraction of Component 1 is measured along the bottom axis and increases from left to right. The mole fraction of Component 2 is measured along the top axis and increases from right to left. This makes sense because as the mole fraction of one component increases, the mole fraction of the other must consequently decrease.

Now let's observe what is happening with the two point curves. The passage states that the dew and bubble point curves represent the different vapor and liquid mole fractions of each component at different temperatures. This means that as the temperature of the mixture increases, we must move to the right along both curves, since they are moving up and to the right. So as the temperature decreases, we must move to the left along the curves.

As we move right along both curves, we see that the mole fraction of Component 1 increases and that of Component 2 decreases. The opposite is true in the left direction. So, as we move right along the curves, the vapor mole fraction (from the dew point curve) and the liquid mole fraction (from the bubble point curve) must both increase for Component 1 and decrease for Component 2. This is all the information we need to answer the question. Thus, the correct answer is **(D)**.

Note that the number of moles of each component has no significance on the answer of the question. In the question, we start off with 0.5 moles of each component, meaning both of their mole fractions must be 0.5 (since the total is $0.5 + 0.5 = 1.0$). But we could've started off with mole fractions of 0.1 and 0.9 for Components 1 and 2, respectively. The result would still be the same.

We also did not need to concern ourselves with the dashed "vapor" and "liquid" lines in the diagram, as well as the *Example isotherm*. These are all examples of extraneous information that may be included to intimidate you. DON'T LET THEM. If they are not required to answer a question, just skip over them and move on.

sP8A

Directions: The following two passages are similar to real ACT test passages. Read each passage and answer the questions that follow. Use the methods and techniques that you learned in the instructions of this lesson.

PRACTICE PASSAGE 1 (TIME: 4 MINUTES)

Sports medicine is the study of how the body reacts to physical activity, as well as of the treatment and prevention of injuries. Numerous studies conducted on the three energy systems used by the body during physical stress have shown that different types of physical activity elicit different physiological responses from the body. Table 1 shows a summary of the systems, their energy sources, time durations during physical activity, and examples of activities that use each system.

Table 1

Energy System	Energy Source	Time Duration	Activity
Phosphagen	Stored ATP + creatine phosphate	First several seconds	100-m sprint
Glycogen-lactic acid	Glucose	First 60-90 seconds	400-m swim
Aerobic	Oxygen + glucose	From two minutes after onset of activity onwards	15-km marathon

In addition to using different energy systems, the human body utilizes different muscle fibers depending on the type of activity taking place. A summary of the fibers and their characteristics is shown in Table 2.

Table 2

Muscle Fiber	Contractile Velocity	Resistance to Fatigue	Metabolism
Type I	Slow	High	Aerobic
Type II	Fast	Low	Anaerobic
Type IIa	Fast	Medium	Aerobic + Anaerobic
Type IIb	Very fast	Very low	Anaerobic

Experiment 1

To study the effects of diet on athletic performance, an experimenter placed three groups of athletes on various diets for 24 hours: high protein/high fat; high carbohydrate; and fasting. He recorded their initial muscle glycogen levels and engaged them in strenuous physical activity for 2 hours. The athletes' muscle glycogen levels were recorded during each phase as a measure of muscle fatigue and recovery. The results are shown in Figure 1 below.

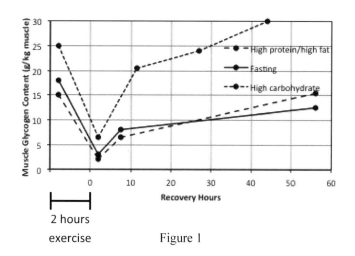

Figure 1

1. Two athletes run in a 10 km race. Runner 1 has the more efficient phosphagen and glycogen-lactic acid systems (together called the *anaerobic system*), but Runner 2 has the more efficient aerobic system. Which of the following would most likely happen?

   (A) Runner 2 is ahead of Runner 1 at first, but Runner 1 wins the race.
   (B) Runner 1 is ahead of Runner 2 at first, but Runner 2 wins the race.
   (C) Both runners start off even, but Runner 2 wins the race.
   (D) Runner 1 is ahead of Runner 2 at first, but both runners finish at approximately the same time.

2. A swimmer swims as quickly as he can for two minutes, and then swims at a sustainable pace for thirty minutes. Which types of muscle fibers was his body most likely using?

   (A) Type I for the first two minutes, then Type II for the remainder of the swim.
   (B) Type II for the first two minutes, then Type I for the remainder of the swim.
   (C) Type I only for the entire swim.
   (D) Type II only for the entire swim.

3. From the results of Experiment 1, the scientist could conclude that:

   (A) exercise depletes the muscles' glycogen more rapidly for someone on a high carbohydrate diet than for someone on a high protein/high fat diet.
   (B) exercise depletes the muscles' glycogen more slowly for someone on a high carbohydrate diet than for someone on a high protein/high fat diet.
   (C) exercise depletes the muscles' glycogen at approximately the same rate regardless of diet.
   (D) exercise depletes the muscles' glycogen for someone on a high protein/high fat diet, but increases glycogen for someone on a high carbohydrate diet.

4. Approximately how many hours did it take athletes on the high carbohydrate diet to recover to half of their initial muscle glycogen levels?

   (A) 0-4
   (B) 5-9
   (C) 10-14
   (D) 15-19

5. Experiment 1 is repeated with the addition of a group of athletes who are given a drug that maintains the body's muscle glycogen levels in the same state as in the absence of food, regardless of diet. At the beginning of the period of physical activity, what should the experimenter expect this group's glycogen content to be?

   (A) 15 g/kg muscle
   (B) 18 g/kg muscle
   (C) 20 g/kg muscle
   (D) 25 g/kg muscle

PRACTICE PASSAGE 2 (TIME: 4 MINUTES)

Over the course of millions of years, *hominids*, or "The Great Apes," have evolved significantly from their apelike ancestors. Bipedalism, or walking upright on two feet, is a basic adaptation of the hominid line and is estimated to have been present as early as 6 to 7 million years ago in the genus Sahelanthropus. Since then, fundamental changes have occurred in the human body as a result of changing environments and human behaviors. For instance, among other influences, colder climates led to the development of bigger hominid brains. Figure 1 plots the average cranial size for one lineage of hominids over time.

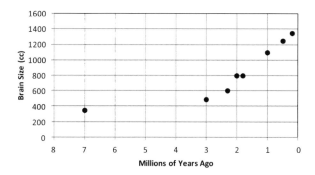

Figure 1

Larger and more complex brains allowed later species of hominids to complete more sophisticated tasks, such as constructing and using tools for hunting and daily living. These new behaviors, in turn, caused a shift in hominid diet patterns and body structure. Table 1 lists various tools used by hominids and their first dates of appearance. Table 2 lists hominid body characteristics and diet types for different time periods.

Table 1

Time (years ago)	Tool
2.6 million	Hammerstones
1.7 million	Stone Handaxes
790,000	Fire
500,000	Wooden Spears
100,000	Bone needles
70,000	Harpoons
26,000	Pottery

Table 2

Time (years ago)	Body Type	Gut Length	Diet
6 million	Short	Long	Plants
1.9 million	Tall	Short	Plants and Raw Meat
400,000	Compact	Short	Plants and Cooked Meat

Accessibility to new tools for protection and food storage led to hominid migration into new areas and the development of cultural practices, such as sharing resources and gathering around campfires. Table 3 lists several hominid species, not necessarily in the same lineage, their times of existence, and their geographic locations.

Table 3

Time (millions of years ago)	Species	Geographic Location
2.3 – 1.4	*H. habilis*	Africa
1.9	*H. rudolfensis*	Kenya
1.9 – 1.4	*H. ergaster*	Eastern and Southern Africa
1.8 – 0.2	*H. erectus*	Africa, China, India, Caucasus, Java
1.2 – 0.8	*H. antecessor*	Spain
0.6 – 0.35	*H. heidelbergensis*	Europe, Africa, China
0.5 – 0.35	*H. cepranensis*	Italy
0.35 – 0.03	*H. neanderthalensis*	Europe, Western Asia
0.2 – present	*H. sapiens*	Worldwide

6. Which of the following set of tools were most likely NOT used by *H. erectus*?

    (A) Hammerstones and stone handaxes
    (B) Stone handaxes and fire
    (C) Fire and wooden spears
    (D) Bone needles and harpoons

7. Using the data in the passage, one CANNOT make which of the following assumptions?

   (A) Stone handaxes may have been made by *H. habilis* in Africa.
   (B) Fire may have been made by *H. erectus* in China.
   (C) Bone needles may have been made by *H. ergaster* in Eastern Africa.
   (D) Harpoons may have been made by *H. neanderthalensis* in Europe.

8. *H. antecessor* may have had larger brains than which of the following hominids?

   (A) *H. habilis, H. ergaster,* and *H. erectus*
   (B) *H. habilis, H. erectus,* and *H. cepranensis*
   (C) *H. cepranensis, H. heidelbergensis,* and *H. ergaster*
   (D) *H. ergaster, H. rudolfensis,* and *H. neanderthalensis*

9. Using the data in the passage, one can most likely assume that *H. neanderthalensis* may have had:

   (A) compact bodies, short guts, and plant-based diets.
   (B) compact bodies, short guts, and plant and cooked meat-based diets.
   (C) compact bodies, long guts, and plant-based diets.
   (D) compact bodies, long guts, and plant and raw meat-based diets.

10. Which of the following is the best conclusion one can draw regarding the development of the hominid brain as time progressed?

   (A) The trend shows a directly proportional relationship.
   (B) The trend shows an inversely proportional relationship.
   (C) The trend shows a direct exponentially proportional relationship.
   (D) The trend shows an inverse exponentially proportional relationship.

sP8B

Directions: The following two passages are similar to real ACT test passages. Read each passage and answer the questions that follow. Use the methods and techniques that you learned in the instructions of this lesson.

HOMEWORK PASSAGE 1 (TIME: 4 MINUTES)

For a science project, a chemistry student is studying the relationships between temperature, pressure, volume, and number of particles for different gases.

Experiment 1

The student adds, to a sealed vacuum chamber kept at a constant volume and constant temperature of 300 K, 25 particles of the heavy gas A and 25 particles of the light gas B. He then measures the total pressure inside the chamber and average speeds of the different gases as a function of time for three minutes. His data are recorded in Figure 1. The average speeds of the light and heavy gases are measured along the axis to the left, and the pressure in the chamber along the axis to the right.

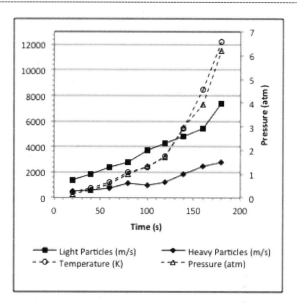

Figure 2

Experiment 3

The student then adds 25 particles each of gas A and B into a new sealed vacuum chamber held at a constant temperature of 300K. He manipulates the volume of the chamber and measures the corresponding change in pressure of the gas particles for three minutes. His data are shown in Table 1.

Table 1

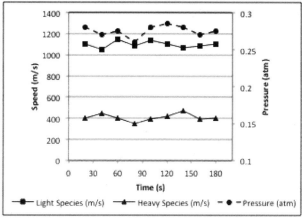

Figure 1

Experiment 2

In a new sealed vacuum chamber with an initial pressure of 0.16 atm, the student then adds 25 particles of both gases A and B. Keeping the volume of the chamber constant, he adds more particles of each gas continuously for three minutes, periodically measuring the temperature, pressure, and speeds of the gases. Figure 2 plots the data. The particle speeds and temperature are measured on the unlabeled axis to the left, and the pressure on the pressure axis to the right.

Time (s)	Volume (L)	Pressure (atm)
0	5.0	0.50
20	4.5	0.56
40	4.0	0.63
60	3.5	0.71
80	3.0	0.83
100	2.5	1.00
120	2.0	1.25
160	1.5	1.67
180	1.0	2.50

1. Which of the following hypotheses could have been tested in Experiment 1?

(A) Average speed of gas particles can increase over time even if volume, temperature, and number of particles are kept constant.
(B) When the number of particles increases, the average speed of the particles increases.
(C) When temperature is kept constant, pressure is inversely proportional to volume.
(D) When volume, temperature and number of particles are kept constant, light particles have a higher pressure than heavy particles.

2. The student repeats Experiment 2, with the addition of another gas, C, which is lighter than gas B. The average speed of the particles of gas C would be:

(A) lower than that of gas A and gas B.
(B) lower than that of gas A, but higher than that of gas B.
(C) higher than that of gas A, but lower than that of gas B.
(D) higher than that of gas A and gas B.

3. Based on the results of Experiments 2 and 3, if the student continued Experiment 3 after the first three minutes by steadily removing the gas particles while keeping the volume constant at 1.0 L, which of the following would be expected to happen?

(A) Pressure would increase.
(B) Pressure would decrease.
(C) Pressure would decrease, and then increase.
(D) Pressure would stay constant.

4. If the student continued Experiment 3 by decreasing the volume of the chamber to 0.5 L, the pressure of the gas particles would be:

(A) 2.00 atm.
(B) 2.25 atm.
(C) 2.50 atm.
(D) 5.00 atm.

5. The student wants to determine the relationship between the volume and temperature of the gases. Which of the following experiments should he perform?

(A) Keeping volume constant, manipulate the temperature in the container over time.
(B) Keeping temperature constant, manipulate the volume of the container over time.
(C) Keeping pressure and number of particles constant, manipulate the volume of the container and measure the temperature at each volume.
(D) Keeping volume and temperature constant, manipulate the pressure and number of particles in the container.

Homework Passage 2 (Time: 4 minutes)

Recently, scientists have discovered the reason for radioactive decay. Like electrons, nucleons (the protons and neutrons in a nucleus) exist at certain energy levels arranged in "shells." Nuclei that have precisely filled shells are more stable and less prone to decay.

While an element's name and atomic number are determined by protons, every element has different isotopes. Isotopes of a given element all have the same proton count, but different isotopes of the same element will have different numbers of neutrons.

Scientists have observed a variety of isotopes of different elements to note which are the most stable and which decay the most quickly. They observed a 1-kg sample of each isotope, noting the number of decay events each second and the total time for the entire sample to decay. Their findings are summarized in Table 1.

Table 1

Time to Decay Completely	Atomic Mass of Sample	Decay Events per Second
Infinite	4	None
7613.36 sec	24	8.56×10^{22}
806.39 sec	45	4.25×10^{23}
321.73 sec	91	5.14×10^{23}
0.315 sec	132	1.45×10^{25}
1.7×10^{-3} sec	216	6.20×10^{28}

The scientists then observed isotopes of krypton to note how decay rates progressed to see if they could find any samples that might be more stable. Their findings are summarized in Table 2.

Table 2

Time to Decay Completely	Isotope's Atomic Mass	Decay Events per Second
9663.10 sec	75	2.15×10^{22}
1.66×10^5 sec	77	1.24×10^{21}
Infinite	78	None
Infinite	84	None
6.05×10^5 sec	85	3.45×10^{20}
Infinite	86	None
3.84×10^5 sec	88	5.44×10^{20}
1213.34 sec	90	1.70×10^{23}
321.73 sec	91	5.14×10^{23}

6. If the number of decay events per second of an isotope of an element used in Table 1 were 4.87×10^{23}, then the atomic mass would be closest to which of the following?

(A) 38
(B) 73
(C) 103
(D) 289

7. If an isotope of an element took 503.13 seconds to fully decay, then, according to Table 1, its atomic mass would be closest to which of the following?

(A) 24
(B) 70
(C) 89
(D) 240

8. According to Table 2, the isotopes of krypton are:

(A) most stable when their atomic masses are 85.
(B) most stable when their atomic masses are between 78 and 86.
(C) most stable when their atomic masses are 75.
(D) least stable when their atomic masses are between 78 and 86.

9. From Table 1, you can conclude that:

(A) as atomic mass increases, the elements become more stable.
(B) as atomic mass increases, decay events per second decrease.
(C) as atomic mass increases, the elements become less stable.
(D) as decay events per second increase, the elements become more stable.

10. The isotopes of krypton represented in Table 2 are:

(A) least stable when the atomic mass is 85.
(B) most stable when the atomic mass is 91.
(C) least stable when the atomic mass is 91
(D) the least stable at atomic masses of 78, 84, and 86.

sP9: RESEARCH SUMMARIES

Directions: Read the explanation and examples below to learn about this lesson's topic.

TOPIC OVERVIEW

There are three Research Summary passages on each ACT Science Test, each containing six questions. Research summary passages consist of an introduction followed by descriptions of one or more related experiments. Most experiment descriptions will also feature charts or graphs that show the results of the experiment.

Questions in this section focus on the design of experiments and the interpretation of the experimental results. This may require you to identify the purpose of the research, the structure of the experiment(s), and the information represented by each variable. However, most of the questions will focus specifically on interpreting the results of the experiments.

An experiment or question may be complicated by a changed procedure or result. You must read each question carefully to understand exactly what is being asked.

Remember not to read the passage in great detail the first time through. Skim the text and get an idea of the charts and graphs. You will understand what details to look for in the passage after you read the questions.

For a demonstration of these techniques, read the sample passage below and explanation that follows.

SAMPLE PASSAGE

Friction is the force resisting the relative motion of solid or liquid surfaces against each other. A group of physics students study the effects of friction and angle of elevation on motion of various objects.

Experiment 1

The group places different massed objects on a 10 m long ice ramp at various angles from the ground. It releases the objects and counts the time they take to reach the end of the ramp. Table 1 lists the data.

Table 1

Mass (kg)	Angle	Time (s)
10	30°	2.0
25	45°	1.8
50	60°	1.6
10	45°	1.8
25	60°	1.6
50	30°	2.0
10	60°	1.6
25	30°	2.0
50	45°	1.8

Experiment 2

The students now cover the surface of their ramp with a 2 cm layer of oil. They again measure the times of various masses to travel down the ramp at different angles. Their results are shown in Table 2.

Table 2

Mass (kg)	Angle	Time (s)
25	30 °	4.5
10	45 °	4.0
50	60 °	3.5

Explanation

Focus on ideas that help you understand the design of the research experiments and their results. This will help you avoid getting stuck on unfamiliar vocabulary or ideas that might not be useful in answering the questions that follow.

Let's start by interpreting the experimental design. These experiments were conducted to investigate the effects of friction, angle of elevation, and mass on the movement of objects.

It is easier to interpret the results presented in the tables if you understand the experimental design. For example, an ice ramp was used in Experiment 1, while a ramp covered with oil was used in Experiment 2. Since the introduction states the students are measuring the effects of friction, you should assume that the ice and oil will likely cause different amounts of friction. To determine how much, however, you would have to look at the tables.

1. The students placed a fourth object on the ramp in Experiment 1 and found the time needed to travel down the ramp to be 1.9 s. Which of the following could MOST likely be the mass and angle of elevation for this trial?

    (A) 20 kg and 13°
    (B) 20 kg and 27°
    (C) 40 kg and 38°
    (D) 40 kg and 50°

Explanation:

If we look at Table 1, we see that the same three masses and the same three angles are used throughout. Thus, we can compare the times of any two trials while keeping one of the variables constant to figure out the effect of the other. If we do this, we'll find that time is independent of mass but varies indirectly with the angle. So to answer this question, we can ignore the different mass values in the answer and just focus on the angle values. Since 1.9 s is between 1.8 s and 2.0 s from the experiment, we can conclude that the angle for this trial must be between 45° and 30°. Thus, the answer is **(C)**.

2. The students conduct a new experiment in which they cover the surface of a new ice ramp of the same length with a 2-cm layer of sand. They find the time for a 30-kg object to slide down the ramp at a 35° angle to be 3.5 s. Which of the following shows the correct relationships among the friction forces F of the surfaces in the three experiments?

    (A) $F_{oil} > F_{sand} > F_{ice}$
    (B) $F_{sand} > F_{oil} > F_{ice}$
    (C) $F_{ice} > F_{sand} > F_{oil}$
    (D) $F_{sand} > F_{ice} > F_{oil}$

Explanation:

From the previous explanation, we know that mass has no effect on the time for an object to travel down a ramp, so we just have to pay attention to the angle. Since 35° is not an angle used in the passage, we have to look at the range it falls in—30° to 45°. According to Table 1, the times for these angles down an ice ramp are 2.0 s and 1.8 s, respectively. Table 2 shows the times down the oil ramp to be 4.5 s and 4.0 s, respectively. The question states that the time for the sand-covered ramp at 35° was 3.5 s. This falls directly between the time ranges for the ice- and oil-covered ramps.

But how do we determine which ramp had the greatest friction? The passage introduction states that friction is a force that *opposes* motion. Therefore, a greater friction will result in a greater resistance to motion. This opposition or resistance can be studied using the different times in the tables. An object will take longer time to travel a certain distance when facing greater resistance in its motion. Thus, we know that because the ice ramp gave us the smallest times, it must have caused the least resistance against motion. In other words, it had the least friction. By the same reasoning, we can figure out that the oil ramp had the greatest friction, and the sand-covered ramp a value in between the two. The answer is **(A)**.

sP9A

Directions: The following two passages are similar to real ACT test passages. Read each passage and answer the questions that follow. Use the methods and techniques that you learned in the instructions of this lesson.

PRACTICE PASSAGE 1 (TIME: 5 MINUTES)

Viruses have some of the most varied and obscure features known to scientists. For instance, whereas most living organisms only have one type of nucleic acid—*double stranded* (ds) linear DNA, viruses can have multiple types, including ds or *single stranded* (ss) linear, or circular DNA or RNA. In addition, viruses can have numerous *capsid* (structure containing the genetic material and proteins) shapes, including helical, polyhedral, or rod-shaped.

Viruses are combated in mammal species by special immune cells called *cytotoxic*, or killer, *T-cells*. These cells are made in the bone marrow and mature, or specialize, in an organ called the thymus.

Experiment 1

A scientist working in a laboratory infects each of his experimental mice with one of the four viruses listed below. To treat the mice with the proper vaccines, another scientist isolates the individual viruses to obtain characteristics to help identify them. Traits of the four viruses the mice have are listed in Table 1, and the second scientist's observations are recorded in Table 2.

Table 1

Virus Name	Capsid Shape	Genetic Material	Size (nm)
TMV	Helical	ss RNA	300
Adenovirus	Polyhedral	ds DNA	90-100
Influenza	Helical	various RNAs	80-120
Bacteriophage T4	Complex	ds DNA	25-200

Table 2

Virus Sample	Capsid Shape	Genetic Material	Size (nm)
Mouse 1	—*	ds DNA	—*
Mouse 2	Polyhedral	—	95
Mouse 3	—*	ss RNA	—*
Mouse 4	Helical	—*	100
Mouse 5	—*	ds DNA	98
Mouse 6	Helical	ss RNA	—*

*No data obtained.

Experiment 2

The scientist uses the character traits of his virus strains to administer equal amounts of a specific vaccine to each mouse. He records whether the reaction improved the health of (+) or had no effect (—) on the mice.

Table 3

Mouse	Vaccine Type	Reaction
1	Adenovirus	+
2	Adenovirus	—
3	TMV	—
4	Influenza	—
5	Bacteriophage T4	+
6	Influenza	—

Experiment 3

The scientist then extracts blood samples from the four mice to determine their virus and killer T-cell concentrations (*ppm* indicates "parts per million").

Table 4

Blood Sample	Virus Concentration	Killer T-Cell Concentration
Mouse 1	23 ppm	24×10^4 cells/mL
Mouse 2	55 ppm	24×10^4 cells/mL
Mouse 3	25 ppm	30×10^4 cells/mL
Mouse 4	57 ppm	22×10^2 cells/mL
Mouse 5	36 ppm	28×10^4 cells/mL
Mouse 6	22 ppm	35×10^4 cells/mL

1. Based on Experiments 1-3, which virus did Mouse 1 most likely have?

   (A) TMV
   (B) Adenovirus
   (C) Influenza
   (D) Bacteriophage T4

2. What is the most likely reason that the vaccine had no effect on Mouse 2?

    (A) It was not the correct vaccine.
    (B) The vaccine dosage was too low.
    (C) The virus concentration in the mouse was too high.
    (D) The killer T-cell concentration in the mouse was too low.

3. What is the most likely reason that the influenza vaccine did not work for Mouse 4 or Mouse 6?

    (A) Neither mouse had influenza.
    (B) Mouse 4 did not have influenza; Mouse 6 did, but its killer T-cell concentration was too low.
    (C) Mouse 4 did not have influenza; Mouse 6 did, but its virus concentration was too high.
    (D) Mouse 6 did not have influenza; Mouse 4 did, but its T-cell concentration was too low.

4. If the scientist knows that a virus is one of the types presented in Table 1, which of the following is true?

    (A) Knowing the capsid shape is always sufficient to identify the virus.
    (B) Knowing the type of genetic material is always sufficient to identify the virus.
    (C) Knowing the type of genetic material and virus size is always sufficient to identify the virus.
    (D) Knowing the capsid shape and size is always sufficient to identify the virus.

5. Which of the following conclusions can be drawn from Experiments 1-3?

    (A) Virus concentration and killer T-cell concentration are not factors in the effectiveness of a vaccine.
    (B) In a single mouse, as T-cell concentration increases, virus concentration decreases.
    (C) Influenza vaccine is less effective than adenovirus vaccine.
    (D) The effectiveness of a vaccine is dependent on factors other than the type of vaccine.

6. The scientist finds that a seventh mouse is infected with a virus that has a helical shape and measures about 292 nm in length. The mouse's virus and T-cell concentrations are similar to those of Mouse 1. If the scientist administers influenza vaccine to the mouse, should the mouse's health be expected to improve?

    (A) Yes, because it is the correct vaccine.
    (B) No, because it is not the correct vaccine.
    (C) Yes, because the mouse's T-cell concentration is high.
    (D) No, because the mouse's virus concentration is high.

PRACTICE PASSAGE 2 (TIME: 5 MINUTES)

Many modern mountain bikes feature rear suspension, which allows the rear wheel to move up and down relative to the rider and the rest of the bike. The rear *wheel travel* provided by suspension decreases the impact of rough terrain and increases tire traction, allowing riders to go at faster speeds for longer periods of time. Rear wheel suspension requires at least two parts: a shock, which is a spring that can compress and extend; and a pivot linkage, which connects the rear wheel and the shock to the rest of the bike. A calculation called the *leverage ratio*, which is found by dividing rear wheel travel by maximum shock travel (called *stroke*), can help determine key characteristics of the suspension. A low leverage ratio typically means less maximum rear wheel travel, but also a softer ride that absorbs smaller bumps and puts less stress on the shock. Conversely, a high leverage ratio typically means more maximum rear wheel travel, but also a harsher ride that bounces over smaller bumps and puts more stress on the shock. Table 1 below shows data on the rear suspensions of bikes offered by one company. Figure 1 shows the leverage ratios for all eight bike models. Figure 2 shows customer satisfaction data for the first four bike models.

Table 1

Bike Model	Rear Wheel Travel (mm)	Maximum Shock Stroke (mm)
Previous Model Year		
Stub (A)	80	30
Jack (B)	110	40
Pit (C)	145	55
Cliff (D)	210	75
Upcoming Model Year		
HF (A)	90	35
MC (B)	115	45
TH (C)	150	60
RA (D)	215	80

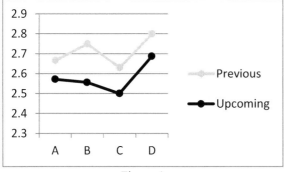

Figure 1

Warranty and Customer Satisfaction Data from Previous Model Year

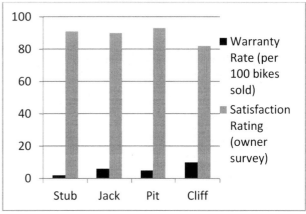

Figure 2

7. The bike company suspects that the Cliff model was taken in for warranty service so frequently because there was too much mechanical stress on the shock and pivot linkage. What data would support this conclusion?

(A) Cliff had the lowest satisfaction rating of all the bikes offered that year.
(B) Cliff had the highest leverage ratio of all the bikes offered that year.
(C) Cliff had the most rear wheel travel of all the bikes offered that year.
(D) Cliff had the most shock stroke of all the bikes offered that year.

8. In the upcoming model year, the bike company is planning to replace the Cliff model with the RA model. One of the reasons for the replacement is that many bike racers who used the Cliff complained that the bike lost traction over smaller bumps. Which aspect of the RA model will likely fix this problem?

(A) RA decreases wheel travel by 5 mm, compared to Cliff.
(B) RA uses a shock with 5 mm more stroke than Cliff does.
(C) RA has a leverage ratio of 2.69, compared to 2.8 in Cliff.
(D) There is insufficient data to make this conclusion.

9. One negative side effect of low leverage ratios is the tendency for rear suspension to activate while riders are pedaling hard. When this happens, a phenomenon referred to as *pedal bob* occurs—a rider's pedaling energy ends up being used to move the wheel up and down, rather than to move the bike forward. High leverage ratios can help limit pedal bob. Which type of rider could benefit from a high leverage ratio rear suspension?

    (A) A downhill racer who competes on bumpy and steep courses
    (B) A recreational rider who wants to limit stress on her joints
    (C) A cross country racer who competes on flat and uphill courses
    (D) A stunt rider who rides on or jumps over stairs and other obstacles

10. The bike company does not exceed a leverage ratio of 3 on any of its bikes because of performance and maintenance concerns. If this company created a special edition of the HF model, which maximized wheel travel using the same 35 mm shock, what would be the resulting travel?

    (A) 35 mm
    (B) 90 mm
    (C) 105 mm
    (D) 270 mm

11. A competitor in the bike market is planning to release a new model called the Batty. Spies for the original bike company have reported that early prototypes of the Batty used a 45 mm shock, but the most recent test bike uses a 40 mm shock instead. Based on this information, the original bike company has concluded that:

    (A) the Batty model will be a direct competitor for the MC model.
    (B) the early Batty prototypes put less stress on shocks than the newest test bikes.
    (C) the Batty will have a rear suspension that has less problems with pedal bob.
    (D) it needs more data before trying to evaluate the Batty's suspension design.

12. One of the biggest goals the bike company has for the upcoming model year is to produce bikes with satisfaction ratings all above 90%. Based solely on the data provided for the new suspension designs, does the company have a good chance of reaching this goal?

    (A) Yes, because only the Cliff model had a low satisfaction rating, and it is not going to be offered again.
    (B) Yes, because the leverage ratios on all the bikes are lower for the upcoming model year.
    (C) No, because increasing wheel travel and shock stroke results in heavier, slower bikes.
    (D) No, because the company will be charging more for its bikes in the upcoming model year.

sP9B

Directions: The following two passages are similar to real ACT test passages. Read each passage and answer the questions that follow. Use the methods and techniques that you learned in the instructions of this lesson.

HOMEWORK PASSAGE 1 (TIME: 5 MINUTES)

Single replacement reactions are reactions in which one element replaces another in a compound. In the following reaction:

$$A(s) + BC(aq) \rightarrow B(s) + AC(aq)$$

Solid metal A must have a greater oxidation potential than aqueous species B to replace it. As a result, A is considered the more "active" metal. Such reactions can only occur spontaneously if the *net potential* (the sum of the solid metal's oxidation potential and the aqueous species' reduction potential) is positive.

Table 1 shows the *reduction potentials* of several aqueous species. The *oxidation potentials* of the corresponding solid metals can be found by taking the opposite of the reduction potentials: e.g., since the reduction potential of Mg^{2+}(aq) is –2.37 V, the oxidation potential of metal Mg(s) is +2.37 V.

Table 1

Aqueous species	Reduction Potential (V)
$Mg^{2+}(aq)$	–2.37
$Al^{3+}(aq)$	–1.66
$Mn^{2+}(aq)$	–1.18
$Co^{2+}(aq)$	–0.28
$Pb^{2+}(aq)$	–0.13
$2H^{+}(aq)$	0.00
$Cu^{2+}(aq)$	+0.34
$Ag^{+}(aq)$	+0.80
$Br_{2}(l)$	+1.07
$Au^{3+}(aq)$	+1.50

In a set of experiments, a group of chemistry students carries out a series of single-replacement reactions using different metal elements.

Experiment 1

The students mix four unknown solid metals with four unknown aqueous metals (aq) in different combinations and observe whether reactions occurred. An X indicates the presence of a reaction. Table 2 shows their results.

Table 2

Metal	Aqueous Species			
	I	II	III	IV
A	-	X	X	X
B	-	-	X	X
C	-	-	X	X
D	-	-	-	X

Experiment 2

The students then set up four electrochemical cells with four known metals and four unknown aqueous solutions. They observe the formation of solid in cells A and B, but no solid in cells C and D. Table 3 lists their data.

Table 3

Cell	Metals	Solid Formed Spontaneously?
1	Mg(s)	Yes
2	Cu(s)	Yes
3	Au(s)	No
4	Co(s)	No

1. Based on the data in Table 1, which of the following lists metals from most to least active?

    (A) Mg(s), Co(s), Al(s)
    (B) Co(s), Cu(s), Mn(s)
    (C) Al(s), Pb(s), Au(s)
    (D) It cannot be determined, because Table 1 only includes the reduction potentials of aqueous species, not the oxidation potentials of solid metals.

2. Based on the information in the passage and Table 1, which of the following reactions would NOT occur spontaneously?

    (A) Al(s) with Au(aq)
    (B) Mg(s) with Al(aq)
    (C) Ag(s) with Au(aq)
    (D) Au(s) with Ag(aq)

3. Metals with greater oxidation potentials react more easily with aqueous species. Based on the data in Tables 1 and 2, if Metal A was Mn(s), then Metal B could NOT have been:

   (A) Au(s)
   (B) Pb(s)
   (C) Cu(s)
   (D) Al(s)

4. Based on the data in Tables 1 and 3, Cell 3 in Experiment 2 could have contained an aqueous species:

   (A) with a reduction potential less than +1.50 V.
   (B) with an oxidation potential less than −1.50 V.
   (C) with a reduction potential greater than +1.50 V.
   (D) with an oxidation potential greater than −1.50 V.

5. In Cell 4 of Experiment 2, the aqueous species could have been:

   (A) Au(aq), but not Mg(aq) or 2H(aq).
   (B) Mg(aq) or 2H(aq), but not Au(aq).
   (C) Au(aq), Mg(aq) or 2H(aq).
   (D) none of the above.

6. One of the students determines that the aqueous species in Cell 4 of Experiment 2 is Mg(aq). If the student added +4.0 V to the reaction to increase its net potential, would that be sufficient to cause the reaction to occur spontaneously?

   (A) Yes, because the net potential of the reaction would be positive.
   (B) No, because the net potential of the reaction would be negative.
   (C) Yes, because that would increase the reduction potential of Co(aq).
   (D) No, because that would decrease the oxidation potential of Mg(aq).

HOMEWORK PASSAGE 2 (TIME: 5 MINUTES)

Photoperiodism is the physiological reaction of plants or animals to the length of day or night. *Short day plants* (SD) flower when growing in short days and long nights. *Long day plants* (LD) flower when growing in long days and short nights. *Day neutral plants* (DN) are unaffected by the lengths of day and night in their flowering patterns.

Florigen is the hormone hypothesized to trigger and control the flowering in plants. It is produced in the leaves but acts in the *shoot apical meristem* (SAM) of buds and growing tips, the region of the plant where cell division occurs. The gene Flowering Locus T (FT) is thought to be involved in the flowering mechanism of long day plants, and its analogue, Heading date 3a (Hd3a), in short day plants.

Experiment 1

Three different plants of the same age growing in identical soil composition are kept under a series of constant light and dark periods. Each plant is grown at a constant 25°C under a constant light intensity of 300 mW. Table 1 shows the data collected.

Table 1

Plant	Day Length (Hours)	Night Length (Hours)	Flowering
1	15	9	Yes
	9	15	No
	12	12	No
2	15	9	Yes
	9	15	Yes
	12	12	Yes
3	15	9	No
	9	15	Yes
	12	12	No

Experiment 2

Plant 1 was kept under periods of 15 hours of light and 9 hours of dark, starting with a dark period. Temperature was kept constant at 25°C. Levels of FT in the SAM were measured and are plotted in Figure 1.

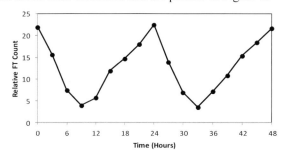

Figure 1

Experiment 3

Plant 3 was kept under a series of constant 9-hour light and 15-hour dark periods at a constant 25°C. Levels of Hd3a in the SAM were measured and are recorded in Figure 2.

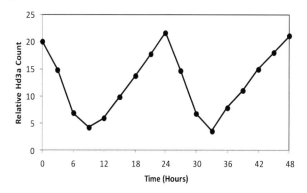

Figure 2

Experiment 4

The leaves of several samples of Plant 1 were injected with equal quantities of FT, after which they were cut off at the shoot apical meristem at different times. The concentrations of FT in the leaves and SAM were measured immediately after cutting, and the occurrence of flowering was recorded. Table 2 shows the results.

Table 2

Hours before cut	Relative Leaf [FT]	Relative SAM [FT]	Flowering
1	25	5	No
2	18	12	No
3	11	19	No
4	4	26	Yes
5	0	30	Yes

The procedure was repeated with several samples of Plant 3, and the relative [Hd3a] were measured. Table 3 lists the data.

Table 3

Hours before cut	Relative Leaf [Hd3a]	Relative SAM [Hd3a]	Flowering
1	20	6	No
2	14	12	No
3	8	18	Yes
4	2	24	Yes
5	0	30	Yes

7. Based on the results in Experiment 1, one can conclude that Plants 1, 2, and 3 are respectively:

   (A) short day, long day, and day neutral plants.
   (B) long day, short day, and day neutral plants.
   (C) short day, day neutral, and long day plants.
   (D) long day, day neutral, and short day plants.

8. If in Experiment 3, Plant 3 flowered at 24 and 48 hours, but not at 9 or 33 hours, one can most likely assume that:

   (A) high Hd3a levels trigger flowering in short day plants during the day.
   (B) high Hd3a levels trigger flowering in long day plants during the day.
   (C) high Hd3a levels trigger flowering in short day plants at night.
   (D) high Hd3a levels trigger flowering in long day plants at night.

9. Based on the results in Experiment 4, which of the following could most likely be the amount of time required for sufficient Hd3a to be transported from the leaves to the shoot apical meristem to cause flowering?

   (A) Two hours
   (B) Three hours
   (C) Four hours
   (D) Five hours

10. Which of the following is the most likely explanation as to why flowering did not occur in Plant 3 two hours before the SAM was cut?

    (A) The concentration of Hd3a in the leaves was too low.
    (B) The concentration of Hd3a in the SAM was too low.
    (C) The concentration of Hd3a in the leaves was too high.
    (D) The concentration of Hd3a in the SAM was too high.

11. Which of the following is most likely true regarding the photoperiodism of Plant 2?

    (A) Flowering requires more than 12 hours of daylight and less than 12 hours of darkness.
    (B) Flowering requires less than 12 hours of daylight but at least 12 hours of darkness.
    (C) Flowering requires less than 12 hours of daylight but less than 12 hours of darkness.
    (D) Flowering is independent of the amount of daylight and darkness.

12. Based on the results of Experiment 4, which of the following most likely represents the relative concentration range of Hd3a required in the SAM for Plant 3 to flower?

    (A) 4 to 12
    (B) 12 to 20
    (C) 20 to 28
    (D) None of the above

sP10: CONFLICTING VIEWPOINTS

Directions: Read the explanation and examples below to learn about this lesson's topic.

TOPIC OVERVIEW

The Conflicting Viewpoints passage on the ACT Science Test feels less like a science passage and more like a reading passage. Instead of charts, tables, graphs, or other visual representations, most of the data are in the form of reading passages. Each passage gives a short introductory paragraph about the general topic of the passage, followed by short statements by two or more scientists, students, or other individuals giving their opinions on the topic at hand. You should read these passages carefully to make the best use of your time; simply skimming the passages won't work here like it does in the other passage types. While reading the passages, keep these five points in mind:

1. Identify the point of conflict.
2. Identify the position of each scientist. (Read the passages separately and come to a decision at the end of each part.)
3. What problems does Scientist 1 have with the argument of Scientist 2?
4. What problems does Scientist 2 have with the argument of Scientist 1?
5. About what, if anything, do the scientists agree?

SAMPLE PASSAGE

Two astronomers below discuss the Big Bang theory, the cosmological theory describing the origins of the universe.

Astronomer 1

The Big Bang theory states that the universe arose from nothing, but this violates one of the most fundamental laws in physics—the 1st Law of Thermodynamics, which states that energy can neither be created nor destroyed. In addition, the 2nd Law of Thermodynamics states that *entropy*, the amount of disorder in a system, of the universe can only increase. Yet, the formation of stars and galaxies suggests decreasing entropy.

Einstein's Theory of Relativity posits that nothing can travel faster than the speed of light. However, data suggests that during its early expansion, the universe surpassed the speed of light.

Astronomer 2

The Big Bang theory is not meant to address the creation of the universe, but rather its evolution. Furthermore, all of the current laws and theories of

physics break down as you approach the beginning of the universe, so there is no reason to believe the 1st Law of Thermodynamics or other laws or theories would have even applied at the time.

It is true that entropy of the universe must always increase, and that the formation of stars and galaxies reduces entropy. However, if viewed from the perspective that the universe is completely homogenous and maintains identical physical properties throughout, then the universe obeys the laws of entropy.

1. ***Identify the point of conflict*** – The two astronomers are arguing about the viability of the Big Bang theory.

2. ***Identify the position of each scientist*** – Scientist 1 provides arguments against the Big Bang theory, saying that it violates various laws and theories in physics. Scientist 2 provides arguments for the Big Bang Theory, stating that it doesn't violate any laws or theories if certain circumstances are taken into consideration.

3. ***What problems does Scientist 1 have with the argument of Scientist 2?*** – Notice that while Scientist 1 argues against the possibility of the Big Bang, he does NOT refute any of the arguments made by Scientist 2 himself. There is a difference between arguing against a theory, and arguing against the arguments made to support that theory. Watch out: some questions may try to use this subtle difference to trick you into choosing wrong answers.

4. ***What problems does Scientist 2 have with the argument of Scientist 1?*** – Notice now that Scientist 2 DOES have issues with the claims of Scientist 1. He states that the laws for energy and entropy are not violated when considered in particular circumstances.

5. ***About what, if anything, do the scientists agree?*** – Both scientists support the 2nd Law of Thermodynamics.

While reading passages, take notes on or underline important parts of the passage. The majority of the questions asked will be based on these five points.

sP10A

Directions: The following two passages are similar to real ACT test passages. Read each passage and answer the questions that follow. Use the methods and techniques that you learned in the instructions of this lesson.

PRACTICE PASSAGE 1 (TIME: 6 MINUTES)

The three domains of life—Archaea, Eukarya, and Bacteria—are said to have originated over two billion years ago. While the domains maintain individual differences among them, their many similarities have researchers contemplating two hypotheses about the evolutionary origins of eukaryotes: vertical gene transfer and lateral gene transfer.

Scientist 1

Eukaryotic organisms (organisms whose cells contain nuclei and other membrane-bound structures, known as organelles) arose through symbiosis between an archaean cell and a bacterial cell. An early archaean cell engulfed a bacterial cell, which eventually served the function of an organelle. According to this theory, the only DNA of bacterial origin we should find in eukaryotes is that of the bacteria engulfed by early archaean cells. The rest of the eukaryotic genome should be inherent to the original archaean host cell. Furthermore, the fact that, over the course of evolution, bacterial DNA was only transferred to eukaryotic cells—the descendants of that first eukaryotic cell—and not to archaean cells, suggests that the three domains of life evolved from a single common ancestor, which was formed when the early archaean cell engulfed the bacteria cell. This is consistent with the vertical gene transfer hypothesis, which proposes that the three domains evolved from one common ancestor, in the process of which genes were passed only from parent organisms to their offspring.

Scientist 2

Eukaryotic nuclear DNA does contain bacterial sequences associated with the functions of specific organelles. However, it also holds bacterial sequences that bear no relation to those organelles at all. In addition, there is evidence that a transfer of DNA occurred not only between bacteria and eukaryotes, but also between bacteria and archaea. The bacterium *Thermotoga maritima*, for instance, contains 24% archaean DNA. Similarly, the archaean *Archaeoglobus fulgidus* contains numerous bacterial genes. The domains of Bacteria, Archaea, and Eukarya all share commonalities, which suggests not a single common ancestor of eukaryotes, but rather a

community of primitive cells that swapped genes freely with each other. This community eventually coalesced into three distinct communities, which evolved to become the three domains we know today. These findings serve as strong evidence for the lateral gene transfer hypothesis, which proposes that the three domains evolved from a loose community of primitive cells, in which genes were passed not only from parent to offspring, but also between unrelated organisms.

1. Which of the following would Scientist 1 most likely disagree with?

   (A) In a diagram representing the evolution of the three domains, the branches for all three domains should converge at some point in the past.
   (B) The fact that bacterial DNA was transferred to eukaryotic cells suggests that the ancestors of today's organisms formed a community of cells that exchanged DNA with each other.
   (C) The evolution of the three domains did not necessarily involve the transfer of an organism's genes to organisms that were not its offspring.
   (D) Similarities between archaea and bacteria can be explained by the theory that archaea and bacteria were once involved in a mutually beneficial relationship.

2. Scientist 2 would most likely agree that:

   (A) in a diagram representing the evolution of the three domains, the branches for all three domains should converge at some point in the past.
   (B) the evolution of the three domains involved the transfer of early organisms' genes to organisms that were not their offspring.
   (C) the fact that eukaryotic nuclear DNA contains bacterial sequences associated with organelles proves the theory that eukaryotes evolved from early cells that engulfed bacteria.
   (D) bacteria and archaea are too similar to not have a single common ancestor.

3. To accept Scientist 1's argument, one must assume that:

   (A) bacterial DNA was not transferred to eukaryotic cells through lateral gene transfer.
   (B) the earliest eukaryotes arrived before the earliest bacteria and archaea.
   (C) bacterial DNA was transferred to archaean cells through vertical gene transfer.
   (D) eukaryotic nuclear DNA contains only bacterial sequences associated with the functions of specific organelles.

4. Which of the following, if true, would most weaken Scientist 2's hypothesis?

   (A) Several more strains of bacteria are discovered that contain archaean DNA.
   (B) Ancestors of *Thermotoga maritima* are discovered that lived one million years ago and contained no archaean DNA.
   (C) Organisms that existed two billion years ago do not fall into three domains as distinctly as organisms that exist today; rather, they all have traits from all three domains.
   (D) Early bacteria could not have survived in the environment inside of early archaean cells.

5. A scientist places a strain of bacteria similar to early bacteria into an environment that simulates the environment inside of early archaean cells, and discovers that the bacteria cannot survive in the new environment. How would this discovery affect the two hypotheses?

   (A) It would support Scientist 1's hypothesis, and weaken Scientist 2's hypothesis.
   (B) It would support Scientist 2's hypothesis, and weaken Scientist 1's hypothesis.
   (C) It would weaken both hypotheses.
   (D) It would have no effect on either hypothesis.

6. According to Scientist 2's definition of lateral gene transfer, which of the following would NOT be an example of lateral gene transfer?

   (A) One bacterial cell acquires resistance to a specific drug and transfers the resistance genes to several other species of bacteria.
   (B) A fly acquires genetic material from a type of parasitic bacteria living inside it, which gives it resistance to certain viruses.
   (C) Human siblings all share traits from genes acquired from the same set of parents.
   (D) A malaria-causing pathogen acquires genetic material from humans that helps it to survive for longer periods of time in the human body.

7. How might Scientist 1 respond to Scientist 2's claim that *Thermotoga maritima* and *Archaeoglobus fulgidus* support the hypothesis that lateral gene transfer was involved in the evolution of the three domains?

   (A) The exchange of genetic material between archaea and bacteria is not an example of lateral gene transfer.
   (B) Lateral gene transfer may have occurred between archaea and bacteria at some point after the evolution of the three domains from a common ancestor.
   (C) The discovery of bacterial DNA in archaea has been shown by more recent observations to be false.
   (D) Lateral transfer was not necessarily involved because a *Thermotoga maritima* cell could have engulfed an *Archaeoglobus fulgidus* cell, forming the first ancestor of today's eukaryotes.

PRACTICE PASSAGE 2 (TIME: 6 MINUTES)

Between 12,000 and 10,000 years ago, North America experienced the extinction of approximately 45 species of large animals, better known as *megafauna*. Two scientists debate the possible causes of this last extinction event of the Quaternary period.

Scientist 1

Throughout Earth's history, cataclysmic extinction events have threatened, but never quite managed to wipe out, life on the planet. Although several of these extinction events' origins remain mysteries, paleontologists and geologists have succeeded in deciphering the likely causes of others. Some of the largest extinction events, such as the Permian-Triassic event 251 million years ago, the Devonian event 370 million years ago, and the famous, dinosaur-ending Cretaceous-Paleogene event 65 million years ago appear to have stemmed from cataclysmic meteorological, tectonic, and astronomical episodes. Likewise, there is evidence that the last extinction event of the Quaternary period resulted from environmental factors.

The Permian-Triassic event approximately 251 million years ago seems to have been caused by a combination of volcanic activity, changes in the atmosphere, and a loss of dissolved oxygen in the oceans. Likewise, the Late Devonian extinction about 370 million years ago seems to have stemmed from a loss of oxygen in the water and the loss of carbon dioxide in the atmosphere thanks to the explosive growth of terrestrial plants. Most famously, the Cretaceous-Paleogene extinction that destroyed the dinosaurs has conclusively been linked to a meteor strike in the Gulf of Mexico. All of these had a large scale, environmental cause and there's little reason to believe that the extinction of North American megafauna at the end of the last ice age was any different.

The large Pleistocene mammals that dominated the world thrived in ice age conditions because larger animals retain heat more effectively. Unfortunately, bodies this massive require comparable amounts of food and territory. Although the ice ages lowered sea levels and opened up large amounts of land to foragers, the rising sea levels after the ice ages destroyed much of this essential habitat. Rising temperatures—as much as 6 degrees Celsius over 5000 years—reduced habitat and led to the downfall of many species of megafauna and the predators that hunted them.

Scientist 2

The megafauna of the Pleistocene demonstrated remarkable fortitude in enduring 22 of the 23 known ice ages of the era, but the final ice age proved the undoing of dozens of species of large animals. Why should so many perish when before very few had succumbed to the frigid temperature fluctuations? These mammals had to endure a unique and catastrophic stress previously unknown: humans.

Analysis shows that the majority of these now-extinct animals were diurnal (active during the day) and could not take refuge in trees, making them easy prey for early hunters. In addition, many of these species were what might be considered "preferred prey"—easily hunted herbivores. Animal remains at kill sites, such as Dent, Colorado, reveal not only the butchery of animals, but also the mass killings of immense herbivores that would provide far more meat than could be used by a small group of hunter-gatherers. Even a modest exploitation of a large prey species with a low rate of reproduction might gradually lead to its, and its predators, demise.

North America was not the only land mass to lose a substantial number of large mammals in a short time period. Australia's megafauna began their rapid demise about 50,000 years ago, Madagascar's large animals faded away about 2,000 years ago, and New Zealand's flightless moa vanished in less than a century. All of these dates coincide almost exactly with the islands' colonization by humans, and North America's commonly accepted colonization date of 11,000 years ago overlaps perfectly with the local megafauna's extinction.

8. Which of the following would Scientist 2 NOT hypothesize?

   (A) Edible animals such as tortoises would coexist peacefully alongside the human settlers of a small island.
   (B) The extinction of bison, large foraging animals, from a great plains area would cause the wolves that feed on those bison to also become extinct.
   (C) Nocturnal animals, such as raccoons, are less likely to be hunted by humans than diurnal animals, such as squirrels.
   (D) The hunting of immense herbivores, like wooly mammoths, could allow humans to expand into societies larger than small hunter-gather groups.

9. Which of the following could NOT be part of the defense of Scientist 1's theory about changes in climate leading to the downfall of megafauna?

    (A) Rising temperatures caused many coastal areas to become flooded and unsuitable for megafauna.
    (B) Environmental factors drove humans to hunt more animals because of a lack of edible plant matter.
    (C) The large animals that thrive in ice age conditions could not survive rapid changes to environmental conditions.
    (D) Many animals have an easier time finding food during ice ages.

10. An excavation uncovers a dozen wooly mammoth skeletons that all show signs of disease at the end of the animals' lives. Which Scientist's hypothesis does this new data support?

    (A) Scientist 1's
    (B) Scientist 2's
    (C) Both Scientist 1's and Scientist 2's
    (D) Neither Scientist 1's nor Scientist 2's

11. An excavation uncovers the skeleton of a giant beaver, an animal native to forested areas, that shows signs of having been butchered. Soil analysis shows that the region was a grassy plain at the time. Which Scientist's hypothesis does this new data support?

    (A) The atypical environment supports Scientist 1's hypothesis.
    (B) The signs of hunting support Scientist 2's hypothesis.
    (C) The animal being native to forests supports Scientist 2's hypothesis.
    (D) The atypical environment and signs of hunting support the hypotheses of both scientists.

12. Both scientists agree that:

    (A) most megafauna have the endurance to survive small climate changes.
    (B) a large number of animals became extinct during the Pleistocene era.
    (C) humans are responsible for the majority of megafauna extinction events.
    (D) reduced habitats are responsible for the majority of megafauna extinction events.

13. Which of the following would Scientist 1 most likely do to study the extinction of the moa mentioned by Scientist 2?

    (A) Analyze fossil remains of Haast's Eagle, the moa's only known natural predator.
    (B) Analyze historical records on the human settling of New Zealand.
    (C) Analyze soil samples of the area to determine possible changes to the moa's habitat.
    (D) Analyze thermodynamic data regarding how much heat the moa's body could retain.

14. What would Scientist 1 most likely say about Scientist 2's claim that "megafauna of the Pleistocene demonstrated remarkable fortitude in enduring 22 of the 23 known ice ages of the era"?

    (A) The conditions of 22 ice ages in which these megafauna did survive were not as harsh as the one that ended in mass extinction.
    (B) The large herbivores that died out during the 23rd ice age did so because they became "preferred prey."
    (C) The Pleistocene megafauna became extinct as a result of the temperature increasing after the 23rd ice age, not because of the ice age itself.
    (D) The introduction of human hunters was the determining factor of the extinctions during the Pleistocene period.

sP10B

Directions: The following two passages are similar to real ACT test passages. Read each passage and answer the questions that follow. Use the methods and techniques that you learned in the instructions of this lesson.

HOMEWORK PASSAGE 1 (TIME: 6 MINUTES)

Organic foods are those that are cultured without the use of synthetic pesticides or chemical fertilizers. They are also not processed using industrial solvents, chemical food additives, or irradiation. Two scientists below discuss the use of organic foods in the food industry.

Scientist 1

Organic foods have significant advantages over inorganic foods. First, they are much safer to consume than their inorganic counterparts since the latter are grown using dangerous synthetic chemicals. Some studies have linked these chemicals in our food to everything from headaches to birth defects to cancer. This can easily raise health and even litigation concerns among the general public and food providers. The absence of synthetic pesticides and fertilizers in organic plants also helps them boost their production of vitamins and antioxidants to strengthen their resistance to bugs and weeds, thus, preventing the transfer of dangerous elements from unwanted critters into our bodies. This is significant because even low levels of these chemicals pose a threat to fetuses and children due to their premature immune systems and to pregnant women by increasing the burden on their already strained organs.

Organic foods also impact the health of our bodies by indirect means, such as through farm animals. Many scientists are already concerned that some farm animals are being given excessive amounts of growth hormones and antibiotics, many of which are the same ones used by humans. This can lead to the development of antibiotic resistance bacteria, which not only infect the farm animals in which they grew, but also spread across species and infect other animals and human beings.

Organic foods are beneficial not only for our bodies, but also for the environment. Organic farming reduces the number of pollutants in our groundwater and creates soil richer in minerals to aid plant growth, all while helping to reduce erosion. Cultivation of organic foods also reduces the number of pesticides present in our drinking water and even uses as much as fifty percent less energy than does growth of conventional foods, thus, providing an environmentally-friendly option for those who care for Earth's precious resources.

Scientist 2

Organic foods have no significant impacts on human beings—except on our wallets. While conventionally grown foods may contain minor levels of synthetic chemicals and pesticides, these levels are far below those needed to cause noticeable or significant health changes in adults. Children too display significantly lower levels of pesticides when consuming organic foods, but those that do not are still not at risk of acquiring any major types of diseases or infections. After all, most kids in the 1940s and 50s did not have access to organic foods growing up, but their life expectancies today are gradually increasing.

Some studies have also found that there is no significant difference in nutrient levels between organic foods and inorganic foods. Someone who eats organic foods is not necessarily healthier than someone who does not. So a person on an organic food diet may have the same risk of developing heart disease or diabetes or any other disease as someone who is not. Health is not and should not be classified as a function of how many organic foods one consumes. Rather, it is an exercise of eating healthful, balanced meals containing fruits, grains, vegetables, and proteins, while maintaining an active lifestyle.

1. Scientist 1 believes that:

    (A) Organic foods are much safer to consume than inorganic ones because inorganic foods contain very little amounts of pesticides and synthetic chemicals.
    (B) The consumption of organic plants helps to boost antioxidant levels in humans to strengthen their resistance to bugs and weeds.
    (C) Organic farming is an inexpensive process that helps reduce the number of pollutants in our ground and drinking water.
    (D) Birth defects due to contaminants in inorganic foods can lead people to file lawsuits against food providers.

2. Which of the following claims is NOT supported by Scientist 1?

   (A) The synthetic chemicals in inorganic compounds can lead to the development of cancer.
   (B) Organically grown plants may have greater levels of vitamins and antioxidants than conventionally grown plants.
   (C) Organic farming completely eliminates the pollutants in our ground and drinking water and helps create richer soil.
   (D) Organic farming may require only as half as much energy expenditure as conventional farming.

3. Which of the following claims is NOT supported by Scientist 2?

   (A) Kids who grew up in the 1940s and 1950s are healthier than the kids growing up today.
   (B) An adult consuming only organic foods may have the same risk of developing Alzheimer's as an adult consuming only inorganic foods.
   (C) Children who do not consume organic foods are at no greater risk of acquiring infectious diseases than children who do consume organic foods.
   (D) Organic foods are very expensive.

4. Scientist 1 would MOST agree with Scientist 2 on which of the following?

   (A) Levels of pesticides and synthetic chemicals in conventionally grown foods are not dangerous.
   (B) Children consuming only organic foods have greater risks of acquiring infections than adults consuming only organic foods.
   (C) Conventionally grown foods contain some levels of pesticides and synthetic fertilizers.
   (D) Organic farming may be more beneficial for the environment than conventional farming.

5. Bovine somatotropin is a growth hormone secreted by the pituitary gland in cows. Some food producers, however, inject artificial growth hormones (AGH) into cows to rear larger cows that produce more milk. Some studies have found that AGH-treated cows produce milk that may turn sour more quickly than milk produced by AGH-untreated cows. How does this finding affect the arguments made in the passage?

   (A) It strengthens Scientist 1's argument because it shows that artificial chemicals lower the quality of food obtained from farm animals.
   (B) It weakens Scientist 2's argument because it shows that synthetic chemicals cause observable physical changes in the foods people consume.
   (C) It strengthens Scientist 2's argument because it shows that while synthetic chemicals may alter the foods we consume, they do not cause infection inside our bodies.
   (D) It has no effect on the arguments of either Scientist 1 or 2.

6. The main point of contention between the arguments of Scientists 1 and 2 is:

   (A) Scientist 1 believes that conventionally grown foods should not be consumed.
   (B) Scientist 2 believes that organically grown foods should not be consumed.
   (C) Scientist 1 believes that organic foods are more beneficial than inorganic foods.
   (D) Scientist 2 believes that inorganic foods are more beneficial than organic foods.

7. Carbapenem-Resistant Enterobacteriaceae, CRE, are bacteria that have grown resistant to even some of the strongest antibiotics available. If it was found that their antibiotic resistance was due to natural genetic mutations, and not to exposure to antibiotics themselves, this finding would:

   (A) Weaken Scientist 1's argument because it shows that most bacteria acquire antibiotic resistance through natural mechanisms, and not through exposure to antibiotics.
   (B) Strengthen Scientist 1's argument because it shows that the use of synthetic chemicals in conventionally grown foods can cause the emergence of antibiotic resistant bacteria.
   (C) Strengthen Scientist 2's argument because it shows that bacteria have just as much capability to acquire resistance from natural mechanisms as from exposure to antibiotics.
   (D) None of the above.

HOMEWORK PASSAGE 2 (TIME: 6 MINUTES)

Two scientists at a regulatory meeting in Berlin, Germany discuss the severity of the radioactive contamination around the Fukushima Daiichi nuclear plant two years after the earthquake, tsunami, and subsequent meltdown of 3 of its 6 reactors.

Scientist 1

The area around the Fukushima Daiichi nuclear plant is still incredibly unsafe. What's worse, though, is that radioactive material continues to leak from the plant. This disaster was, after all, the only other event in human history to rank a 7 on the International Nuclear Event Scale. Things have gotten no better; if anything, they've gotten worse.

The containment vessels for the fissile cores remain breached. Small amounts of radioactive material can still enter the atmosphere or the Pacific Ocean. Furthermore, radioactive isotopes deposited on the surrounding soil after the accident are entering the groundwater or flowing into the ocean as rainwater gathers these particles. While the radioactive materials that flow into the ocean may dilute, any that sink deep enough and come into contact with the water table will not. Not only would people end up drinking the contaminated groundwater, but it would also be used to water crops. It could take up to two years for all of the nuclear waste in the groundwater to be cycled out.

The disaster released 500 Petabecquerels (PBq) of radioactive material into the air. The plant is still releasing 200 million Bq of radioactive material into the air every hour. 4700 Terabecquerel (TBq) were released into the water during the accident. That's 520 tons of radioactive water and 20,000 years of dumping at the legal limit. 300,000 tons of radioactive water have since continued to leak from the plant. Even today, the ground around the plant, even half a kilometer away, shows 530kBq per kg of soil. This is a background of radiation similar to the testing grounds of atomic bombs. The groundwater of Fukushima has 10,000 times the legal limit for radioactive materials. Fukushima Daiichi's meltdown not only was an enormous disaster, but continues to be one.

Scientist 2

While it is true that the Fukushima Disaster was devastating at the time, the residual effects are nowhere near as worrisome as many alarmists would have us think. True, a great deal of radioactive material was released at the moment of meltdown, but these totals are nowhere near those of Chernobyl. Of the radioactive isotopes tested, only cesium-137 approached the levels seen in the Chernobyl disaster. The total radiation emissions were likely one-tenth of the values seen in the nearby town of Pripyat after Chernobyl. Moreover, while the legally allowed amounts of radiation may sound intimidating, they are nowhere close to what it would actually take for a person to be negatively impacted by exposure to them. Although Fukushima's meltdown is the only disaster apart from Chernobyl rated a 7 on the International Nuclear Event Scale, the scale is entirely qualitative and more a public relations gimmick than a legitimate scientific tool.

Both preventative policies and technological aids make this situation completely different from Chernobyl. Filters have been placed in the Fukushima reactors cutting radioactive emissions by a factor of 4 million, and the quick evacuation of the surrounding areas has limited human exposure. The Pacific Ocean will also carry and dilute the majority of the radiation, so background levels will barely read above normal. Furthermore, the exclusion zone is nowhere near as wide as that of Pripyat, nor should it be. The radiation released was a fraction of that seen in Chernobyl, and any contamination will likewise be limited. Finally, the half-life for the radioactive materials is only a few months; so no matter where the radioactivity ended up, it will be gone in less than a year.

What's more, the Japanese government was much more proactive than the Soviet Union about informing the public of any dangers. While the danger is not zero, individuals who follow government guidelines should not experience any problems. The Chernobyl reactor core exploded, while nothing more than some minor hydrogen gas ignition occurred in Fukushima. The comparison simply is not valid. The danger and degree of the disaster at Fukushima has been grossly overstated.

8. It is discovered that radioactivity can retain its toxicity for thousands of miles in the ocean. This fact weakens:

   (A) Scientist 1's argument.
   (B) neither scientist's argument.
   (C) both scientists' arguments.
   (D) Scientist 2's argument.

9. Which of the following would Scientist 1 *not* use as supporting evidence?

   (A) It is discovered that 500 Petabecquerels of radioactive materials is actually not very harmful.
   (B) Several years after the Fukushima disaster, a substantial number of people in a community a hundred miles from the site suffer effects of radiation poisoning.
   (C) Amounts of radiation have been detected in the groundwater near neighboring communities.
   (D) It is discovered that the ocean does not dilute radioactivity nearly as much as scientists previously thought it did.

10. Both scientists would agree that:

    (A) the amounts of radiation emissions in Fukushima matched the amounts of emissions in Pripyat after the Chernobyl incident.
    (B) the potential for human radiation poisoning after Fukushima has been exaggerated.
    (C) traces of radioactive materials will probably end up in the Pacific Ocean.
    (D) the lack of preventative measures taken by the Japanese government has put many people's lives in danger.

11. What would Scientist 2 say about Scientist 1's observation that, "The disaster released 500 Petabecquerels (PBq) of radioactive material into the air?"

    (A) The radioactive materials could potentially work their way into the local drinking water.
    (B) This number may sound shocking, but it is actually nowhere near the toxic amount.
    (C) The people at Fukushima are in danger of being contaminated.
    (D) These amounts only measured the cesium-137 in the area, which is actually a relatively safe isotope.

12. Which of the following facts would Scientist 1 use as supporting evidence?

    (A) The Fukushima nuclear plant had structural advantages that Chernobyl did not.
    (B) The amounts of radiation that have been deemed legally dangerous are actually not harmful.
    (C) The massive flooding in Japan has caused the water table to rise, thus, leaving it more vulnerable to contamination.
    (D) Chernobyl had no way of cooling the radioactive materials while Fukushima did.

13. It is found that the International Nuclear Event Scale is an ineffective method of measuring the degree of nuclear disasters. This discovery would benefit:

    (A) neither scientist's argument.
    (B) both scientists argument.
    (C) Scientist 1's argument.
    (D) Scientist 2's argument.

14. How would Scientist 2 respond to Scientist 1's statement that, "It could take up to two years for all of the nuclear waste in the groundwater to be cycled out?"

    (A) This poses no threat since the radioactive material's half-life is only a few months.
    (B) The groundwater will pull the radioactive materials out to the Pacific Ocean; the ocean will dilute it and render the radioactive materials harmless.
    (C) If there were any amounts of radioactivity present in the groundwater, it would be far below the legal limit.
    (D) The Japanese government took extra precaution to rid the groundwater of radioactive materials.

sP11A

Directions: The following two passages are similar to real ACT test passages. Read each passage and answer the questions that follow. Use the methods and techniques that you have learned throughout the workbook to help you answer the questions.

PRACTICE PASSAGE 1 (TIME: 4 MINUTES)

Through a process known as *translation*, RNA codes for the production of proteins. A strand of RNA consists of a sequence of bases, each of which can be adenine (A), guanine (G), cytosine (C), or uracil (U). Each set of three consecutive bases, called a *codon*, corresponds to an amino acid, so that the product of translation of a strand of RNA is a sequence of amino acids, the building blocks of proteins.

Table 1 shows all the possible codons and their corresponding amino acids (abbreviated). For example, the codon AUG yields the amino acid methionine (Met) and functions as a "start" signal for translation. UAA, UAG, and UGA designate "STOP" codons, which signal the end of translation.

Table 1

	Second Base				
		U	C	A	G	
First Base	U	Phe	Ser	Tyr	Cys	U
		Phe	Ser	Tyr	Cys	C
		Leu	Ser	STOP	STOP	A
		Leu	Ser	STOP	Trp	G
	C	Leu	Pro	His	Arg	U
		Leu	Pro	His	Arg	C
		Leu	Pro	Gln	Arg	A
		Leu	Pro	Gln	Arg	G
	A	Ile	Thr	Asn	Ser	U
		Ile	Thr	Asn	Ser	C
		Ile	Thr	Lys	Arg	A
		Met	Thr	Lys	Arg	G
	G	Val	Ala	Asp	Gly	U
		Val	Ala	Asp	Gly	C
		Val	Ala	Glu	Gly	A
		Val	Ala	Glu	Gly	G

(Third Base column: U, C, A, G repeating)

Mutations may occur if there are mistakes in the copying of RNA or if the base sequence is altered. Table 1 lists types of mutations with a brief description of each.

Table 2

Mutation	Description
Missense	One base is replaced by another and produces a different amino acid.
Silent	One base is replaced by another, but produces the same amino acid.
Nonsense	One base is replaced by another to produce a stop codon.
Frameshift	Bases are inserted or deleted not in multiples of 3, shifting the reading frame so that every codon that follows is incorrect.
Inversion	One base switches position with another.

A scientist studies the types of mutations that occur during RNA transcription in a species of roundworm. She creates 100 different experimental lines of the roundworm, maintains each line for several hundred generations, and examines some RNA sequences from each generation of roundworms.

Table 3 shows one specific fragment of RNA, and its corresponding sequence of amino acids, in one of the original organisms from the first generation of the experiment (Specimen 0), along with the same fragment from four different specimens (numbered 1 through 4), all from the last generation of roundworms. The left column indicates which specimen the fragment was taken from.

Table 3

0	Bases	UAC-GGU-UAA-AAG-UUA-GCG
	Amino acids	Tyr - Gly - STOP - Lys - Leu - Ala
1	Bases	UAC-GGU-UAA-AAG-UUA-GUG
	Amino acids	Tyr - Gly - STOP - Lys - Leu - Ala
2	Bases	UAC-GGU-UAA-AAG-UGA-GAG
	Amino acids	Tyr - Gly - STOP - Lys - STOP - Glu
3	Bases	UAU-GGU-UAA-CAG-UUA-GCG
	Amino acids	Tyr - Gly - STOP - Gln - Leu - Ala
4	Bases	UAC-GUU-AAA-AGU-UAG-CG
	Amino acids	Tyr - Val - Lys - Ser - STOP - No Last Amino Acid

1. According to Table 1, how many different codons could produce the amino acid serine (Ser)?

   (A) 2
   (B) 4
   (C) 6
   (D) 8

2. In Table 3, which type of mutation does Fragment 1 contain, and in which codon does it occur (numbered from the left)?

   (A) None
   (B) Silent; 6th codon
   (C) Nonsense; 3rd codon
   (D) Frameshift; 6th codon

3. Based on the data in Tables 2 and 3, which type of mutation would potentially be the most harmful?

   (A) Frameshift at the beginning of a sequence
   (B) Nonsense at the end of a sequence
   (C) Missense at the beginning of a sequence
   (D) Inversion at the end of a sequence

4. Which of the following conclusions can be drawn from the data in Table 3?

   (A) Fragment 3 contains one mutation, because one of its amino acids differs from the original.
   (B) Fragment 4 contains a missense mutation, because part of the sequence has been replaced by RNA from a different strand.
   (C) Fragment 1 contains no mutations, because none of its amino acids differ from the original.
   (D) Fragment 2 contains two different types of mutations.

5. The scientist wants to know whether the frequency of mutation in roundworms increases with each successive generation. Which of the following representations of her data would be the most helpful?

   (A) A graph of the rate of change of mutation frequencies (vertical axis) over the number of mutations (horizontal axis)
   (B) A graph of the number of amino acids that differ from the original (vertical axis) over time (horizontal axis)
   (C) A graph of the number of amino acids that differ from the original (vertical axis) over the number of codons that differ from the original (horizontal axis)
   (D) A graph of number of mutations (vertical axis) over time (horizontal axis)

PRACTICE PASSAGE 2 (TIME: 5 MINUTES)

Thermodynamics is the study of energy changes in chemical reactions. Exergonic reactions are those that release energy, and endergonic reactions are those that absorb energy.

Two experiments are conducted to compare energy changes of different reactions. Both occurred at a room temperature of 25°C.

Experiment 1

50 mL of hydrochloric acid (*HCl*) were added into a thermally insulated styrofoam cup containing 100 mL sodium hydroxide (*NaOH*) at 25°C. The temperature inside the cup was recorded at regular 10-second intervals as it equilibrated to that of the surrounding environment. The data are plotted in Figure 1.

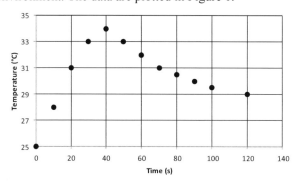

Figure 1

Experiment 2

The procedure from Experiment 1 was repeated, this time adding 50 mL of sodium carbonate (*Na_2CO_3*) to a styrofoam cup containing 100 mL acetic acid (*$C_2H_4O_2$*) at 25°C. The data are shown in Figure 2.

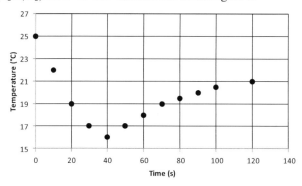

Figure 2

6. In both Experiments 1 and 2, the temperature is at its highest or lowest point when the reaction ends, and then the solution equilibrates to the temperature of the surrounding environment. When did each reaction end?

   (A) Between 0 and 40 seconds
   (B) At 40 seconds
   (C) At 120 seconds
   (D) The reaction in Experiment 1 ended after 40 seconds and the reaction in Experiment 2 ended after 120 seconds.

7. The temperatures at which of the following times would give the LOWEST change in temperatures of the system?

   (A) 0 seconds and 40 seconds in Experiment 1
   (B) 40 seconds and 120 seconds in Experiment 1
   (C) 0 seconds and 40 seconds in Experiment 2
   (D) 40 seconds and 120 seconds in Experiment 2

8. How does the temperature of the surrounding environment in Experiment 1 compare with that in Experiment 2?

   (A) It is higher in Experiment 1 than in Experiment 2.
   (B) It is higher in Experiment 2 than in Experiment 1.
   (C) It is the same in both Experiments 1 and 2.
   (D) It cannot be determined from the given information.

9. Surrounding temperature increases when energy is released from a system, and decreases when energy is absorbed by the system. According to the definitions of exergonic and endergonic reactions in the passage, are the reactions in Experiments 1 and 2 exothermic or endothermic?

   (A) Experiment 1 is exergonic, and Experiment 2 is endergonic.
   (B) Experiment 1 is endergonic, and Experiment 2 is exergonic.
   (C) Experiments 1 and 2 are exergonic.
   (D) Experiments 1 and 2 are endergonic.

10. A third experiment is performed, in which the initial temperature in the cup is the same as the final temperature (after 120 seconds) of Experiment 2, but the temperature changes identically as that observed in Experiment 1. The highest temperature measured in the cup should be approximately:

   (A) 21°C
   (B) 25°C
   (C) 30°C
   (D) 34°C

11. Enthalpy is a measure of the total energy of a thermodynamic system. Enthalpy decreases when surrounding temperature increases, because energy is being released from the system, and enthalpy increases when surrounding temperature decreases, because energy is being absorbed by the system. The enthalpy change is:

   (A) positive in Experiment 1 and negative in Experiment 2.
   (B) negative in Experiment 1 and positive in Experiment 2.
   (C) positive in Experiments 1 and 2.
   (D) negative in Experiments 1 and 2.

sP11B

Directions: The following two passages are similar to real ACT test passages. Read each passage and answer the questions that follow. Use the methods and techniques that you have learned throughout the workbook to help you answer the questions.

HOMEWORK PASSAGE 1 (TIME: 4 MINUTES)

The *index of refraction*, n, is a property of a medium that has to do with how light is refracted, or bent, when passing into or out of the medium.

A generic diagram of light passing from one medium to another is shown below. Medium 1, above the horizontal line, has an index of refraction n_1, and Medium 2, below the horizontal line, has an index of refraction n_2. A ray of light passing through Medium 1 hits the surface of Medium 2 at the angle of incidence θ_1 (as measured from the normal line, which is perpendicular to the surface) and is refracted at an angle θ_2, also measured from the normal.

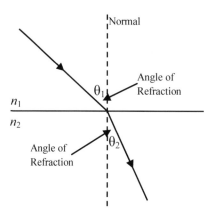

Figure 1

When n_1 is equal to n_2, the ray is not refracted at all, and passes into the second medium in a straight line. When n_1 is greater than n_2, and the angle of incidence is large enough, the light can fail to pass into Medium 2 at all. Instead it is reflected back into Medium 1, a phenomenon known as *total internal reflection*.

White light is shone from air into various media at an incident angle of 45°, and then from each medium into air at the same incident angle. The resulting angles of refraction are listed in Table 1. The index of refraction of air is 1.00.

Table 1

Medium	Index of Refraction	Refraction angle (from air into medium) (°)	Refraction angle (from medium into air) (°)
Nickel	1.08	41	50
Aerogel	1.15	38	54
Porous Silica	1.20	36	58
Acetone	1.36	31	74
Glycerol	1.47	29	None
Glass	1.50	28	None
Sodium chloride	1.54	27	None

The index of refraction of a material can vary depending on the wavelength of light that passes through it. The different colors of visible light, for example, have different wavelengths and, thus, can refract at different angles in the same material. Table 2 lists the visible colors of light, their corresponding wavelengths, and the index of refraction of glass for light of each wavelength. (Each color actually spans a range of wavelengths, but only a single representative wavelength is listed here.)

Table 2

Color	Wavelength (nm)	Index of refraction of glass
Red	640	1.509
Yellow	590	1.511
Green	510	1.515
Blue	490	1.517
Indigo	430	1.521

1. Based on the data in Table 1, regardless of which medium light passes into or out of, as the difference between indices of refraction of two media increases:

   (A) the angle of refraction must increase.
   (B) the angle of refraction must decrease.
   (C) the positive difference between the angle of refraction and the angle of incidence increases.
   (D) none of these; the effect varies depending on which medium the light passes into and out of.

2. If the angle of incidence of a ray of light exceeds what is known as the *critical angle*, the light will experience total internal reflection. The critical angle varies depending on which media the light is passing from and into. For light traveling from the medium into air, the critical angle is:

   (A) greater than 74° for acetone and smaller than 74° for glycerol.
   (B) greater than 45° for acetone and smaller than 45° for glycerol.
   (C) smaller than 74° for acetone and greater than 74° for glycerol.
   (D) smaller than 45° for acetone and greater than 45° for glycerol.

3. Yellow light passing from air into glass would be refracted at an angle of:

   (A) less than 28°.
   (B) exactly 28°.
   (C) greater than 28°.
   (D) None of these; the light would experience total internal reflection.

4. Light that has a wavelength shorter than that of indigo light is shone from one of the media from Table 1 into glass. Which medium or media would have to be used for the light to pass through unrefracted?

   (A) Glass, because light can only pass through unrefracted if the medium does not change.
   (B) Sodium chloride, because with light of a shorter wavelength, the glass could have an index of refraction high enough to equal that of sodium chloride.
   (C) Any of the media other than glass or sodium chloride, because with light of a shorter wavelength, the glass could have an index of refraction low enough to equal any of theirs.
   (D) None of them, because the light experiences total internal reflection.

5. If blue light traveling from air into sodium chloride is refracted at a certain angle A, red light traveling through the same media would be expected to have an angle of refraction:

   (A) less than A.
   (B) greater than A.
   (C) equal to A.
   (D) that does not exist. Refraction does not occur.

HOMEWORK PASSAGE 2 (TIME: 6 MINUTES)

Assisted migration is the act of helping plant and animal species colonize new habitats after their removal from their historical ones due to rapid environmental change. Three scientists discuss the utility of assisted migration.

Scientist 1

All plants and animals possess some natural capacity to migrate and adapt to new environments; however, continuing climate change is currently occurring at a rate with which many species cannot cope. To continue to flourish and grow, these precious life forms must be removed from their current environments and introduced to new habitats.

Using general niche models, some researchers have predicted that without this assisted migration, roughly a quarter of Earth's living species would become extinct by the end of this century. It is, therefore, imperative that these transfer efforts occur as soon as possible. While niche models and predictions specific to individual species would be more accurate, time is extremely limited, and action must be taken now rather than later. It might even benefit to conduct exclusively broad species movements and forego time-consuming and tedious monitoring efforts. Nature has the ability to adapt to different environments, so we can let ecosystems sort themselves out.

Scientist 2

While the impact of Earth's continuing climate change on its habitats is certainly alarming, the potential risks of assisted migration preclude any chances of its application in nature. A significant concern is the plausibility of newly introduced species becoming invasive in their new habitats and driving out native ones, a scenario that has happened time and again during accidental introductions in nature.

Furthermore, the niche models used to plan the migratory processes make unrealistic assumptions, thereby, rendering their predictions useless in nature. For instance, they do not take into account the possibility that some species may be able to tolerate new climates through adaptation or acclimatization. They do not consider the possibility that some species may thrive better or worse in their new habitats than in their current ones depending on the community of species present there, such as predators and prey. In addition, the models do not account for

the existence of considerable variability among climate parameters, such as average annual precipitation and monthly high and low temperatures. These inaccuracies in determining the future suitability of different habitats severely limit the practicality of assisted migration.

Scientist 3

Undoubtedly, climate change is accelerating the rate at which the habitats of numerous species are transforming and disappearing. Preserving the existence of as many species as possible should be a top priority, but not at the expense of the lives of others. Assisted migration certainly has positive intentions and multiple positive points, but it would behoove scientists to use caution and careful planning before exercising such large-scale migrations. They must possess substantive evidence of habitats on the brink of disappearance, robust and quantitative models of predicted habitat and species outcomes, and carefully constructed and organized management plans examined by experts in the field. Assisted migration is a significant issue and one that should be treated as such. We should not make hasty decisions that can potentially cause more harm than good. Our efforts should be focused on minimizing negative outcomes while maximizing positive ones.

6. Scientists 1, 2, and 3 all agree that:

    (A) assisted migration has both good and bad sides to it.
    (B) niche models need further examination and modification to provide more accurate predictions about different species and their habitats.
    (C) all species have the ability to adapt to changing and new environments.
    (D) climate change is a significant threat to the Earth's species and natural habitats.

7. Scientist 1 would MOST agree with Scientist 2 on which of the following?

    (A) The current niche models are not completely accurate.
    (B) The transfer of species from one habitat to another is a possible measure against the growing number of disappearing habitats.
    (C) All plants and animals have the remarkable ability to adapt to new surroundings.
    (D) Earth's changing climates are causing extinctions of numerous species habitats.

8. Suppose new niche models were constructed that accurately take into account the variability among numerous climate parameters, including average annual precipitation and monthly temperatures. Scientist 2 would most likely respond to this new development by:

   (A) being more open to the possibility of assisted migration.
   (B) being more supportive of the validity of niche models and their predictions.
   (C) questioning whether the models consider the variability in different species' ability to adapt to different environments.
   (D) exactly two of the above statements would be true.

9. The main point of difference between the views of Scientist 1 and the views of Scientist 3 is that:

   (A) Scientist 1 believes that preserving the existence of as many species as possible is vital, but not the top priority.
   (B) Scientist 3 calls for more data collection and planning before implementing assisted migration.
   (C) Scientist 1 believes that the construction of more accurate niche models will have very little benefit.
   (D) Scientist 3 believes that most species cannot quickly adapt to new environments.

10. Suppose new and more accurate niche models found that a quarter of Earth's species will become extinct not by the end of the century, but within the next 50 years. How would this change the views of Scientist 3?

    (A) He would be more likely to favor the implementation of assisted migration now rather than later.
    (B) He would question the validity of the data in the new niche models.
    (C) He would call for further evidence collection and development of organized management plans.
    (D) It cannot be determined.

11. Which of the following claims is supported by Scientist 1?

    (A) After large-scale assisted migrations are conducted, it may be best to leave species and their habitats alone.
    (B) Assisted migration should be implemented as soon as more accurate niche models are developed.
    (C) Without any sort of action, a quarter of Earth's species will become extinct by the turn of the century.
    (D) Time-consuming planning and monitoring efforts will have very little impact on the effectiveness of assisted migration.

12. Suppose new and more accurate niche models found that a quarter of Earth's species will become extinct not by the end of the century, but by the next 200 years. How would this change the views of Scientist 1?

    (A) He would be more in favor of implementing assisted migration now rather than later.
    (B) He would be more likely to favor further data collection and development of new niche models specific to individual species.
    (C) He would feel less pressured to adopt time-consuming and tedious monitoring efforts after the implementation of assisted migration.
    (D) Exactly two of the above statements would be true.

sP12A

Directions: The following two passages are similar to real ACT test passages. Read each passage and answer the questions that follow. Use the methods and techniques that you have learned throughout the workbook to help you answer the questions.

PRACTICE PASSAGE 1 (TIME: 4 MINUTES)

Chemical kinetics involves the study of rates of reactions, which can be affected by factors including reactant concentration, temperature of the reaction, surface area of the reacting molecules, and the catalyst used in the reaction.

Reaction orders are used to determine the overall *molecularity* of a reaction, a measure of the number of molecules required per reaction. A reaction that requires one reactant molecule is *unimolecular*, a reaction that requires two reactant molecules is *bimolecular*, and so on.

Various initial concentrations of the following four reactions were used, and the initial rates of the respective reactions measured.

Reaction 1 $Cl + CH_4 \rightarrow HCl + CH_3$

Reaction 2 $O_3 \rightarrow O_2 + O$

Reaction 3 $H_2 + Cl_2 \rightarrow 2HCl$

Reaction 4 $O + NO + N_2 \rightarrow N_2 + NO_2$

All reactants were in their liquid phases, and all reactions occurred at 25°C. Tables 1 through 4 show the data found for Reactions 1 through 4, respectively.

Table 1

Trial	$[Cl]$ (M)	$[CH_4]$ (M)	Initial Rate (M/s)
1	.120	.120	1.2×10^{-5}
2	.060	.120	6.0×10^{-6}
3	.060	.030	1.5×10^{-6}

Table 2

Trial	$[O_3]$ (M)	Initial Rate (M/s)
1	.120	2.4×10^{-5}
2	.060	1.2×10^{-5}
3	.240	4.8×10^{-5}

Table 3

Trial	$[H_2]$ (M)	$[Cl_2]$ (M)	Initial Rate (M/s)
1	.120	.120	2.4×10^{-5}
2	.060	.120	2.4×10^{-6}
3	.120	.240	2.4×10^{-4}

Table 4

Trial	$[O]$ (M)	$[NO]$ (M)	$[N_2]$ (M)	Initial Rate (M/s)
1	.120	.120	.120	2.4×10^{-5}
2	.360	.120	.120	7.2×10^{-5}
3	.360	.030	.120	1.8×10^{-5}
4	.120	.120	.240	4.8×10^{-5}

Reaction 1 was again carried out under various conditions. The initial concentrations of both Cl and CH_4 are kept constant for each trial at .120 M. Table 5 lists the data.

Table 5

Trial	Reactant Phase	Temperature (°C)	Initial Rate (M/s)
1	Liquid	65	6.0×10^{-4}
2	Liquid	0	1.2×10^{-6}
3	Large Solid Chunks	65	1.0×10^{-9}
4	Fine Solid Grains	0	1.2×10^{-8}
5	Gas	65	4.8×10^{-2}

1. Based on the data in Table 1, a fourth trial with the same concentration of Cl as Trial 3, but twice the concentration of CH_4 as Trial 3, should be expected to have an initial rate of:

(A) 1.5×10^{-6} M/s.
(B) 3.0×10^{-6} M/s.
(C) 6.0×10^{-5} M/s.
(D) 6.0×10^{-6} M/s.

2. Reaction 1 is bimolecular because it requires two reactant molecules, while Reaction 2 is unimolecular because it requires one reactant molecule. If Reactions 1 and 2 were each reversed, and the reversed reactions called Reactions 1' and 2', respectively, which of the following would be true?

    (A) Reaction 1' would have the same molecularity as Reaction 1, and Reaction 2' would have a different molecularity from Reaction 2.
    (B) Reaction 1' would have the same molecularity as Reaction 1, and Reaction 2' would have the same molecularity as Reaction 2.
    (C) Reaction 1' would have a different molecularity from Reaction 1, and Reaction 2' would have the same molecularity as Reaction 2.
    (D) Reaction 1' would have a different molecularity from Reaction 1, and Reaction 2' would have a different molecularity from Reaction 2.

3. Based on the data in Table 3, a fourth trial with .030 M H_2 and .060 M Cl_2 should be expected to have an initial rate of:

    (A) 1.2×10^{-7} M/s
    (B) 2.4×10^{-8} M/s
    (C) 3.0×10^{-6} M/s
    (D) 2.4×10^{-4} M/s

4. A scientist with O_3 at the same concentration from Trial 1 of Reaction 2 wants to repeat the reaction, but at the same rate as Trial 2 of Reaction 3. What should he do?

    (A) Use 1/10th the concentration of O_3.
    (B) Use 10 times the concentration of O_3.
    (C) Use 10 times the concentration of O_3, and 1/10th the concentration of O_2.
    (D) Nothing; the two reactions already occur at the same rate.

5. Based on the data presented in Tables 1 and 5, Reaction 1, if repeated at 45°C using .120 M of Cl and .120 M of CH_4, should have an initial reaction rate:

    (A) lower than 1.2×10^{-6} M/s.
    (B) between 1.2×10^{-6} and 1.2×10^{-5} M/s.
    (C) between 1.2×10^{-5} and 6.0×10^{-4} M/s.
    (D) higher than 6.0×10^{-4} M/s.

PRACTICE PASSAGE 2 (TIME: 5 MINUTES)

Heat capacity is the measure of a substance's ability to store energy without changing its own temperature. The more energy a substance can store per unit change in temperature, the greater its heat capacity.

The following experiments were conducted to measure the heat capacities of four different metals and liquids.

Experiment 1

20.0-gram samples of each of five metals are placed into five separate insulated heating chambers at identical temperatures with uniform heat distribution. The initial temperature of each metal was recorded before it was placed into its chamber. Each metal was heated for 10 minutes, after which it was removed and its temperature immediately recorded. Table 1 shows the initial and final temperatures for each metal.

Table 1

Metal	Initial Temperature (°C)	Final Temperature (°C)
I	40	84
II	40	63
III	50	75
IV	60	72
V	60	83

Experiment 2

A 20.0-gram block of Metal II is heated to 60°C from an initial temperature of 25°C. The metal is then fully submerged in a 50.0-gram sample of unknown Liquid I at 25°C in an insulated container and allowed to sit until the final temperatures of the liquid and metal equilibrate. The procedure was then repeated with four other different liquids. No heat was lost from or added to the container during any of the experiments. The data are shown in Table 2.

Table 2

Liquid	Final Temperature (°C)
I	35
II	39
III	42
IV	50
V	44

Experiment 3

20.0 grams of each of the five liquids in Experiment 2 were then mixed with 20.0 grams of water at 25°C to form five different solutions. The initial temperature of the liquids before mixing was 20°C. Assume the final temperature of the water equaled the final temperature of the solution.

Experiment 4

Varying masses of Metal III are placed into separate insulated heating chambers at identical temperatures with uniform heat distribution. Table 3 gives the initial temperature of each mass, as well as the final temperature after 10 minutes.

Table 3

Trial	Mass (g)	Initial Temperature (°C)	Final Temperature (°C)
1	10	20	26
2	20	20	23
3	30	25	27
4	40	25	26.5

6. Which of the following lists the metals from Experiment 1 from least to greatest heat capacity?

   (A) I, V, III, IV, II
   (B) II, IV, III, V, I
   (C) IV, II/V, III, I
   (D) I, III, II/V, IV

7. A sixth metal is added to Experiment 1 that has a heat capacity greater than that of Metal I but less than that of Metal III. It could have had initial and final temperatures of:

   (A) 30°C and 80°C.
   (B) 40°C and 70°C.
   (C) 50°C and 70°C.
   (D) 40°C and 90°C.

8. Which liquid in Experiment 3 would be expected to undergo the greatest change in temperature?

    (A) I
    (B) II
    (C) III
    (D) IV

9. A mixture of two liquids would be expected to reach equilibrium at a temperature between the initial temperatures of the two liquids, unless a reaction occurs between them. If one of the solutions in Experiment 3 has a final temperature of 30°C, does this indicate that a reaction occurred?

    (A) Yes, because the final temperature of the solution is higher than that of either liquid initially.
    (B) No, because the final temperature of the solution is higher than that of either liquid initially.
    (C) Yes, because the final temperature of the solution is lower than that of either liquid initially.
    (D) No, because the final temperature of the solution is the same as that of both liquids initially.

10. Which of the following conclusions can be drawn from the results of Experiment 4?

    (A) As mass of the metal increases, its final temperature increases.
    (B) The change in temperature varies, but the temperature always changes at a constant rate.
    (C) As mass of the metal increases, temperature change of the metal decreases.
    (D) As mass of the metal increases, temperature change of the metal increases.

11. If Experiment 4 were repeated using Metal IV from Experiment I, how would the results differ from those of Metal III?

    (A) With Metal IV, the initial temperatures would be higher than with Metal III.
    (B) With Metal IV, the change in temperature would be greater than with Metal III.
    (C) With Metal IV, the final temperatures would be higher than with Metal III.
    (D) With Metal IV, the change in temperature would be smaller than with Metal III.

sP12B

Directions: The following two passages are similar to real ACT test passages. Read each passage and answer the questions that follow. Use the methods and techniques that you have learned throughout the workbook to help you answer the questions.

HOMEWORK PASSAGE 1 (TIME: 5 MINUTES)

Magma mixing is the process by which two magmas of different composition mix to form magma of intermediate composition between the two. When cooled, the mixture can be identified by distinct layers from both magma sources. This process occurs inside volcanic magma chambers, as well as in deeper levels of the crust, and forms intermediate rocks such as andesite and monzonite. Examples of the three major rock types are given in Table 1.

Table 1

Type	Examples
Igneous Intrusive	Batholiths, stocks, sills
Igneous Extrusive	Basalt, pumice, obsidian
Sedimentary	Sandstone, breccia, shale
Metamorphic	Quartzite, marble, slate

The rock cycle describes the dynamic transition among three rock types over the course of geologic time: sedimentary, igneous, and metamorphic. Igneous rocks are formed through the cooling and solidification of magma. When cooled slowly deep below the earth's surface, they form coarse-grained intrusive rocks containing crystals. When cooled quickly above the earth's surface, they form fine-grained extrusive rocks containing no crystals. Sedimentary rocks are formed through the deposition of material either at the earth's surface or underwater. Minerals found in sea or ground water become enmeshed in the rock to help "glue" it together, a process called cementation. Metamorphic rocks form from the transformation of other rock types through heat and pressure. Figure 1 gives an overview of the rock cycle.

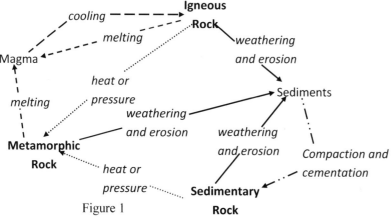

Figure 1

In a geology class, a high school student studies the rock cycle using white and dark chocolate as different rock materials. White chocolate contains a larger percentage of cocoa butter and, thus, possesses a different composition than dark chocolate.

Experiment 1

Equal amounts of white and dark chocolate were melted, mixed, and left to cool over an ice bath to solidify into Mixture A. The procedure was repeated with another similar mixture using an ice bath at a different temperature to form Mixture B. After cooling, Mixture B was found to contain significantly more sugar crystals than was Mixture A.

Experiment 2

The hardened Mixtures A and B were each cut and grated into small chunks and flakes. Each mixture was tightly wrapped in a separate piece of aluminum foil and placed under a heavy textbook of equal weight until each mixture coalesced into one piece.

Experiment 3

Mixtures A and B were then wrapped in separate pieces of wax paper to create two small, tightly packed envelopes. The envelopes were then tightly squeezed with a clamp until the size of the samples could be shrunk no more. After removal from the wrapping papers, both samples were seen to possess a marbled pattern.

1. Based on the information in the passage, a pumice rock was most likely formed through:

   (A) cooling and solidification of magma above the earth's surface.
   (B) cooling and solidification of magma below the earth's surface.
   (C) the deposition of material at the earth's surface.
   (D) the transformation of shale through heat and pressure.

2. Based on the information in the passage, a breccia rock was most likely formed through:

   (A) cooling and solidification of magma above the earth's surface.
   (B) cooling and solidification of magma below the earth's surface.
   (C) the deposition of material underwater.
   (D) the transformation of marble through heat and pressure.

3. At the end of Experiment 1, Mixture B would most resemble which type of rock?

   (A) Igneous intrusive
   (B) Igneous extrusive
   (C) Metamorphic
   (D) Sedimentary

4. Which of the following would best represent the classification of Mixtures A and B, respectively, at the end of Experiment 1?

   (A) Igneous intrusive and igneous extrusive
   (B) Igneous extrusive and igneous intrusive
   (C) Sedimentary and igneous extrusive
   (D) Sedimentary and igneous intrusive

5. The procedure in Experiment 3 best represents which transformation in the rock cycle?

   (A) Cooling
   (B) Weathering and erosion
   (C) Heat or pressure
   (D) Compaction and cementation

6. Which of the following transformations could change the type of Mixture A at the end of Experiment 2 into a basalt type rock?

   (A) Pressure and melting, followed by cooling.
   (B) Heat followed by weathering and erosion.
   (C) Weathering and erosion, followed by compaction.
   (D) Melting followed by cooling.

HOMEWORK PASSAGE 2 (TIME: 6 MINUTES)

The critical period hypothesis states that there exists an ideal window of time during early development in which to acquire a first language if presented with adequate stimuli reinforcing that language. Studies have shown this critical period to last for the first thirteen years of life in humans, during which exposure to language later in the period results in lower mastery than exposure earlier in the period. After this critical period, language acquisition becomes much more difficult and effortful. Two hypotheses below describe the evolutionary functionality of the critical period in language acquisition.

Hypothesis 1

The language acquisition model for evolving species generations is based on three assumptions:

I. Language is an evolutionary benefit that is naturally selected for, or favored genetically from one generation to the next.
II. A person's individual language can be quantitatively measured.
III. Multiple factors in maturation and development are genetically controlled. This affects the timing for critical periods for specific capacities.

Collectively, these assumptions lead to the conclusion that language acquisition is an adaptation that has evolved over time to benefit the survival of humans. Therefore, knowing a language correlates positively with an individual's reproductive success, or ability to produce viable offspring, which will then live and continue to propagate their species.

This model is supported by the notion that language is a complex design that serves a specific function, one that cannot be substituted by any other existing capacity. Thus, language is a trait that was naturally selected for over the course of human history.

Furthermore, the critical period of language acquisition is not an adaptation, but rather a control on language that arose due to a lack of selection pressures favoring the learning of multiple languages. This signifies that the acquisition of more than one language did not confer any evolutionary advantage over the period of human history.

Hypothesis 2

The language acquisition model for animal populations of constant size is based on the three following assumptions:

I. Knowing a language correlates positively with an individual's reproductive success.
II. The ability to learn a language is inherited.
III. Learning a language bears with it certain costs.

Language acquisition is an evolutionary stable strategy due to two competing selection pressures. One, if the critical period for language learning is too short, language does not develop well and results in an evolutionary disadvantage to an individual. On the other hand, if the critical period for language acquisition is too long, the learning becomes too costly by reducing opportunities for reproduction by the individual, thereby reducing reproductive success. These variations lead to the conclusion that the critical period for language learning is an evolutionary adaptive mechanism that keeps these pressures in equilibrium, while providing optimal reproductive success to the individual.

7. Hypotheses 1 and 2 both state that:

(A) the knowledge base one has of a language can be quantitatively measured.
(B) speaking a language will result in greater reproductive success for an individual.
(C) language serves a unique function and cannot be replaced by any other existing capacity.
(D) learning multiple languages during the critical period may result in a decrease in reproductive success.

8. Suppose a child learns two languages in her home during the first thirteen years of her life. According to Hypothesis 1, this would:

(A) increase the reproductive success of that individual.
(B) decrease the reproductive success of that individual.
(C) reduce the evolutionary advantage of language acquisition in that child's progeny.
(D) have no effect on the evolutionary advantage of language acquisition in that child's progeny.

9. The main point of difference between Hypothesis 1 and Hypothesis 2 is that:

   (A) Hypothesis 1 describes language acquisition as an evolutionary benefit, while Hypothesis 2 does not.
   (B) Hypothesis 1 considers the ability to learn a language as an acquired trait, while Hypothesis considers it an inherited trait.
   (C) Hypothesis 2 considers the costs of learning a language, while Hypothesis 1 does not.
   (D) Hypothesis 2 considers the length of the language learning critical period to be favorable, while Hypothesis 2 considers the length to be unfavorable.

10. Feral children are those that grow up living in isolation with animals instead of people, and without exposure to or practice with the human language. How would the reproductive success of feral children living in isolation for fifteen years be affected according to Hypotheses 1 and 2?

   (A) Reproductive success will decrease according to Hypothesis 1 and be unaffected according to Hypothesis 2.
   (B) Reproductive success will decrease according to Hypothesis 2 and be unaffected according to Hypothesis 1.
   (C) Reproductive success will decrease according to both Hypotheses 1 and 2.
   (D) Reproductive success will be unaffected according to both Hypotheses 1 and 2.

11. Suppose an individual continues to learn a language in his home past the critical period up to twenty years of age. According to Hypothesis 2, this would:

   (A) reduce his opportunities for reproduction and, therefore, his reproductive success.
   (B) put him and his progeny at an evolutionary advantage even greater than the one if he had just learned for thirteen years.
   (C) have no effect on his reproductive success only.
   (D) have no effect on his reproductive success nor affect his and his progeny's evolutionary adaptation.

12. A boy is born and raised in Russia for twenty years, learning and only being exposed to the Russian language during that time. He then moves to the United States for the remainder of his life, where he is exposed to and learns English for the first time. According to the information presented in the passage, by the end of his lifetime, the boy will have experienced which of the following?

   (A) A difficult time learning English only
   (B) A difficult time learning both English and Russian
   (C) A decrease in reproductive success only
   (D) A decrease in reproductive success and an evolutionary disadvantage for him and his progeny

13. In one study, the linguistic performance of deaf children exposed to and learning American Sign Language (ASL) at three different periods during development was studied. Individuals were grouped according to when they were first exposed to and began learning ASL: since birth, since 2 years old, since 6 years old, and since 12 years old. According to the information presented in the passage, which of the following statements is true?

   (A) Those first exposed to ASL at 6 years of age will have a greater reproductive success than those first exposed at 2 years of age.
   (B) Those first exposed to ASL at 2 years of age will perform better on ASL tests than those first exposed at 6 years of age.
   (C) Those first exposed to ASL at 12 years of age will have the greatest evolutionary advantage for them and their progeny.
   (D) Those first exposed to ASL at birth will have a lower evolutionary advantage than those first exposed at 6 years of age.

sP13A

Directions: The following two passages are similar to real ACT test passages. Read each passage and answer the questions that follow. Use the methods and techniques that you have learned throughout the workbook to help you answer the questions.

PRACTICE PASSAGE 1 (TIME: 4 MINUTES)

Heat is the transfer of energy from an object of warmer temperature to one of colder temperature via thermal interactions. For the following experiments on the properties of heat, assume heat flows in a straight line from one surface of a block to its corresponding surface on the opposite side of the block. Thus, the distance the heat crosses is the block's thickness.

Experiment 1

Four rectangular prisms made from various metals but with identical dimensions are heated with equal amounts of energy at one surface, after which the difference in temperatures (ΔT) is measured between the heated surface and its corresponding surface on the opposite side of the block. The blocks are then left to sit until both surfaces reach the same temperature—that is, until the heat travels from one side of the block to the other. The difference in temperatures and time needed to reach equilibrium are shown in Table 1.

Table 1

Metal	ΔT (°C)	Time (s)
I	50	40
II	40	30
III	30	20
IV	20	10

Experiment 2

The block of Metal I is then cut into four separate parts labeled A through D. Each part has a different thickness but the same width and height. The procedure from Experiment 1 is then repeated with each block. Table 2 shows the data.

Table 2

Part	Thickness (cm)	ΔT (°C)	Time (s)
A	5	30	4
B	10	30	8
C	15	15	24
D	20	30	16

Experiment 3

The procedure from Experiment 1 is then repeated with three new blocks of a different metal, Metal V, each with identical dimensions. Each block is heated on one of its three surfaces: A, B, or C. The data are shown in Table 3.

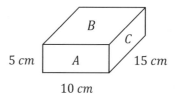

Figure 1

Table 3

Surface	Area (cm^2)	ΔT (°C)	Time (s)
A	50	20	45
B	150	20	5
C	75	40	10

1. Given that a greater time required to reach equilibrium means a lower rate of energy transfer, which of the following hypotheses is supported by the results of Experiment 2?

(A) Rate of energy transfer is directly proportional to thickness and inversely proportional to temperature difference.
(B) Rate of energy transfer is affected by thickness, but not temperature difference.
(C) Rate of energy transfer is inversely proportional to thickness and directly proportional to temperature difference.
(D) Rate of energy transfer is dependent on the type of metal used.

2. If a fifth prism were added to Experiment 1 with dimensions identical to those of the other four, but made from a fifth metal, and it had a temperature difference of 10°C, the time needed for it to reach equilibrium would be closest to:

(A) 0 s
(B) 5 s
(C) 10 s
(D) It cannot be determined from the given information.

3. In Experiment 2, if Part C were altered to have a different thickness and/or temperature difference but took the same amount of time to reach equilibrium, its new thickness and temperature difference could be:

(A) 30 cm and 30°C
(B) 7.5 cm and 30°C
(C) 30 cm and 7.5°C
(D) It cannot be determined from the given information.

4. Which of the following conclusions can be drawn from the results of Experiment 3?

(A) Thickness has no effect on the time needed for opposite surfaces to reach equilibrium.
(B) Doubling the surface area has a greater effect on the rate of energy transfer than reducing the thickness by half.
(C) The smaller the surface area, the higher the rate of energy transfer.
(D) The greater the surface area, the higher the rate of energy transfer.

5. Experiment 3 is repeated with a fourth block also made from Metal V, but with the length and width of surface A both doubled, and the depth unchanged. If surface A is heated and the temperature difference is 20°C, the time needed for it to reach equilibrium would be closest to:

(A) 3 s
(B) 11 s
(C) 45 s
(D) 180 s

6. Which of the following statements is true about Experiments 1-3?

(A) Experiments 2 and 3 examine individual metals from Experiment 1 more closely.
(B) Experiment 3 uses prisms with dimensions identical to those in Experiment 1, while Experiment 2 does not.
(C) Experiments 1 and 3 each examine a factor related to the rate of heat transfer that is not examined in Experiment 2.
(D) Experiments 1, 2, and 3 each examine the same factors related to the rate of heat transfer.

PRACTICE PASSAGE 2 (TIME: 6 MINUTES)

In the following passage, two physiologists debate the most beneficial forms of physical training.

Physiologist 1:

Today, there is tremendous emphasis on aerobic and endurance exercise for better cardiovascular health. While some cardiovascular exercise is essential to health, this emphasis can often ignore another key component to fitness: strength (anaerobic) training. Strength training—which includes weightlifting and movements such as sprinting and jumping—will greatly improve overall health when combined with cardiovascular exercises; strength training is not just for professional athletes. Strength training improves health in a few broad ways. It increases muscle tone and mass, which fortifies bones and helps provide protection from injuries. It also makes the body break down and use food more efficiently, which means higher energy levels and lower body fat levels. And, it uses the type of physical stress (short bursts of high intensity movement) that the body, especially the heart and other muscles, can recover and augment from best. Strength training is an effective component of any training program that seeks to improve overall and long-term health.

Physiologist 2:

Cardiovascular exercises are widely promoted because training programs that emphasize them are appropriate for the majority of the population. Cardiovascular exercises are based on movement and activity; when a person is sedentary, his health will improve drastically simply by introducing the regular activity that cardiovascular exercises provide. Other than a poor diet, the main obstacle to better health for most individuals is a lack of activity. An additional benefit of emphasizing cardiovascular training is that it is accessible to nearly everyone: no special equipment is required for most exercises (for example, walking, jogging, and cycling) and the amount of initial training is minimal. Finally, cardiovascular training is the foundation for all physical activities, whether one is just trying to lose weight or training to become an Olympic champion. Emphasizing cardiovascular training does not ignore the benefits of other forms of exercise, but it does put the focus on training that is the simplest and most efficient way to improve health.

7. What is the main point of disagreement between the two physiologists?

   (A) Whether strength training or cardiovascular exercise results in more injuries
   (B) Which physical movements promote the fastest recovery
   (C) Which types of physical training are most beneficial for overall health
   (D) Whether improving diet or increasing activity is the best solution for improving overall health

8. Physiologist 1 claims that strength training is not being emphasized and used enough to promote overall health, while Physiologist 2 claims that:

   (A) diet is the biggest obstacle to improving the health of most individuals.
   (B) cardiovascular training is emphasized strongly because it is simple and benefits the most people.
   (C) short, intense workouts throughout the day are the solution to sedentary lifestyles.
   (D) only aspiring Olympic champions do not need cardiovascular training.

9. Which of the following statements is a critique Physiologist 1 has for the position of Physiologist 2?

   (A) Physiologist 1 argues that emphasizing cardiovascular training always leads to the exclusion of strength training in an exercise program.
   (B) Physiologist 1 implies that strength training provides the same benefits as cardiovascular training.
   (C) Physiologist 1 claims that cardiovascular training does not lead to higher energy levels and lower body fat levels.
   (D) Physiologist 1 asserts that strength training is safer and easier on the body than cardiovascular training.

10. Which of the following is a critique Physiologist 2 has for the position of Physiologist 1?

    (A) Physiologist 2 argues that cardiovascular training in more accessible than strength training.
    (B) Physiologist 2 implies that strength training is costly to integrate into exercise programs.
    (C) Physiologist 2 claims that cardiovascular training is the best means to compensate for poor diets.
    (D) Physiologist 2 asserts that cardiovascular training is not promoted as widely as strength training.

11. What, if anything, do the physiologists agree on?

    (A) They agree that poor diets are the main obstacle to overall health and fitness.
    (B) They agree that some cardiovascular training is needed for overall health.
    (C) They agree that some strength training is necessary in any exercise program.
    (D) The physiologists do not agree on anything.

12. What would NOT be an example of the "short bursts of high intensity movement" that Physiologist 1 alludes to?

    (A) Sprints at a local track
    (B) Pull-ups at a park jungle gym
    (C) Walking up a steep hill
    (D) Jumping up and down a ledge repeatedly

13. What would be an example of experimental results that strengthen Physiologist 2's position?

    (A) A researcher reports that running elevates the risk of cartilage degeneration in knees.
    (B) A researcher reports that sprinters have higher energy levels than cyclists.
    (C) A study finds that activity and diet are the only factors in overall health.
    (D) A study finds that walking throughout the day decreases body fat levels.

sP13B

Directions: The following two passages are similar to real ACT test passages. Read each passage and answer the questions that follow. Use the methods and techniques that you have learned throughout the workbook to help you answer the questions.

HOMEWORK PASSAGE 1 (TIME: 4 MINUTES)

Two biologists have proposed a broad scheme for classifying organisms according to their life histories. *Life history* refers to an organism's patterns or habits of reproduction and growth. Beyond shedding light on how particular organisms and populations live, the study of life history strategies has become vital to evaluating solutions for problems such as invasive species and habitat conservation. Table 1 summarizes the two general life history strategies that the two scientists proposed. Table 2 below lists some North American animals along with information on several of these categories.

Table 1

Category	Strategy A	Strategy B
Development	Fast	Slow
Offspring Number	High	Low
Time to Fertility	Early	Late
Reproductive Frequency	Once	Repeated
Body Size	Small	Large
Lifespan	Short	Long
Competitive Ability	Weak	Strong
Survivorship	High mortality of young	High mortality of old
Dispersal Ability	Strong	Weak
Habitat Type	Frequently changing	Stable
Population Size	Highly Variable	Fairly Constant

Table 2

Category	Raccoon	American Alligator	Blue Jay	Eastern Cottontail	Fruit Fly
Body Weight	3.5 to 9 kg	300 to 350 kg	70 to 100 g	0.8 to 2 kg	<1 mg
Body Length	40 to 70 cm	3.2 to 4 m	22 to 30 cm	36 to 48 cm	2.5 mm
Offspring Number	2 to 5	20 to 50 eggs	4 to 5 eggs	Approximately 5	100 eggs
Reproductive Frequency	Once per year	Once per year	Once per year	3 to 5 times per year	Once per day
Time to Fertility	Males: 2 years Females: 1 year	10 to 12 years	1 year	2 to 3 months	7 days
Lifespan	2 to 3 years	Up to 50 years	Up to 7 years	15 months	Up to 30 days
Survivorship	50% live at least 1 year	20% reach adulthood	15% reach adulthood	20% reach adulthood	Very low

1. A polar bear requires a wide habitat range in order to have steady access to food, which in turn allows maintenance of its proper body size. Which strategy does this animal likely belong to?

    (A) Strategy A
    (B) Strategy B
    (C) Either Strategy
    (D) Neither Strategy

2. A tide pool, which is often battered by waves and subject to tides on a daily basis, is a habitat that would likely be full of organisms following which strategy?

    (A) Strategy A
    (B) Strategy B
    (C) Either Strategy
    (D) Neither Strategy

3. Some cultivated grasses are known to grow better and to resist invasion by weeds the more frequently the lawn area is mowed. Which strategy and life history category pair best explains these grasses?

(A) Strategy A and Lifespan because regular mowing shortens how long the grasses live.
(B) Strategy A and Habitat Type because regular mowing frequently changes the habitat.
(C) Strategy B and Survivorship because regular mowing kills mostly the older grass.
(D) Strategy B and Reproductive Frequency because regular mowing makes the grass reproduce quickly.

4. Many animals that are endangered and in captive breeding programs follow life history Strategy B. When they are finally released back into the wild, what would be important considerations when creating their nature preserve?

(A) A small area with a stable climate
(B) A small area with a variable climate
(C) A large area with a stable climate
(D) A large area with a variable climate

5. Some organisms seemingly switch strategies, depending on their life stage. For example, green sea turtles (*Chelonia mydas*) have seemingly contradictory features: young hatchlings are likely to be eaten by predators while trying to cross a sandy beach, but mature turtles can easily cross thousands of miles of open ocean safely; female sea turtles take years to reach reproductive maturity but produce hundreds of eggs; and, while their population sizes increase dramatically shortly after mating season, their population sizes tend to remain constant over time. Are green sea turtles switching strategies and, if so, in what direction?

(A) No, they follow Strategy A their whole lives.
(B) No, they follow Strategy B their whole lives.
(C) Yes, they follow Strategy A initially and then switch to Strategy B as they age.
(D) Yes, they follow Strategy B initially, then switch to Strategy A as they age.

HOMEWORK PASSAGE 2 (TIME: 4 MINUTES)

A dam is a massive barrier built across a river or stream to regulate the flow of water for human purposes. Some uses of dams include generation of hydroelectricity, irrigation, and flood control during seasons of high rain or snowfall.

Changing reservoir levels upstream of, or before, the dam affects the water levels in the river downstream, or after the dam. These changes can also have an impact on activities dependent upon the reservoir levels, such as boating and rafting. Each year from 1990–2010, city officials from City A raised reservoir levels for a dam by one meter. Figure 1 plots the dam's recreation sales and fish catch for the same time period. Note that a change in mean depth is a reflection of a change in year.

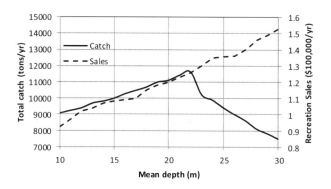

Figure 1

Some species of fish, such as tilapia and catfish, live near shore in shallow waters and are collectively known as *littoral species*. Others, such as sardines or cyprinids, live offshore in deeper waters and are known as *pelagic species*. Shallow reservoirs typically only possess littoral species, while deeper reservoirs usually possess both littoral and pelagic species. Figure 2 plots the total littoral and pelagic species count as a function of nutrient level in City A's dam reservoir.

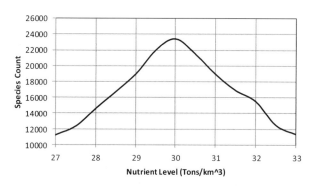

Figure 2

Officials of City A want to make optimum use of their dam by minimizing negative environmental impacts and maximizing recreation profits. They conducted a survey of 10,000 people living in the city to find out in which months most people favor to engage in aquatic activities that utilize the dam's upstream reservoir or downstream river. The results are listed in Table 1. Each person was allowed to vote for multiple periods.

Table 1

Month	People
January – February	223
March – May	2,468
June – August	9,845
September – October	3,210
November – December	890

In addition, they counted the number of littoral and pelagic species residing in the dam reservoir during the same periods. Table 2 lists the data.

Table 2

Month	Littoral	Pelagic
January – February	2,451	3,954
March – May	8,421	11,023
June – August	15,245	19,324
September – October	6,423	8,465
November – December	4,123	5,419

6. Based on the data presented in the passage, which conditions would be MOST optimal for total fish count in City A's reservoir?

    (A) Mean depth of 20 m and nutrient level of 30 tons per km^3
    (B) Mean depth of 22 m and nutrient level of 30 tons per km^3
    (C) Mean depth of 30 m and nutrient level of 20 tons per km^3
    (D) Mean depth of 30 m and nutrient level of 22 tons per km^3

7. Suppose the total fish catch one year from City A's reservoir was 9,000 tons. Based on the information presented in the passage, most of these fish could be:

    (A) Tilapia.
    (B) Sardines.
    (C) Catfish and cyprinids.
    (D) Two of the above.

8. Over the time period from 1990 to 2010, in which month and year might the reservoir have yielded the greatest fish catch?

    (A) June of 1990
    (B) March of 2000
    (C) August of 2002
    (D) July of 2010

9. Over the time period from 1990 to 2010, in which month and year might the reservoir have yielded the lowest recreation sales?

    (A) January of 1990
    (B) January of 2000
    (C) February of 2002
    (D) February of 2010

10. During the count of littoral and pelagic species plotted in Figure 2, the count recorded at a nutrient level of 28 tons/km^3 could have been during which month?

    (A) February
    (B) July
    (C) October
    (D) November

sP14A

Directions: The following two passages are similar to real ACT test passages. Read each passage and answer the questions that follow. Use the methods and techniques that you have learned throughout the workbook to help you answer the questions.

PRACTICE PASSAGE 1 (TIME: 4 MINUTES)

Marine iguanas are a unique species of lizards that live close to the shore and feed off algae from the ocean. The following maps indicate the location of populations of marine iguanas over a 50 year time span on the same tropical island.

Tropical Island in 1955

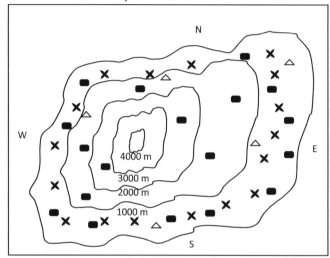

Tropical Island in 2005

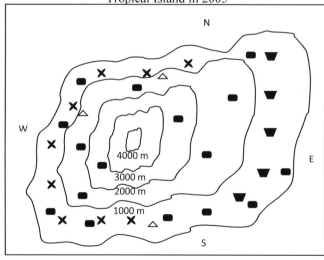

✘ Population of marine iguanas
▪ Local vegetation
△ Predators
▼ Human activity

1. From 1955 to 2005 what happened to the distribution of marine iguanas?

   (A) The distribution increased.
   (B) The distribution decreased.
   (C) The distribution remained constant.
   (D) There is not enough information to answer the question.

2. From 1955 to 2005 what happened to the total amount of vegetation on the island?

   (A) The amount of vegetation increased.
   (B) The amount of vegetation decreased.
   (C) The amount of vegetation remained constant. (D) There is not enough information to answer the question.

3. What is the most likely explanation for the change in marine iguana distribution?

   (A) Lack of food caused by decreases in local vegetation
   (B) Over predation
   (C) Increasing human activity
   (D) Increasing global temperatures

4. What is the most likely explanation for the distribution of marine iguanas with regards to elevation on the island?

   (A) Marine iguanas live at higher elevation where they can avoid predators.
   (B) Marine iguanas live at lower elevations but will move to higher elevations if pressured to.
   (C) Marine iguanas are unlikely to survive at locations away from the sea.
   (D) Marine iguanas were forced to live at lower elevations due to human activity.

5. With regards to the survival of marine iguanas, the best place for continued human expansion on the island would be?

   (A) The Northern area of the island
   (B) The Western area of the island
   (C) The central area of the island
   (D) The Southern area of the island

PRACTICE PASSAGE 2 (TIME: 6 MINUTES)

Animal testing, also known as animal research or *in vivo* testing, is the use of non-human animals in experiments and has been commonplace for almost two centuries of biomedical research. Two scientists below discuss the use of animal testing.

Scientist 1

Animal testing to some may seem harmful and unethical, but those individuals must realize that most of the major biomedical treatments and cures we have today are possible because of animal testing. Claude Bernard, known as the father of physiology, argued that "experiments on animals…are entirely conclusive for the toxicology and hygiene of man…The effects of these substances are the same on man as on animals, save for differences in degree."

Before a compound is introduced into any living species, it is carefully tested and altered to a point where it should not fail by any means. However, a certain risk is involved in the procedure and the potential side effects. Therefore, animal testing is used as a final measure to ensure the safety and efficacy of a substance before it is introduced into the human body. If not for animal testing, the health and lives of millions of individuals would be in danger to unknown potential side effects of any number of drugs or treatments.

Most people do not realize that animal testing benefits not only humans, but also other animals. Veterinarians, zookeepers, pet owners, and others who care for animals all rely on medicines and procedures initially tested on laboratory animals like rats or mice, which are commonly known as house "pests." If one would not hesitate to kill a mouse in his home, would it not be preferable to obtain some good from the rodent before ending its life?

A universal truth exists that humans take the highest priority as species. Before preserving the life of any other species, we must preserve our own, even if at the expense of another. Fortunately, however, we can replenish the species we are harming, as done with numerous endangered species like the Siberian Tiger. We can also take solace in the fact that our advancement of biomedical knowledge, as well as accomplishments, through animal testing causes enough good to counter the harm that may result.

Scientist 2

Animal testing on vertebrates, especially mammals, has misled researchers since its very beginning, confounding our understanding of the human body and the diseases that plague it. Many vertebrates react differently to drugs than do humans, even if some like chimpanzees and other primates share 99.9% of their DNA with us. This fact itself questions the validity of animal testing, making it unreliable. Furthermore, animals in a laboratory setting are in a stressful environment and would, therefore, exhibit different physiological reactions to drugs than would humans in their natural, unstressful settings, again questioning the utility and benefits of animal testing.

Even if humans maintain the highest priority of all species, they must exercise the same level of respect and compassion toward other species that they give to fellow human beings. Currently, millions of rats, mice, rabbits, and primates, among other vertebrates, are trapped in cold, barren cages in laboratories across the world, only to be operated on or manipulated upon release. The stress, sterility, and boredom lead these animals to develop neurotic, hurtful behaviors, such as spinning in circles incessantly, pulling out their hair, and biting their own skin—or even those of other animals confined in the same cage. It is evident that these innocent creatures feel immense pain, loneliness, and terror, all of which any human being would never wish on his loved ones.

There exist several alternatives to animal testing that are not only more humane and safe, but also more economical and reliable, such as cloning of human organs and stem cell research. These methods should be considered and implemented more in biomedical research to prevent further wrongful manipulation of animals than what has already occurred.

6. Scientist 1 believes that:

    (A) animals are the best substitute for humans with which to test different drugs and procedures.
    (B) animal testing is the last step in ensuring that a drug works safely and effectively.
    (C) more rats and mice are killed in homes than killed in laboratory experiments.
    (D) humans have an inherent duty to preserve the lives of other humans before their own.

7. Scientists 1 and 2 would most agree on which of the following?

(A) Primates share 99.9% of their DNA with humans.
(B) Cloning of human organs and stem cell research can be effective ways to research and develop drugs and treatments.
(C) Humans take the highest priority of all species.
(D) The lack of animal testing over the past two centuries may have resulted in the deaths of millions of individuals.

8. One point of difference between the views of Scientists 1 and 2 is that:

(A) Scientist 1 believes animal testing is the best method for testing drugs and procedures, while Scientist 2 believes that organ cloning or stem cell research should be more favored.
(B) Scientist 1 believes that humans should be given the top priority from all species, while Scientist 2 believes that all species deserve the same basic rights.
(C) Scientist 1 believes that animals do not feel pain, while Scientist 2 believes that they do.
(D) Scientist 1 believes *in vivo* testing provides significant benefits that warrant its continued use, while Scientist 2 believes it should be substituted with alternative methods.

9. Which of the following does Scientist 1 NOT cite as a reason for animal testing?

(A) It serves as a final test to ensure the safety and efficacy of drugs in humans.
(B) Efforts are being made to conserve endangered species and reintroduce them into the wild.
(C) Humans are the highest priority of all species and must preserve the lives of fellow human beings before any other species.
(D) Animal testing benefits not only humans, but also other animals.

10. Because of similarities between the innate immune system of insects and mammals, insects like fruit flies and moths, which are not vertebrates, have replaced mammals in certain types of studies. How would Scientist 2 most likely react to this fact?

(A) He would disapprove of the practice since insects are still animals that deserve the same respect humans give to other humans.
(B) He would approve of the practice since insects, unlike humans, do not feel pain, loneliness, and terror.
(C) He would approve of the practice since insects are not vertebrates and are much more abundant in nature.
(D) It cannot be determined.

11. In 2009, *Nature* magazine reported that most animal tests either under- or overestimate the risk of chemical compounds or do not reflect their toxicities well in humans. How does this report affect the strengths of the arguments of Scientists 1 and 2?

(A) It weakens the argument of Scientist 1 and supports the argument of Scientist 2.
(B) It has no effect on the argument of Scientist 1 and supports the argument of Scientist 2.
(C) It supports the argument of Scientist 1 and weakens the argument of Scientist 2.
(D) It has no effect on the arguments of either Scientist 1 or 2.

12. Which of the following does Scientist 2 NOT cite as a reason against animal testing?

(A) Animals react differently to drugs than do humans, undermining the understanding of drug reactions in humans.
(B) Many animals are treated without respect and are kept in cold, barren cages only to be removed when used for experiments.
(C) Vertebrates are the top priority of all species and should be treated accordingly.
(D) Many alternatives to animal testing exist that are safer and provide more reliable data.

sP14B

Directions: The following two passages are similar to real ACT test passages. Read each passage and answer the questions that follow. Use the methods and techniques that you have learned throughout the workbook to help you answer the questions.

HOMEWORK PASSAGE 1 (TIME: 4 MINUTES)

In a chemical reaction, the starting materials (often called *reactants*) must be furnished with energy before they can react to form the *products*. The minimum amount of energy needed to start the reaction is called the *activation energy*.

The figures below illustrate two possible ways that a particular reaction could occur. Additionally, they focus on *Gibbs free energy* (G), which is energy that can be used to perform work in biological systems such as muscle cells.

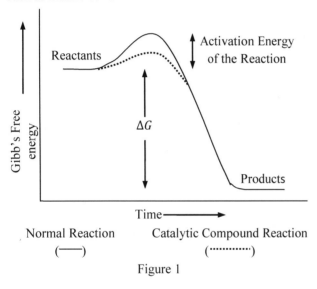

Figure 1

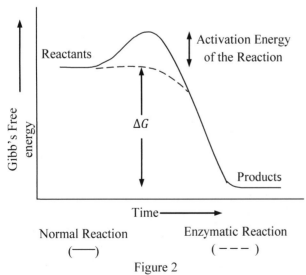

Figure 2

1. $\Delta G = G_{products} - G_{reactants}$

   In the above equation, ΔG stands for the change in Gibbs free energy of a reaction. If ΔG is negative, energy is released and available to perform work; if ΔG is positive, energy is stored for later work. In these reactions:

   (A) ΔG is positive and energy is stored.
   (B) ΔG is positive in the first and negative in the second.
   (C) ΔG is negative in the first and positive in the second.
   (D) ΔG is negative and energy is released.

2. Based on Figure 1, one can conclude that the catalytic compound:

   (A) decreases the amount of reactants needed in the reaction.
   (B) decreases the activation energy needed for the reaction to occur.
   (C) decreases the ΔG of the reaction.
   (D) decreases the amount of products created.

3. Which of the following reactions is expected to occur spontaneously—that is, as soon as the reactants are mixed together?

   (A) The normal reaction
   (B) The reaction with the catalytic compound
   (C) Neither reaction
   (D) Both reactions

4. The *net energy change* of a reaction is the Gibbs free energy released or stored, minus the activation energy need to start it. Which reaction has the greatest net energy change?

   (A) The normal reaction
   (B) The reaction with the catalytic compound
   (C) The reaction with the enzyme
   (D) All reactions have the same net energy change.

5. A scientist needs to create the products depicted
    in these figures, but has a limited volume in
    which to perform the reaction. Which reaction
    should he perform in order to maximize the
    products created in a certain volume?

    (A) The normal reaction
    (B) The reaction with the catalytic compound
    (C) The reaction with the enzyme
    (D) Cannot be determined from the information
         given.

HOMEWORK PASSAGE 2 (TIME: 5 MINUTES)

Germination is the emergence of plants from seeds to begin plant growth. It is affected by factors including water content, oxygen levels, and temperature. *Herbicides* are chemical agents used to kill undesired plants. Some herbicides are selective and are used to kill specific target plants while leaving the desired plants unharmed. Others are unselective and kill all plant material with which they come into contact. The following experiments were conducted to study the effects of herbicides on germination and seedling development of three grass types.

Experiment 1

Twenty-five seeds of buffalograss were added to a petri dish, which was then left to grow under 16 hours of light at 30°C and 8 hours of darkness at 25°C each day for 28 days. The dish was watered daily and kept under humid conditions to ensure optimum water and oxygen levels for germination and growth. The procedure was then repeated with two other grasses: Blue grama and Sideoats grama. Germination results are listed in Table 1.

Table 1

Grass	% Seed Germination
Buffalograss	40
Blue grama	57
Sideoats grama	86

Experiment 2

Six concentrations of the herbicide 245T were added to distilled water: 0.3, 0.6, 1.1, 2.2, 4.5, and 9.0. Two mL of the solution were then added to each petri dish containing 25 seeds of buffalograss. The dishes were then grown under conditions identical to those in *Experiment 1*. The procedure was then repeated using Blue grama and Sideoats grama. The final percentage of seed germination for each plant is shown in Figure 1.

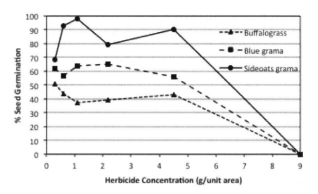

Figure 1

Experiment 3

The procedure from *Experiment 2* was repeated using the herbicide picloram. Figure 2 plots the results.

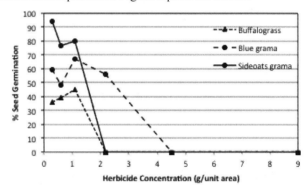

Figure 2

The percentage of final seedling growth of the plants (taken at day 28) in the different herbicide conditions is listed in the tables below as a percentage of the seedling growth of the control.

Table 2: % Buffalograss Seedling Growth

Herbicide	Herbicide Concentration (g/unit area)					
	0.3	0.6	1.1	2.2	4.5	9.0
245T	67.9	63.3	65.4	60.4	41.4	36.5
Picloram	50.3	45.7	43.0	40.9	39.8	35.1

Table 3: % Blue Grama Seedling Growth

Herbicide	Herbicide Concentration (g/unit area)					
	0.3	0.6	1.1	2.2	4.5	9.0
245T	77.6	79.8	70.6	70.7	49.3	39.8
Picloram	76.2	79.4	67.8	63.1	59.7	50.2

Table 4: % Sideoats Grama Seedling Growth

Herbicide	Herbicide Concentration (g/unit area)					
	0.3	0.6	1.1	2.2	4.5	9.0
245T	67.9	68.5	48.9	43.4	37.0	36.1
Picloram	56.8	56.0	48.4	35.9	38.5	30.1

6. Which of the following correctly describes the observations for buffalograss seed germination as a function of 245T herbicide concentration?

    (A) The percent germination increases, then decreases, then increases, and again decreases.
    (B) The percent germination increases, then remains constant, and then decreases.
    (C) The percent germination decreases, then increases, and then decreases.
    (D) None of the above.

7. Which of the following correctly lists the grasses used in Experiment 2 in order of increasing percent seed germination as a function of 245T herbicide concentration?

    (A) Buffalograss, Blue grama, Sideoats grama
    (B) Sideoats grama, Blue grama, buffalograss
    (C) Buffalograss, Sideoats grama, Blue grama
    (D) Sideoats grama, buffalograss, Blue grama

8. Based on the results of Experiments 2 and 3, one can conclude that:

    (A) Buffalograss germinates better in a 2.2 g/unit area of picloram than of 245T.
    (B) Blue grama germinates better in a 4.5 g/unit area of picloram than of 245T.
    (C) Sideoats grama germinates better in a 0.3 g/unit area of picloram than of 245T.
    (D) Buffalograss germinates better in a 0.3 g/unit area of picloram than of 245T.

9. A gardener wants to grow grasses in her backyard but also wants to prevent the growth of any undesired plants. Which of the following combinations of grass and herbicide will NOT give her at least a 50% seedling growth yield?

    (A) Growing buffalograss in 2.2 g/unit area of 245T.
    (B) Growing sideoats grama in 0.6 g/unit area of picloram.
    (C) Growing blue grama in 9.0 g/unit area of picloram.
    (D) Growing buffalograss in 4.5 g/unit area of 245T.

10. Experiments 1, 2, and 3 were conducted with sideoats grama and a new herbicide, triclopyr. The results showed that at 0.3 g/unit area, it produced a greater percentage of seedling growth at Day 28 than did either 245T or picloram at the same concentration. Which of the following could be the final percentage growth observed with the triclopyr?

    (A) 65.5%
    (B) 58.1%
    (C) 69.7%
    (D) 59.1%

11. Experiments 1, 2, and 3 were conducted with buffalograss and a new herbicide, chlopyralid. The results showed that as an average for all the concentrations of herbicide used, the percentage of seedling growth was second highest after the average percentage growth using 245T. Which of the following concentrations of herbicide would yield the greatest percentage of final seedling growth for buffalograss?

    (A) 0.3 g/unit area of chlopyralid
    (B) 0.3 g/unit area of 245T
    (C) 0.3 g/unit area of picloram
    (D) It cannot be determined.

sP15A

Directions: The following two passages are similar to real ACT test passages. Read each passage and answer the questions that follow. Use the methods and techniques that you have learned throughout the workbook to help you answer the questions.

PRACTICE PASSAGE 1 (TIME: 4 MINUTES)

The human body does not always maintain constant levels of carbon dioxide (CO_2) and oxygen (O_2). For instance, during times of strenuous physical activity, CO_2 levels rise while O_2 levels fall. The body possesses a mechanism that compensates for such changes to resume normal functioning.

Myoglobins are proteins found in muscle cells that carry oxygen molecules. They are composed of a single polypeptide chain and possess a very strong affinity for oxygen. The oxygen saturation curve of myoglobin is shown in Figure 1.

Hemoglobins are proteins found in red blood cells that also bind to oxygen. However, these proteins are composed of four polypeptide chains that allow them to bind up to four oxygen molecules simultaneously. When CO_2 levels in the body rise, hemoglobin affinity for oxygen decreases, causing the release of bound oxygen molecules. When CO_2 levels fall, hemoglobin affinity for oxygen increases, and the proteins take up more oxygen from the surrounding blood vessels.

Other factors produce similar phenomena in hemoglobin binding affinity. Levels of 2,3-Bisphosphoglycerate (2,3-BPG) and body temperature are inversely related to hemoglobin affinity for oxygen. Conversely, blood pH is directly related to hemoglobin affinity for oxygen. Figures 2 and 3 illustrate the saturation curve of hemoglobin at different carbon dioxide levels and body temperatures, respectively.

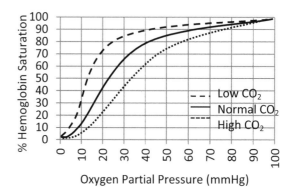

Figure 2

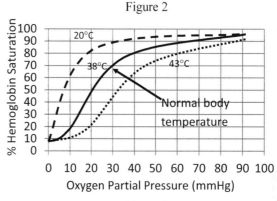

Figure 3

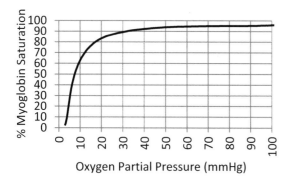

Figure 1

1. The range of oxygen partial pressures in which the smallest difference in oxygen pressure causes the largest difference in myoglobin saturation is:

   (A) 0-10 mmHg
   (B) 10-20 mmHg
   (C) 40-50 mmHg
   (D) 90-100 mmHg

2. Hemoglobin affinity for oxygen is most similar to myoglobin affinity for oxygen in conditions of:

   (A) low CO_2
   (B) normal CO_2
   (C) high CO_2
   (D) normal body temperature

3. The range of oxygen partial pressures in which CO_2 levels have the greatest effect on hemoglobin affinity for oxygen is:

   (A) 0-10 mmHg
   (B) 15-25 mmHg
   (C) 40-50 mmHg
   (D) 65-75 mmHg

4. In chemistry, pH is a measure of the concentration of hydrogen ions in a substance. The relationship between concentration of hydrogen ions in a substance and hemoglobin affinity for oxygen:

   (A) is similar to that of 2,3-BPG levels, CO_2 levels, and body temperature.
   (B) is similar to that of 2,3-BPG levels and body temperature, but not CO_2 levels.
   (C) is similar to that of CO_2 levels, but not 2,3-BPG levels or body temperature.
   (D) is not similar to that of 2,3-BPG levels, CO_2 levels, or body temperature.

5. In blood with 20 mmHg of oxygen, which of the following lists the proteins, from most to least saturated?

   (A) Hemoglobin with low CO_2, hemoglobin with high body temperature, myoglobin
   (B) Myoglobin, hemoglobin with low body temperature, hemoglobin with low CO_2
   (C) Hemoglobin with high CO_2, hemoglobin with normal body temperature, myoglobin
   (D) Hemoglobin with high body temperature, myoglobin, hemoglobin with normal CO_2

PRACTICE PASSAGE 2 (TIME: 6 MINUTES)

Antibiotics are not created equal. An *antibiotic* is a drug designed to kill *pathogens*, harmful organisms that can cause illness; bacteria are common pathogens so most antibiotics target them. The way an antibiotic works against pathogens is called its *mechanism*. Generally, antibiotics can be classified into two categories based on mechanism: broad spectrum and narrow spectrum. Broad spectrum antibiotics typically puncture the cells walls that protect bacteria and work against many types of bacteria. Narrow spectrum antibiotics, on the other hand, typically attack the unique proteins bacteria use to live and grow; therefore, each narrow spectrum antibiotic is limited to a specific group or family of bacteria.

Below, two *immunologists* (scientists who study how to defeat pathogens) debate the merits of broad and narrow spectrum antibiotics, as well as their proper uses.

Immunologist 1:

It is good that broad-spectrum antibiotics are more frequently used. First, their mechanism permits their use for illnesses in which we do not know—or do not have time to determine—the pathogenic cause. Speed of treatment is important, especially when there is risk of rapid death. Second, illnesses can have more than one pathogenic cause. This may be the result of exposure to multiple pathogens initially or inability to fight off new pathogens once already sick. By using a broad spectrum antibiotic, we can help ensure that the treatment is effective for the entire course of the illness. Yes, there have been problems with antibiotic resistance and indiscriminate use of broad spectrum antibiotics may be the cause, but this does not mean such antibiotics are ineffective or lack a place in medical treatment.

Immunologist 2:

Both broad and narrow spectrum antibiotics have legitimate roles in treatments. The main problem is that their roles are reversed: broad spectrum ought to be used less and narrow spectrum ought to be used more. While narrow spectrum antibiotics are limited in the bacteria they can kill, they provide three benefits that broad spectrum antibiotics do not. First, narrow spectrum antibiotics are more effective and efficient at killing the specific bacteria they were designed for. Second, they often require smaller doses, which lessen the risk of poisoning patients. Third, by killing specific bacterial groups, they are

far less likely to ravage the beneficial bacteria (*commensals*) we have, such as the intestinal bacteria that aid digestion. This drastically reduces recovery time after antibiotic treatment. It takes a little extra effort to properly diagnose the cause of an illness, but being able to use narrow spectrum antibiotics is worth it.

6. Based on the information in the introduction, which of the following would NOT be considered a broad spectrum antibiotic?

   (A) Azithromycin inhibits protein synthesis by binding to the 50S subunit of the bacterial ribosome.
   (B) Daptomycin disrupts cell membrane integrity in Gram-positive cocci bacteria.
   (C) Rifampicin inhibits RNA synthesis by binding to RNA polymerase in specific viruses and multiple genera of bacteria.
   (D) Penicillin weakens cell walls by disrupting the structure of peptidoglycan that bacteria produce.

7. Immunologist 1 would most likely state that the frequent prescription of broad spectrum antibiotics by doctors is a result of:

   (A) their low cost compared to narrow spectrum antibiotics.
   (B) illnesses that continue for long periods of time.
   (C) the weak immune systems of more and more patients.
   (D) not being able to quickly or accurately diagnose the cause of an illness.

8. Which of the following best explains why Immunologist 2 mentioned "intestinal bacteria that aid digestion?"

   (A) Such bacteria can drastically reduce recovery time after antibiotic treatment.
   (B) Such bacteria illustrate the need to be judicious with which antibiotics are chosen for treatments.
   (C) The presence of those bacteria precludes the use of broad spectrum antibiotics.
   (D) The presence of those bacteria precludes the use of narrow spectrum antibiotics.

9. Which of the following generalizations is most consistent with Immunologist 1's statement?

   (A) Bacterial illnesses with an unknown pathogen are best treated with broad spectrum antibiotics.
   (B) Increasing antibiotic resistance means that broad spectrum antibiotics are gradually becoming less effective and losing their place in medical treatment.
   (C) Illnesses with more than one pathogenic cause are a common occurrence.
   (D) The course of an infection does not tend to change over time.

10. Both immunologists would most likely agree that broad spectrum antibiotics are an appropriate treatment in which of the following situations?

    (A) The doctor has ample time to diagnose the pathogen causing the illness.
    (B) The patient is highly sensitive to medication, so only small doses of antibiotics can be used.
    (C) The doctor has discovered that the patient tests positive for four different species of pathogenic bacteria.
    (D) The patient wants to recover as quickly as possible in order to return to work.

11. Vancomycin-resistant *S. aureus* (VRSA) is a pathogenic bacterial strain that is resistant to nearly all antibiotics. The only accepted treatment available is the drug Trimethoprim/sulfamethoxazole, which is also used against fungi, protozoans, and other classes of bacteria. What effect does the emergence of VRSA have on the immunologists' viewpoints, if at all?

    (A) It would weaken Immunologist 1's viewpoint only.
    (B) It would strengthen Immunologist 2's viewpoint only.
    (C) It would strengthen both immunologists' viewpoints.
    (D) It would have no effect on either immunologist's viewpoint.

12. There is a third, hotly debated class of antibiotics called *bacteriostatics*, which prevent bacteria from growing and reproducing but do not otherwise kill them. It is claimed that bacteriostatics do not pose the same dangers with antibiotic resistance because the immune system is what actually kills the bacteria. Since the immune system would target the pathogenic bacteria almost exclusively, commensals are spared and pathogens would be more likely to develop additional defenses to that immune system, rather than to the drug in general. Which immunologist would likely be in favor of developing more bacteriostatics and promoting their wider use?

    (A) Immunologist 1.
    (B) Immunologist 2.
    (C) Both immunologists.
    (D) Cannot be determined from the information.

sP15B

Directions: The following two passages are similar to real ACT test passages. Read each passage and answer the questions that follow. Use the methods and techniques that you have learned throughout the workbook to help you answer the questions.

HOMEWORK PASSAGE 1 (TIME: 5 MINUTES)

Natural selection is the phenomenon by which species possessing the most favorable traits in a given environment enjoy the greatest reproductive success, or *fitness*. Table 1 lists different selection phenomena observed in nature by their *phenotypes*, or observed characteristics.

Table 1

Selection	Description
Directional	One extreme phenotype favored
Stabilizing	Intermediate phenotype favored
Disruptive	Extreme phenotypes furthest from the mean favored
Frequency-dependent	Phenotype fitness is a function of how common that phenotype is

Experiment 1

A biologist is measuring the changes in color frequencies of her peppered moths. She measures the initial frequencies of the colors and then releases the moths into a temperate deciduous forest. She measures the color frequencies every five generations. Black moths have *genotype*, or genetic makeup, *BB*; gray moths have genotype *Bb*; and white moths have genotype *bb*. The observed color frequencies are shown in Table 2.

Table 2

Generation	BB	Bb	bb
Initial	.35	.55	.10
5	.31	.57	.12
10	.29	.58	.13
15	.25	.59	.16
20	.22	.60	.18

Experiment 2

The biologist then collects the 20th generation moths from the forest and releases them into a heavily polluted city. Again, she measures the color frequencies every five generations. Her data are shown in Table 3.

Table 3

Generation	BB	Bb	bb
Initial	.22	.60	.18
5	.24	.61	.15
10	.27	.61	.12
15	.29	.62	.09
20	.31	.62	.07

Experiment 3

The biologist introduces a new population of white, gray, and black moths into a habitat with a certain species of bat that preys on the moths. She then observes the population count of the moths every 30 days for a duration of 360 days. Figure 1 plots her data for two of the types of moths.

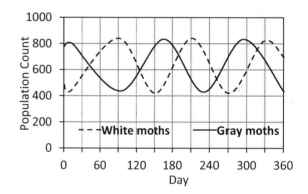

Figure 1

1. Which type of selection does Experiment 2 illustrate?

    (A) Directional
    (B) Stabilizing
    (C) Disruptive
    (D) Frequency-dependent

2. The biologist wants to find out if this species of moth can undergo stabilizing natural selection. Which of the following experiments should she perform?

   (A) Repeat Experiment 1, but in an environment with less neutral colors.
   (B) Collect the 20th generation moths from Experiment 2 and release them into an environment with more neutral colors.
   (C) Repeat Experiment 3, but without introducing bats into the environment.
   (D) Release a new population of all gray moths into the environments of Experiments 1 and 2.

3. In Experiment 3, if the total population of moths remains constant at approximately 1400 for the duration of the experiment, which of the following must be true?

   (A) The population of black moths fluctuates over time.
   (B) The population of black moths remains constant and is greater than zero.
   (C) The population of black moths is always zero.
   (D) There is not enough information to determine what happens to the population of black moths.

4. Which of the following is the most likely explanation for the results of Experiment 3?

   (A) The total population of moths was at its maximum, so an increase in the population of one type caused a decrease in the population of the other.
   (B) The bats learned to look for the color of moth that was most common, which led to a decrease in the frequency of that color.
   (C) The bats learned to look for the color of moth that was least common, which led to a decrease in the frequency of that color.
   (D) Moths of different phenotypes cannot coexist, so an increase in the population of one caused a decrease in the population of the other.

5. Which of the following hypotheses could Experiment 1 have tested?

   (A) The population of moths changes over time as a function of the population of predators in the environment.
   (B) The frequencies of the different phenotypes of moths change over time regardless of the environment they are in.
   (C) Gray moths are better suited than white moths to living in a temperate deciduous forest.
   (D) Black moths are better suited than white moths to living in a heavily polluted city.

6. Which experiment best illustrates the idea that a high frequency of a phenotype does not necessarily indicate high fitness?

   (A) Experiment 1
   (B) Experiment 2
   (C) Experiment 3
   (D) None of them.

HOMEWORK PASSAGE 2 (TIME: 4 MINUTES)

Electrostatics is the study of slow-moving or stationary electrical charges. The forces F between three different point charges $Q1, Q2, Q3$ and point charge P were measured as a function of radius length r. The results are plotted in Figure 1 below.

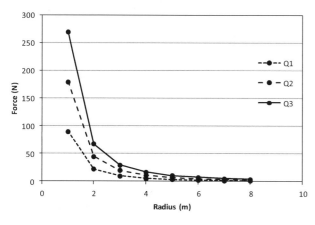

Figure 1

Every point charge Q creates its own electric field in space that is felt by another charge P at a radius r from Q. The strengths of the electric fields generated by point charges $Q1$, $Q2$, and $Q3$ as a function of radius length are plotted in Figure 2.

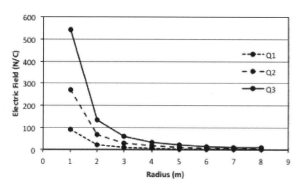

Figure 2

Voltage, or electric potential energy, represents the work done per unit charge against a static electric field to move a point charge from Point A to Point B. The total work done can be calculated as the final potential minus the initial potential. Since the difference in electric potential energy is independent of the path taken by a point charge, voltage is said to be a state function. According to mathematical convention, negatively charged objects are attracted toward higher voltages, and positively charged objects toward lower voltages. Therefore,

conventional current in a circuit flows from higher voltage to lower voltage. However, current may flow from lower to higher voltage if energy is provided to push it against the opposing electric field. The electric potential energy created by a point charge Q at a distance r from the charge is found using:

$$V = \frac{k_e Q}{r},$$

where V is the voltage or electric potential energy, k_e is Coulomb's constant, and Q is the point charge. In Figure 3 below, five point charges A through E were held in initial positions labeled A through E, respectively, at different electric potentials and were released. Their movements were tracked across the different voltages to their final positions (labeled F through J).

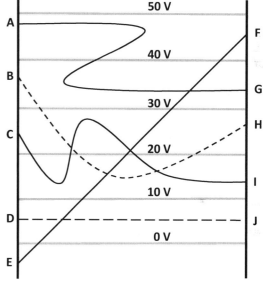

Figure 3

7. If the charge of Q2 in Figure 1 is twice as much as the charge of Q3, which of the following must describe the relationship between the magnitude of charge on a point charge and electrostatic force?

   (A) As charge increases, force increases linearly.
   (B) As charge decreases, force increases linearly.
   (C) As charge increases, force increases exponentially.
   (D) As charge decrease, force increases exponentially.

8. Based on the information presented in the passage, conventional current in a circuit most likely employs:

   (A) protons
   (B) electrons
   (C) neutrons
   (D) It cannot be determined

9. Which of the following could NOT be true about Point charge E in Figure 3?

   (A) It is negatively charged.
   (B) It is positively charged.
   (C) Its final potential is less than the initial potential of Point C.
   (D) Its movement required an input of energy.

10. If the movements of the point charges in Figure 3 were reversed so that they moved from to right to left, which of the following would be true?

    (A) Point charge J would do the most amount of work.
    (B) Point charge F would do the most negative work.
    (C) Point charge I would do twice the amount of work as Point charge F.
    (D) Point charge G would do twice the amount of work as Point charge I.

11. The strength of the electric field generated by Point charge B in Figure 3 at a distance d would be:

    (A) More than three times as strong as the field generated by Point charge D at the same distance.
    (B) More than twice as strong as the field generated by Point charge C at the same distance.
    (C) Less than twice as strong as the field generated by Point charge A at the same distance.
    (D) Less than three times as strong as the field generated by Point charge E at the same distance.

sP16A

Directions: The following two passages are similar to real ACT test passages. Read each passage and answer the questions that follow. Use the methods and techniques that you have learned throughout the workbook to help you answer the questions.

PRACTICE PASSAGE 1 (TIME: 4 MINUTES)

In meteorology, *relative humidity* is used to measure the amount of moisture in the air. It represents the ratio of the partial pressure of water vapor in an air-water mixture to the *saturated*, or maximum, water vapor pressure at a given temperature. At constant pressure, the temperature at which this ratio is 1:1 is called the *dew point*. This occurs when the rate of condensation of water is equal to its rate of evaporation. Figure 1 plots the moisture content in air at different relative humidities as a function of air temperature.

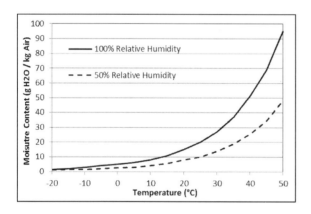

Figure 1

Different conditions in the Earth's atmosphere cause the formation of different weather patterns. A low pressure system occurs when the atmospheric air pressure in an area is lower than that of the air pressure in the surrounding area. This results when warm air rises over cool air due to differences in density, causing the loss of air and air pressure in an area. The greater the difference in air temperatures, the greater the amount of air leaving the area. The difference in air pressure then results in the movement of air from an area of high pressure to one of low pressure, felt as wind. Greater pressure differences produce stronger winds. Figure 2 plots the air pressure and wind speed in a city for a 24-hour period.

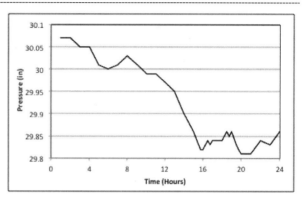

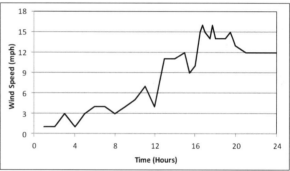

Figure 2

As hot air rises through the Earth's atmosphere, it expands and consequently cools. This cooling eventually results in the condensation of water molecules to form cloud droplets, which coalesce and grow larger with more condensation. If the droplets become too heavy, they fall toward the earth in the form of precipitation. Table 1 lists characteristics for different forms of precipitation, and Table 2 the characteristics of the three major cloud forms.

Table 1

Precipitation	Size	Cloud Type
Mist	0.005 – 0.05 mm	Stratus
Rain	0.5 – 5 mm	Cumulonimbus
Snow	1mm – 2 cm	Nimbus
Hail	5 mm – 10 cm	Cumulonimbus

Table 2

Cloud Type	Approximate Altitude	Appearance
Cirrus	6000 m	White, thin, sheet-like or wispy fibers
Cumulus	4000 m	Globular with flat base and rising domes
Stratus	2000 m	Sheets or layers

1. Based on the data presented in the passage, which of the following best describes the relationship between air pressure and wind speed?

   (A) Wind speed varies directly with air pressure.
   (B) Wind speed varies inversely with air pressure.
   (C) Wind speed varies directly and exponentially with air pressure.
   (D) Wind speed varies inversely and exponentially with air pressure.

2. Which of the following air temperature differences would result in the HIGHEST wind speeds?

   (A) 4°C
   (B) 8°C
   (C) 12°C
   (D) 16°C

3. The precipitation falling in one city was around 0.01 mm. From what height may have this precipitation fallen?

   (A) 500 m
   (B) 1900 m
   (C) 4200 m
   (D) 5800 m

4. Clouds appearing above a city had a gray, flat, layered appearance. Which of the following forms of precipitation may the city experience?

   (A) Mist and hail.
   (B) Mist and rain.
   (C) Mist only.
   (D) Rain only.

5. Based on the data presented in Figure 1, which of the following statements is NOT true?

   (A) The ratio of water to air in water vapor at 50% humidity and 40°C is greater than the ratio of water to air in water vapor at 50% humidity and 20°C.
   (B) The ratio of water to air in water vapor at 100% humidity and 20°C is greater than the ratio of water to air in water vapor at 50% humidity and 40°C.
   (C) The ratio of water to air in water vapor at 50% humidity and 40°C is less than the ratio of water to air in water vapor at 100% humidity and 40°C.
   (D) The ratio of water to air in water vapor at 50% humidity and 20°C is less than the ratio of water to air in water vapor at 100% humidity and 20°C.

PRACTICE PASSAGE 2 (TIME: 5 MINUTES)

A soil scientist investigates the effects of erosion in a river basin over the course of ten weeks to determine what promotes and deters erosive forces.

Experiment 1

Using random sampling, the scientist marked and monitored nine different four-meter square test sites. The average grade of the surface (Slope) and the percentage of the surface covered by vegetation (% Vegetation) were recorded in Table 1. In addition, the scientist measured the initial average depth of the topsoil/humus soil at a typical test site, which is not shown, and the difference between the site and the average after 5 weeks (Δ Depth$_5$) and 10 weeks (Δ Depth$_{10}$).

Table 1

Site	Δ Depth$_5$ (cm)	Δ Depth$_{10}$ (cm)	Slope	% Vegetation
1	−0.5	−0.8	Gentle	20
2	−1.8	−2.0	Gentle	8
3	−0.2	+0.3	Gentle	40
4	−0.8	−1.0	Moderate	37
5	−1.1	−1.5	Moderate	23
6	−3.0	−2.4	Moderate	3
7	−0.1	−0.3	Steep	57
8	−1.9	−2.1	Steep	20
9	0.0	+0.1	Steep	92

Experiment 2

The scientist took 100 mL samples of the topsoil layer from each of the nine test sites and named them to correspond with the site they were taken from. Each sample was placed inside a 250 mL beaker with 100 mL of water, sealed, shaken, and allowed to settle into layers of sand, silt, and clay over 24 hours. The scientist then recorded the height of each of the layers.

Table 2

Sample	Sand height (cm)	Silt height (cm)	Clay height (cm)
1	0.51	0.42	3.17
2	3.17	0.40	0.43
3	1.03	2.18	0.82
4	2.34	0.86	0.81
5	1.51	1.34	1.21
6	3.49	0.52	0.01
7	2.41	0.02	1.59
8	1.55	2.52	0.02
9	0.52	3.11	0.37

6. According to the data in Table 1, which of the following would you expect to be the % Vegetation at the typical test site, provided that plant growth is independent from slope?

(A) Less than 10%
(B) Between 10% and 25%
(C) Between 25% and 50%
(D) Between 50% and 90%

7. Based on the data obtained in Experiment 2, one can assume that which of the following is true about the relationship between % Vegetation and type of topsoil?

   (A) There is a weak positive correlation between the amount of silt in a site's topsoil and the amount of plant life that covers that site.
   (B) There is a strong negative correlation between the amount of silt in a site's topsoil and the amount of plant life that covers that site.
   (C) There is a no correlation between topsoil and the amount of plant life that covers that site.
   (D) There is a strong negative correlation between the amount of clay in a site's topsoil and the amount of plant life that covers that site.

8. A new site was analyzed 20 meters upstream from Site 6. The slope, Δ Depth$_5$, and Δ Depth$_{10}$ of this new site were approximately the same as Site 6, but the site had half the sand content of the sample at Site 6. Instead, all of the sand was replaced by a 4:1 mixture of silt and clay. What would you expect the % Vegetation of this new site to be?

   (A) Less than 3%
   (B) Approximately 3%
   (C) Between 3% and 6%
   (D) Larger than 6%

9. When sediment settles in water, the densest particles will always settle to the bottom. Clay had the lowest density of the 3 types of soil, with a density of 1.20 g/mL. Which of the following is a possible ordering of the 4 substances in the beaker, with the densest material being the furthest to the left?

   (A) Clay, Sand, Silt, Water
   (B) Sand, Silt, Clay, Water
   (C) Clay, Silt, Sand, Water
   (D) Water, Clay, Silt, Sand

10. According to the data found in Experiment 1, which site experienced the most soil erosion, the washing away of layers of soil, over the 10-week period?

    (A) Site 1
    (B) Site 3
    (C) Site 5
    (D) Site 6

11. Soil from two new sites (A and B), located 2 m apart, was collected and analyzed as in Experiment 2. The data obtained is below:

Site	Sand height (cm)	Silt height (cm)	Clay height (cm)	% Vegetation
A	3.68	0.34	0.00	5%
B	2.80	0.80	0.42	45%

What is the most logical reason for the differences in soil makeup of two sites so close together?

    (A) Recent seismic activity caused a fissure to open up beneath Site B, reducing the amount of sand present at the site. Site A was unaffected by seismic activity.
    (B) A recent storm system washed away the topmost layers of soil at Site A, while the presence of plant life at Site B helped keep most of the soil intact.
    (C) Recent seismic activity shifted the layers of soil at both sites, resulting in Sand being the topmost layer at both sites.
    (D) A recent wildfire torched the vegetation at Site A but left Site B untouched.

sP16B

Directions: The following two passages are similar to real ACT test passages. Read each passage and answer the questions that follow. Use the methods and techniques that you have learned throughout the workbook to help you answer the questions.

HOMEWORK PASSAGE 1 (TIME: 6 MINUTES)

Over the past decade, the media has paid increasingly more attention to high fructose corn syrup, which has repeatedly been cited as a major cause of the widespread obesity problem in the United States.

Scientist 1

This heightened focus on high fructose corn syrup has become a distraction from the real cause of obesity in the United States: overconsumption. If Americans learned to eat in moderation, these problems would not exist. High fructose corn syrup contains the same amount of calories as sucrose, common table sugar. This is why the studies on sodas show no significant weight gain when sodas sweetened with sucrose are consumed instead of those sweetened with high fructose corn syrup. The consumption of high fructose corn syrup was irrelevant; high caloric diets always led to a weight increase.

In 31 *isocaloric* tests, participants were given foods with the same amount of calories. One group was given non-fructose carbohydrates, while the other ate solely fructose carbohydrates. Neither group gained a significant amount of weight. Similarly, 16 *hypercaloric* tests were given, in which participants were given either glucose or fructose in excess. Both groups gained relatively the same amount of weight. Thus, the main factor in weight gain is excess.

Scientist 2

High fructose corn syrup alters brain chemistry in ways similar to that of endorphin-releasing drugs like cocaine. Consumers feel elated when they ingest high fructose corn syrup and agitated or depressed when they do not have any. These effects are especially evident in Americans due to their habits of overconsumption. However, the substance causes even more concern when one realizes all of the harmful physical effects of high fructose corn syrup.

There have been a number of experiments that prove the negative effects of high fructose corn syrup. In one experiment, rats were given standard rat food and sweetened water. One group was given water sweetened with sucrose, and the other was given water sweetened with high fructose corn syrup. The rats in the second group gained much more weight than the first. These studies were continued over long periods of time. The rats that were given high fructose corn syrup gained a significant amount of weight.

Furthermore, much of the data used to support the use of high fructose corn syrup is derived from studies that only use fructose. The results from these experiments are irrelevant because there is a significant difference between fructose and high fructose corn syrup. Sucrose and high fructose corn syrup both contain glucose and fructose. However, high fructose corn syrup contains 5% more fructose and 5% less glucose than table sugar does. This is why some scientists think that tests with heavy doses of fructose are the same as tests with doses of high fructose corn syrup. However, high fructose corn syrup is prepared in such a way that the fructose is unbound and readily available for absorption into the body. Very simply, high fructose corn syrup skips a metabolic step that regular fructose and sucrose do not. Thus the impact of high fructose corn syrup on the body is exponentially different than fructose alone. By eliminating high fructose corn syrup from our diet and learning to eat in moderation, we could help solve the obesity problem in the United States.

1. Both scientists would agree that:

    (A) there is no evidence to support the idea that high fructose corn syrup is harmful to the body.
    (B) overconsumption is a contributing factor to the obesity problem in the United States.
    (C) consumption of high fructose corn syrup has severe negative effects on the human body.
    (D) high caloric diets do not lead to a significant weight increase.

2. How would Scientist 2 respond to Scientist 1's claim that in the 16 tests in which participants were given excessive amounts of either glucose or fructose both groups gained relatively the same amount of weight?

   (A) Since the tests were not sustained over a long period of time, the endorphin-releasing effects were not taken into account.
   (B) These results mirror the results from the experiment conducted on the rats.
   (C) These results are unusable since the tests were conducted with fructose and not high fructose corn syrup.
   (D) These results are faulty because the amounts do not reflect Americans' habits of overconsumption.

3. A study came out recently that suggests that high fructose corn syrup could help people who suffer from hypoglycemia by acting as a blood sugar-controlling agent. Whose argument does this weaken?

   (A) Scientist 1.
   (B) Neither scientist.
   (C) Both scientists.
   (D) Scientist 2.

4. Which of the following statements would be most consistent with Scientist 1's argument?

   (A) Since high fructose corn syrup was first put into food as a commercial sweetener in the 1980s, obesity rates have tripled.
   (B) Studies show that the human body processes table sugar and high fructose corn syrup in the same way.
   (C) It has recently been discovered that high fructose corn syrup contains unhealthy doses of mercury.
   (D) Overconsumption of fructose or table sugar has no negative effects on the human body.

5. Scientist 2 mentions all of the following as harmful effects of high fructose corn syrup EXCEPT:

   (A) The effects of high fructose on the brain are similar to that of an endorphin-releasing drug.
   (B) Experiments were conducted that showed that rats who drank water sweetened with high fructose corn syrup gained significantly more weight than rats who drank water sweetened with table sugar.
   (C) Studies have shown that people who consume excessive amounts of high fructose corn syrup are more susceptible to blood sugar diseases like diabetes than those who do not.
   (D) High fructose corn syrup is prepared in such a way that makes it more readily absorbed into the body than fructose alone.

6. Both scientists would agree that which of the following is a solution to the obesity problem in the United States?

   (A) Cutting all sugars out of our diets.
   (B) Regulating the commercial use of high fructose corn syrup.
   (C) Using table sugar as a sweetener instead of high fructose corn syrup.
   (D) Having diets rooted in the principle of moderation.

7. Based on Scientist 2's argument, why is high fructose corn syrup more impactful on the body than fructose alone?

   (A) High fructose corn syrup skips a step in the metabolic process and is absorbed by the body much quicker than fructose.
   (B) High fructose corn syrup contains 10% more fructose than table sugar.
   (C) Fructose has qualities that mimic those of endorphin-releasing drugs.
   (D) High fructose corn syrup leads to overconsumption, especially in Americans.

HOMEWORK PASSAGE 2 (TIME: 4 MINUTES)

Among insects, many different living and feeding strategies exist. One common strategy, especially for wasps, is *parasitism*. In parasitism, one organism, the *parasite*, infects and draws energy or resources from another, the *host*, in order to grow and reproduce, usually killing the latter the process. Parasitism is such a highly successful strategy in nature that it has even been applied commercially. In agriculture, insect parasites have been tried as a means to keep pests under control. One benefit of this approach— called *biocontrol*—is that parasites are usually specific to particular hosts, so they will not attack beneficial organisms, such as pollinating bees. However, this specificity requires some study before application to ensure that only the desired pest is actually attacked.

The two figures below are the results of experiments an entomologist conducted on two parasitic wasp candidates against two species of caterpillar pests, which eat the leaves of valuable crops. In an enclosed greenhouse, the entomologist placed caterpillars on crop plants and then introduced parasitic wasps. After three weeks, the entomologist checked to see what survived. If a caterpillar successfully avoided wasp attack or infection, a butterfly would hatch from the cocoon; without exposure to wasps, over 90% of caterpillars will become butterflies. If a wasp laid eggs inside a caterpillar and the infection successfully completed, wasp offspring would emerge from the cocoon instead. Figure 1 shows how well Wasp S does against certain pest species. Figure 2 shows how well Wasp G does against those same pests.

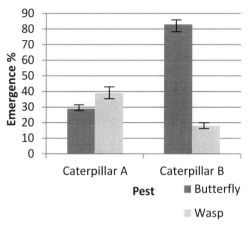

Figure 1

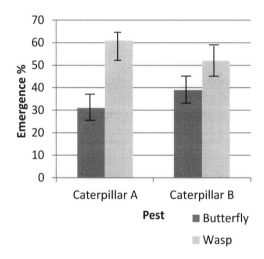

Figure 2

8. Under what condition would Wasp G be a better choice of biocontrol agent against Caterpillar A?

    (A) Wasp G has a longer lifespan than Caterpillar A.
    (B) Caterpillar A tends to flee an area once Wasp G has arrived.
    (C) Caterpillar A has no natural defenses against Wasp G.
    (D) None; Wasp S is always a better choice.

9. In this experiment, a parasite will have done its job if fewer butterflies emerge because butterfly offspring (caterpillars) feed on and damage crops. However, when choosing the appropriate parasite for a particular pest, one has to consider more than just how well the parasite kills the pest. Another important consideration is how well the parasite can persist (reproduce) after initial application; the most effective biocontrols require little maintenance or reapplication and continue to attack pests that survive the first application. Taking both killing effectiveness and persistence into consideration, which would be a better biocontrol parasite for Caterpillar A?

   (A) Wasp S
   (B) Wasp G
   (C) Both have the same effectiveness
   (D) Cannot be determined based on the information given

10. If a farm was infested with both Caterpillar A and Caterpillar B, which would be the better option for controlling both pests?

   (A) Wasp G
   (B) Wasp S
   (C) Both have the same effectiveness
   (D) Cannot be determined based on the information given

11. The lines in the middle of each bar show the *95% confidence interval* for that data. A confidence interval line helps to quickly illustrate how much variation there was the experiment, with longer lines corresponding to more variation. Which combination of wasp and caterpillar had the most variation in the experiment?

   (A) Caterpillar A vs. Wasps S and G
   (B) Caterpillar B vs. Wasps S and G
   (C) Wasp S vs. Caterpillars A and B
   (D) Wasp G vs. Caterpillars A and B

12. A farmer would like to use Wasp G to control caterpillar pests (Caterpillars A and B), but he's worried that the wasps may also harm the caterpillars (Caterpillar C) of a butterfly that helps pollinate his crops. Which experiment would best determine whether Wasp G will be a suitable biocontrol for his farm?

   (A) Allow wasps to access a plant and see if it can also pollinate the flowers.
   (B) Allow wasps to access a plant infected by Caterpillar species A and B and see how many of each are killed.
   (C) Allow wasps to access a plant with only Caterpillar species C and see how many are killed.
   (D) Allow wasps to access a plant with all three caterpillar species on it and see how many of each species are killed.

sP17A

Directions: The following two passages are similar to real ACT test passages. Read each passage and answer the questions that follow. Use the methods and techniques that you have learned throughout the workbook to help you answer the questions.

PRACTICE PASSAGE 1 (TIME: 4 MINUTES)

In any ecosystem, organisms are dependent on one another for survival; changes in one organism are likely to affect others as well. The magnitude of the effect and the time before it is manifested in the ecosystem varies with how closely connected the organisms are. One common way to depict these connections is through a *food web* diagram. In these diagrams, arrows that show the direction of *energy flow* are used to connect the organisms which consume, or are consumed by, each other in an ecosystem. By tracking energy flow, scientists can draw stronger conclusions about what is currently happening in the ecosystem and even make relevant predictions about future outcomes. The two food webs below were constructed by an ecologist managing a nature preserve.

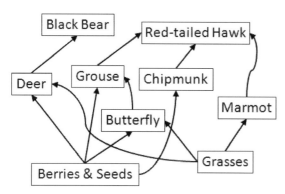

Figure 1: Food Web of Nature Preserve

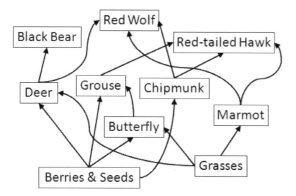

Figure 2: Predicted Food Web of Nature Preserve
after Reintroduction of Red Wolf

1. Animals in different habitats typically have very different feeding patterns. The table below shows some of these feeding patterns for the black bear.

Biome	% Plant Matter Eaten
Temperate Forest	85
Taiga	60
Tundra	10
Sierra	40

Based on this data, the nature preserve shown in Figures 1 and 2 is most likely found in which biome?

(A) Tundra
(B) Taiga
(C) Temperate Forest
(D) Sierra

2. One of the great benefits of food webs is their use as graphical representations of how important organisms are (or are not) in an ecosystem. Often, the organisms most vital to maintaining an ecosystem are at the beginning and end of a food chain. Based on Figure 1, how many other organisms do NOT draw energy from and, thus, rely on berries and seeds?

(A) 0
(B) 2
(C) 4
(D) 8

3. Food webs can be viewed as a collection of *food chains* in an ecosystem. A food chain follows the energy flow directly from start to finish; it usually begins with a *producer* (an organism capable of producing its own food, such as a plant) and ends with an *apex predator* (an organism that consumes other animals, but is not consumed by others). Which of the following is an existing food chain in the habitat shown in Figure 1?

    (A) Grasses, Butterfly, Deer, Black Bear
    (B) Grasses, Marmot, Red Wolf
    (C) Berries & Seeds, Grouse, Red-tailed Hawk
    (D) Berries & Seeds, Chipmunk, Red Wolf

4. An energy pyramid shows the amount of biomass at each *trophic level*, or position, in a food chain or food web. Typically, organisms that make their own food are at the bottom of the energy pyramid, organisms which eat these organisms are at the second level, and so on until you reach the top level, which includes organisms that have no predators. Generally, the total biomass of each level is 10 times greater than that of the level above it. Which of the following is most likely true?

    (A) The energy level that contains the black bear and red-tailed hawk has ten times the biomass of the level that contains the grouse and deer.
    (B) The energy level that contains the butterfly and deer has ten times the biomass of the level that contains grasses, berries, and seeds.
    (C) Black bears have ten times the biomass of deer.
    (D) The energy level that contains the chipmunk and marmot has ten times the biomass of the level that contains the black bear.

5. The introduction of a new apex predator often alters the population of shared prey. For example, prey whose numbers were kept in check by one predator would then have another predator further decreasing their population. In the short term, this can have drastic effects on populations of both the shared prey and the predators that depend on them. Which combination of prey and predator(s), respectively, would likely struggle to maintain their populations after reintroduction of red wolves, in the short term?

    (A) Berries & Seeds; Deer
    (B) Grouses; Red-tailed Hawks
    (C) Chipmunks; Black Bears
    (D) Marmots; Red-tailed Hawks and Red Wolves

PRACTICE PASSAGE 2 (TIME: 5 MINUTES)

Physics student Mary is studying projectile motion for her research project. She uses a 1-meter long cannon to blast off objects in a sealed vacuum chamber with no air.

Experiment 1

Mary first places the cannon at ground level and fires objects of various masses at a 0° angle from the horizontal. She experiments with different initial velocities upon exiting the cannon and records the horizontal distance the objects traveled, as well as the time they took to reach the ground.

Table 1

Mass (kg)	Initial Velocity (m/s)	Range (m)	Flight Time (s)
0.145	25	12.4	0.5
	35	17.3	0.5
	45	22.3	0.5
0.41	15	7.4	0.5
	30	14.8	0.5
	45	22.3	0.5
0.046	20	9.9	0.5
	30	14.8	0.5
	40	19.8	0.5
5.0	15	7.4	0.5
	25	12.4	0.5
	35	17.3	0.5

Experiment 2

The student now decides to fire off one of the objects when placing the cannon at different heights. She keeps the cannon at a 0° angle from the horizontal, varies the initial velocity, and records the range and flight times.

Table 2

Height (m)	Initial Velocity (m/s)	Range (m)	Flight Time (s)
3.0	20	18.6	0.9
	25	23.2	0.9
	30	27.8	0.9
4.0	30	31.0	1.0
	35	36.2	1.0
	40	41.3	1.0
5.0	35	39.3	1.1
	40	44.9	1.1
	45	50.5	1.1

Experiment 3

Mary now decides to investigate the effects of changing the angle from the horizontal at which the objects are fired from the cannon. She places the cannon back at ground level, keeps the initial firing velocity constant at 30 m/s, and records the range and flight time for one of the objects.

Table 3

Angle from horizontal (°)	Range (m)	Flight Time (s)
15	50.0	1.7
30	81.6	3.1
45	93.0	4.4
60	80.2	5.3
75	46.2	6.0

6. If Experiment 3 were to be repeated, which of the following angles, measured from the horizontal, would result in the longest flight time?

   (A) 55°
   (B) 70°
   (C) 100°
   (D) 135°

7. If objects were fired from an identical cannon, which of the following factors would be LEAST important for determining which object would have the greatest range?

   (A) Initial Velocity
   (B) Mass
   (C) Flight time
   (D) Angle from the horizontal

8. Which of the following trials would result in the shortest flight time?

   (A) A 10.0-kg weight fired at a 70° angle from the horizontal with an initial velocity of 10 m/s.
   (B) A 5.0-kg weight fired at a 35° angle from the horizontal with an initial velocity of 20 m/s.
   (C) A 1.0-kg weight fired at a 10° angle from the horizontal with an initial velocity of 40 m/s.
   (D) A 2.0-kg weight fired at a 140° angle from the horizontal with an initial velocity of 5 m/s.

9. Mary decides to repeat Experiment 2 at a height of 6 meters. She accidently sets the cannon to an angle of 15° from horizontal. What is the most likely outcome for the flight time of a projectile fired under these conditions?

   (A) The flight time will be less than that obtained during the 5-m height trial but greater than that from the 4-m height trial.
   (B) The object's flight time will be similar to the flight times obtained in Experiment 1.
   (C) The object's flight time will be longer than any of those obtained during Experiment 2.
   (D) It cannot be determined.

10. Based on the results of the Experiments in the passage, which of the following scenarios would result in the *shortest* range?

   (A) A 10.0-kg object fired from a cannon at a height of 6 m at a 30° angle from the horizontal and an initial velocity of 45 m/s.
   (B) A 1.0-kg object fired from a cannon at ground level at a 170° angle from the horizontal and an initial velocity of 50 m/s.
   (C) A 5.0-kg object fired from a cannon at ground level at a 90° angle from the horizontal and an initial velocity of 40 m/s.
   (D) It cannot be determined.

11. Based on the results of the experiments in the passage, which of the following would result in the longest flight time?

   (A) An 8.5-kg object fired from a cannon at a height of 6 m, a 45° angle from the horizontal with an initial velocity of 45 m/s.
   (B) A 6.0-kg object fired from a cannon at ground level at a 170° angle from the horizontal with an initial velocity of 60 m/s.
   (C) A 4.0-kg object fired from a cannon at a height of 6 m at a 30° angle from the horizontal and an initial velocity of 45 m/s.
   (D) A 10.0-kg object fired from a cannon at ground level at a 20° angle from the horizontal and an initial velocity of 55 m/s.

sP17B

Directions: The following two passages are similar to real ACT test passages. Read each passage and answer the questions that follow. Use the methods and techniques that you have learned throughout the workbook to help you answer the questions.

HOMEWORK PASSAGE 1 (TIME: 6 MINUTES)

With the increasing demand to appear healthier, fitter, and slimmer, new diets are continually being proposed. Two scientists' differing views on the most healthful diets are given below.

Scientist 1

The Mediterranean diet is characterized by moderate to high levels of fruits, vegetables, unrefined grains, fish, and monounsaturated fats. The key components of this diet are the high amount of fiber and complex carbohydrates provided, along with the high levels of monounsaturated fat.

Plant fiber is composed of a carbohydrate chain known as cellulose. Most animals, including human beings, are unable to digest cellulose, even though this indigestible material helps the digestive system function. Plant fibers present in the intestine aggregate food particles and help the passing of food matter through the small and large intestines.

Unrefined grains are complex carbohydrates that contain many varying chains. In contrast, refined grains have had the outer layer of the grain removed and are, thus, lacking the same diversity of carbohydrates that can be found in the unrefined grains. Unrefined grains take longer to digest which leads to a more gradual increase in the levels of carbohydrates, or sugars, in the blood. Thus, unrefined grains provide a more stable source of energy to the body and may protect against sudden spikes in blood sugar levels that could lead to the development of diabetes.

In the Mediterranean diet the source of mono-unsaturated fat is olive oil. Olive oil is a fat that contains one double bond; this double bond causes the olive oil to be liquid at room temperature. In contrast, saturated fats, like butter, are often solid at room temperature. Saturated fats increase the chance of heart attack by forming solid blocks that can clog blood vessels, an issue that is not as concerning with liquid fats. Additionally, olive oil has been shown to be able to decrease the amount of LDL cholesterol, further reducing the risk of heart attack.

Scientist 2

An average American adult will meet roughly 16% of his or her daily energy needs from protein food sources. In contrast, individuals following the all protein diet will derive 50% or more of their daily energy needs from protein food sources.

By meeting an individual's daily energy needs with primarily protein, the all protein diet works to reduce the relative amounts of carbohydrates and fats consumed. Consuming less fat will lead to less fat in the body. Additionally, consuming fewer carbohydrates leads to a decrease in fat acquisition.

The human body is able to synthesize carbohydrates from fat or proteins and vice versa. So even if fat consumption were to be drastically reduced, the body would be able to naturally synthesize some fat from other sources. However, consumption of the same amount of carbohydrates and proteins would result in different amounts of synthesizable fat. The same amount of protein results in much less fat produced when compared to carbohydrates.

Additionally the biosynthesis pathway to produce fat from protein is more energy consuming than is the pathway to produce fat from carbohydrates. Because the body stores excess energy in the form of fat, consuming more energy is better when trying to lose weight, making protein the better food source when trying to lose weight.

In addition to helping an individual lose weight, the all protein diet provides extra health benefits. Protein consumption leads to a gradual increase in blood sugar levels, helping to keep them relatively constant, which can prevent the development of diabetes.

1. Scientists 1 and 2 would most likely agree with which of the following?

   (A) Fat should be a major part of a healthy diet.
   (B) Fluctuating blood sugar levels can lead to the development of diabetes.
   (C) Fats are very difficult to digest.
   (D) Carbohydrates are easy to digest.

2. Scientist 1 would most strongly disagree with which of the following?

   (A) Food can provide health benefits that are not nutrition based.
   (B) A healthy diet is based off consuming a variety of different types of foods.
   (C) Fat is not a beneficial food source.
   (D) Saturated fats can increase the risk of heart attack

3. Scientist 2 would most strongly disagree with which of the following?

   (A) Food can provide health benefits that are not nutrition based.
   (B) A healthy diet is based off consuming a variety of different types of foods.
   (C) Energy inefficiency is beneficial for losing weight.
   (D) Carbohydrates are better than proteins at being converted into fat.

4. Fats are known to yield 9 kcal of energy per gram, while proteins 4 kcal per gram. How does this fact affect the strengths of the arguments of Scientists 1 and 2?

   (A) It strengthens Scientist 1's argument but weakens Scientist 2's argument.
   (B) It weakens Scientist 1's argument but strengthens Scientist 2's argument.
   (C) It strengthens both, Scientist 1's and 2's, arguments.
   (D) It does not affect the argument of either Scientist 1 or 2.

5. Which of the following discoveries would most weaken Scientist 1's position?

   (A) Saturated fats decrease the risk of heart attack.
   (B) Protein consumption leads to an increase in excess energy available for storage.
   (C) Protein consumption leads to lower levels of blood sugar.
   (D) Fiber can be derived from protein food sources.

6. How might Scientist 2 respond to Scientist 1's claim that complex carbohydrates can lower the risk of diabetes?

   (A) Scientist 2 would disagree because carbohydrates are fats, which increase the risk of diabetes.
   (B) Scientist 2 would disagree because complex carbohydrates require more energy to digest, increasing the risk of diabetes.
   (C) Scientist 2 would agree that a slow increase in blood sugar levels decreases the risk of diabetes.
   (D) Scientist 2 would agree because complex carbohydrates are indigestible.

7. How might Scientist 1 respond to Scientist 2's claim that fats are not important for an individual's diet?

   (A) Scientist 1 would agree fats lead to an increased risk of heart attack.
   (B) Scientist 1 would agree, unrefined grains and fiber are much more important.
   (C) Scientist 1 would disagree, saturated fats lower cholesterol levels.
   (D) Scientist 1 would disagree, not all fats are the same and some have important health benefits.

HOMEWORK PASSAGE 2 (TIME: 4 MINUTES)

A mechanical engineer is studying the hydraulics of a sewage system beneath a city. In a large-scale model, shown in Figure 1, the engineer measured the fluid speed and flow of the water in pipes of varying cross-sectional areas.

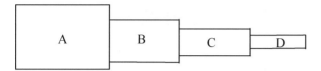

Note: Figure not drawn to scale.

Figure 1

Table 1

Pipe	Area (m^2)	Flow (L/m^{2}s)	Fluid Speed (m/s)
A	9.0	600	0.6
B	6.0	800	0.8
C	3.0	1600	1.6
D	1.0	4800	4.8

In four other pipes made up of the same metal and dimensions, the engineer then examines the pressures of different fluids to determine which fluid would most rapidly wear out the pipe metal. The engineer reasoned that the fluid with the greatest fluid density would exert the greatest pressure on the pipe, thereby causing the greatest corrosion. Figure 2 depicts the pressures of various fluids in the different pipes.

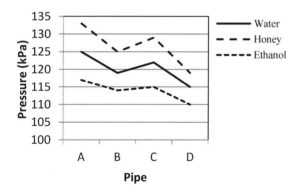

Figure 2

8. The engineer decides to attach a new pipe, Pipe E to the end of Pipe D, shown in Figure 1. Pipe E is larger than Pipe C but smaller then Pipe B. Which of the following would be the expected fluid speed through pipe E?

(A) 1.2 m/s
(B) 3.2 m/s
(C) 4.8 m/s
(D) 5.2 m/s

9. The engineer attaches a new pipe, Pipe F, to the end of Pipe A and discovers that the flow through pipe F is 3,200 L/m^{2}s. Which of the following best describes Pipe F's relative size?

(A) Pipe F is smaller than pipe A but larger than pipe B.
(B) Pipe F is smaller than pipe A but larger than pipe C.
(C) Pipe F is smaller than pipe C but larger than Pipe D.
(D) It cannot be determined from the given information.

10. The pressure generated by a new unknown fluid is measured to be 130 kPa in Pipe B. Which of the following correctly ranks the fluids in order of *decreasing* densities?

(A) Unknown, water, honey, ethanol.
(B) Unknown, honey, water, ethanol.
(C) Ethanol, honey, water, unknown.
(D) Ethanol, water, honey, unknown.

11. The engineer decides to reattach all the pipes
used in the first setup to make a loop such that
A→B→C→D→A. The engineer accomplishes
this without changing the shapes of the pipes.
What effect would this have on fluid speed
through the pipes?

(A) Fluid traveling through large pipes, like A,
would now travel slower than before, while
fluid traveling through small pipes would
now travel faster than before.
(B) Fluid traveling through small pipes, like D,
would now travel slower than before, Fluid
traveling through large pipes, like A, would
now travel faster than before.
(C) There would be no relative change
compared to the previous speeds.
(D) None of the above.

12. The engineer is working on creating a watering
device. The objective is to have the liquid leave
at a high speed. Which of the following setups
would be best for achieving the engineer's
objective?

(A) The watering device should have a small
exit.
(B) The watering device should have a large
exit.
(C) The watering device should have a small
section that leads to a larger exit.
(D) The watering device should have a large exit
and should be filled with honey to achieve
the highest velocity.

sP18A

Directions: The following two passages are similar to real ACT test passages. Read each passage and answer the questions that follow. Use the methods and techniques that you have learned throughout the workbook to help you answer the questions.

PRACTICE PASSAGE 1 (TIME: 4 MINUTES)

To study the relationships between energy and mass, two friends take turns riding a skateboard on a frictionless U-shaped ramp. A schematic of the ramp shown is shown in Figure 1.

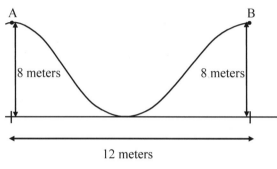

Figure 1

Person A, with a mass of 50 kg, decides to ride down the ramp first and travels once the distance from Point A to Point B. Person B, with a mass of 80 kg, then repeats the procedure. The plots of the potential and kinetic energies at different horizontal positions along the ramp for Persons A and B are shown in Figures 2 and 3, respectively.

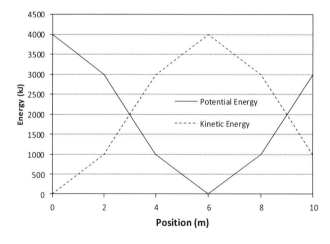

Figure 2

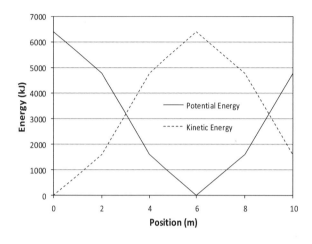

Figure 3

1. The experiment was repeated with Person C who weighed 90 kg. How does the graph of Person C's kinetic energy compare to the graph of Person A's kinetic energy?

   (A) Greater at all positions.
   (B) Identical at all positions.
   (C) Lower at some positions.
   (D) None of the above.

2. If the length of the ramp were truncated from 12 to 8 meters, with the far end of the ramp removed, which of the following would be Person A's new potential energy at the end of the newly shortened ramp?

   (A)   700 kJ
   (B) 1000 kJ
   (C) 2500 kJ
   (D) 3500 kJ

3. A new ramp is created with a height of 8 meters and an extended length of 16 meters. What would Person B's potential energy be at a position of 16 meters? Assume the ramp follows the same design as shown in Figure 1.

   (A) 2000 kJ
   (B) 3500 kJ
   (C) 6400 kJ
   (D) 9000 kJ

4. Person's A velocity was found to be greatest at the 6 m position along the ramp in Figure 2 and lowest at the 0 m position. Which of the following correctly describes the relationship between potential energy and velocity?

   (A) As potential energy increases, velocity increases.
   (B) As potential energy increases, velocity decreases.
   (C) As potential energy increases, velocity stays the same.
   (D) It cannot be determined.

5. Friction is a force that resists a change in motion and, thus, requires the expenditure of energy to overcome. If the data in the passage had taken into account the friction from the ramp, which of the following would NOT be true?

   (A) The potential energy of Person A at Position 0 meters could be 4500 kJ.
   (B) The potential energy of Person B at Position 2 meters could be 3000 kJ.
   (C) The kinetic energy of Person A at Position 8 meters could be 500 kJ.
   (D) The kinetic energy of Person B at Position 10 meters could be 4000 kJ.

PRACTICE PASSAGE 2 (TIME: 5 MINUTES)

The photoelectric effect describes the phenomenon in which energy in the form of photons from electromagnetic radiation strikes a surface, causing the release of electrons from that surface. For electrons to be released from a given metal, the photons must possess a minimum threshold frequency to overcome the electron binding energy of the metal, known as the work function, a property inherent to the metal itself. The relationships among the energy of the photon, the emitted electron, and the work function are given by the following equation:

$$K_{max} = hf - \varphi,$$

where K_{max} represents the maximum kinetic energy possible of the emitted electron, h Planck's constant, f the frequency of the photon, and φ the work function of the metal.

In the following experiment, a physicist connects different metal plates to a 5-Volt battery to study the effects of light intensity and frequency on the ability of a metal to conduct electricity.

Experiment 1

The experimenter shines light of different colors and intensities on a sodium metal plate and records the current passed through the battery.

Table 1

Light	Frequency (×10¹⁵ Hz)	Intensity (%)	Current (A)
Red	0.3	50	0.000
Red	0.3	80	0.000
Red	0.4	80	0.000
Green	0.6	50	0.002
Green	0.6	80	0.004
Blue	0.7	50	0.029
Blue	0.7	80	0.048
Violet	0.75	50	0.066
Violet	0.75	80	0.106
Violet	0.8	80	0.134

Experiment 2

The physicist now repeats the experiment, except this time using a zinc metal plate and altering the voltage of the battery. He finds that even at the highest violet frequency, an increased battery voltage does not produce a current.

Experiment 3

The experimenter switches the zinc metal plate with a calcium plate. While varying the intensity and battery voltage, he again measures the current produced.

Table 2

Light	Frequency (×10¹⁵ Hz)	Intensity (%)	Battery Voltage (V)	Current (A)
Violet	0.75	50	0.00	0.006
Violet	0.75	50	8.00	0.006
Violet	0.8	100	8.00	0.023

6. Which of the following correctly lists the metals in order of *decreasing* work function?

   (A) Zinc, Sodium, Calcium
   (B) Zinc, Calcium, Sodium
   (C) Calcium, Zinc, Sodium
   (D) Calcium, Sodium, Zinc

7. Experiment 1 is repeated with a light frequency of 8×10^{14} Hz, an intensity of 50%, and a 12-Volt battery. Which of the following is the most likely current?

   (A) 0.055
   (B) 0.097
   (C) 0.135
   (D) 0.156

8. Experiment 3 is repeated with an unknown metal. No current is detected when a light frequency 0.3×10^{15} Hz and intensity of 50% is shone onto the unknown metal. Which of the following would be MOST likely to produce a current?

   (A) Increase the light intensity.
   (B) Attach a battery of 8.0 V in a way similar to Experiment 3.
   (C) Use a blue light.
   (D) Replace the unknown metal with zinc.

9. Which of the following is the best way to alter the work function of a metal?

   (A) Increase the frequency of the light.
   (B) Increase the intensity of the light.
   (C) Attach a higher volt battery.
   (D) None of the above.

10. Which of the following correctly describes the effect of increasing light intensity?

    (A) Increasing intensity has no effect on current.
    (B) Increasing intensity increases the work function of the metal.
    (C) Increasing intensity always leads to an increase in current.
    (D) None of the above.

11. Planck's Equation states that the energy of a photon of light is directly proportional to its velocity and inversely proportional to its wavelength. If the wavelength of a photon is inversely related to its frequency, which of the following statements MUST be true?

    (A) A photon of red light will have greater energy than a photon of blue light.
    (B) A photon of green light will have a shorter wavelength than a photon of violet light.
    (C) A photon of violet light will have a greater velocity than a photon of red light.
    (D) None of the above.

sP18B

Directions: The following two passages are similar to real ACT test passages. Read each passage and answer the questions that follow. Use the methods and techniques that you have learned throughout the workbook to help you answer the questions.

HOMEWORK PASSAGE 1 (TIME: 6 MINUTES)

Cancer is one of the leading causes of disease-related death in the United States today, with roughly 600,000 people succumbing to it every year. The scientific and medical communities are united in addressing this disease, but they are not always in agreement over the best solution. Below, two oncologists (people who study cancers) debate the merits of two broad approaches to fighting cancer: detection and treatment.

Oncologist 1:

More research and development needs to be dedicated to earlier and more accurate detection. First, earlier detection aids diagnosis and staging (determining the progression of the cancer), which in turn aids patients and doctors when planning the treatment program. Second, the research behind existing treatments during earlier stages is more robust—the treatment options are clearer and the results of those treatments are easier to evaluate. Third, treatments have a higher success rate at earlier stages of cancer, when the disease is localized, or limited to one area, and easier to monitor. For example, most cancers detected before Stage II (a single, localized, little-developed tumor) have a patient survival rate of greater than 60%; when detected at Stage III (highly-developed tumor, with possible spread to other tissues), the survival rate plummets to about 20%. Finally, on a strictly economic level, earlier and accurate detection can drastically help save and manage resources because treatments at earlier stages of cancer are less expensive than those at later stages.

Oncologist 2:

More research and development needs to be dedicated to safer, more effective treatments. First, earlier detection works only if people are proactive and well-aware of what to look for. Even with the screening and awareness programs that have been implemented over the past two decades, many individuals who seek treatment for cancer do so after it has progressed to more advanced stages. Second, we now have very detailed knowledge on the progression of various cancers, which offers us many potential targets for new treatments. One need only compare the number of cancer drugs, therapies, and clinical trials that are actively being developed today to even that of five years ago to see how far we have progressed. It would be a shame for this progress to be halted by redirecting our attention and resources elsewhere. Finally, some cancers (e.g., breast, prostate) are very likely to occur as one ages, and, not surprisingly, their occurrence has increased as life expectancy has increased. New detection methods would not be as beneficial as new treatment options for such high frequency cancers.

1. Which of the following generalizations about cancer is most consistent with Oncologist 2's viewpoint?

   (A) Cancer science has not progressed far from where it was five years ago.
   (B) The incidence rates of all cancers are very likely to increase as a person ages.
   (C) The number of cancer medicines and therapeutic methods available today is greater than what was available a decade ago.
   (D) The amount of research and development dedicated to cancer treatment today is less than what was dedicated to it in a decade ago.

2. With which of the following statements would both oncologists likely agree?

   (A) The later stages of cancer have a low treatment success rate.
   (B) Early detection is the easiest way to combat high frequency cancers.
   (C) The research behind treatments for later stages of cancer is more robust than for earlier stages.
   (D) Stage IV progression would involve the spread of cancer to other tissues.

3. Given the information from Oncologist 1, what would be a reasonable estimate of the survival rate for a person diagnosed with Stage I breast cancer?

   (A) 25%
   (B) 35%
   (C) 55%
   (D) 65%

4. Which of the following is not addressed by either oncologist in his statement?

   (A) The relative costs of treatment between different stages of cancer.
   (B) The relative accuracy of detection between different stages of cancer.
   (C) The relative knowledge of cancer progression between today and the past.
   (D) The relative ease of determining appropriate treatments based on when cancer is first detected.

5. Suppose a recently approved cancer treatment had a success rate of 90%, as long as it was administered before the cancer progressed to Stage II. How would this development affect the arguments of the oncologists?

   (A) It would strengthen Oncologist 1's viewpoint only.
   (B) It would strengthen Oncologist 2's viewpoint only.
   (C) It would strengthen both oncologists' viewpoints.
   (D) It would have no effect on either oncologist's viewpoint.

6. With each division, the chances of errors occurring in a cell's DNA sequence increases. Thus, rapidly dividing cells, such as those of the intestines and reproductive organs, are expected to accumulate more errors over time than slowly dividing cells, such as nerve cells. As these errors accumulate, the risk of cancer increases. This is likely the rationale for which point made by Oncologist 2?

   (A) Earlier detection works only if people are proactive.
   (B) We now have very detailed knowledge on the progression of various cancers.
   (C) Some cancers have become more common as our life expectancies have increased.
   (D) New detection methods are not as beneficial and new treatment options.

7. Some cancers, such as lung cancer, have both high occurrence and mortality rates. A high occurrence and mortality is often indicative of a rapidly developing, fast spreading cancer. Which oncologist would likely use this fact to support his viewpoint?

   (A) Oncologist 1
   (B) Oncologist 2
   (C) Both oncologists could use this to support his viewpoint.
   (D) This fact would not support either oncologist's viewpoint.

HOMEWORK PASSAGE 2 (TIME: 5 MINUTES)

For a science project, a group of students are investigating the effects of friction and angle of inclination on velocity.

Experiment 1

The students place a 100-kilogram wooden crate at the end of a 7-meter long ice ramp at various heights but a constant angle from the ground and record the time it takes to reach the bottom of the ramp. They do not exert any forces on the ramp but let the crate fall due to gravity. Since the ramp is ice, the students assume negligible forces due to friction.

Table 1

Height of ramp (m)	Time to reach bottom (s)
5	2.02
4	2.35
3	2.67
2	3.25
1	4.53

Experiment 2

The students then attempt to repeat Experiment 1, except this time using a 7-meter long wooden ramp at the same heights and angle. They find that the crate only begins to slide at a height of 5 meters and not at lower heights the others.

Table 2

Height of ramp (m)	Time to reach bottom (s)
5	3.10
4	—

Experiment 3

Finally, the students set out to determine the smallest force they need to exert on the crate to make it slide down the ramp at the remaining heights from Experiment 2.

Table 3

Height of ramp (m)	Force exerted (N)
4	55
3	170
2	285
1	390

8. Which of the following setups would result in the longest time to reach the bottom for a 100 kg crate?

    (A) 7-m long ice ramp at a height of 6 meters.
    (B) 7-m long ice ramp at a height of 2 meters.
    (C) 7-m long wood ramp at a height of 6 meters.
    (D) 7-m long wood ramp at a height of 4 meters.

9. Experiment 1 is repeated with a 5-meter long ramp. If the speed of an object is equal to its distance traveled divided by its travel time, which of the following heights would correspond to the LOWEST speed for the 100-kg crate?

    (A) Height of 2 meters.
    (B) Height of 3 meters.
    (C) Height of 4 meters.
    (D) The speed is independent of height.

10. In all three experiments, which of the following variables were controlled?

    (A) Mass
    (B) Distance
    (C) Height
    (D) Two of the above are correct.

11. Experiment 3 is repeated except with an ice ramp instead of a wooden ramp. How would this affect the amount of force required to get the crate to move?

    (A) The amount of force exerted would increase.
    (B) The amount of force exerted would decrease.
    (C) The amount of force exerted would remain constant.
    (D) It cannot be determined.

12. If the two ramps from Experiment 1 and Experiment 2 were combined to create a 14-meter long ramp, which of the following ramp placements would require less initial force to make the crate slide to the end of the new 14-meter long ramp at a height of 4 meters?

    (A) The crate should start on the ice ramp and go to the wooden ramp.
    (B) The crate should start on the wooden ramp and go to the ice ramp.
    (C) The order does not matter because the crate will have to cross both ramps regardless of order.
    (D) None of the above.

13. The difference in the force exerted on a crate down a 7-meter long wooden ramp at a height of 5 meters and 0.5 meters, respectively, would be:

    (A) Greater than the difference in the forces exerted at heights of 4 meters and 2 meters, respectively.
    (B) Less than the difference in the forces exerted at heights of 1 meter and 3 meters, respectively.
    (C) Greater than the difference in the forces exerted at heights of 6 meters and 0.5 meters.
    (D) Less than the difference in the forces exerted at heights of 5 meters and 1 meter, respectively.

---

sP19A

Directions: The following two passages are similar to real ACT test passages. Read each passage and answer the questions that follow. Use the methods and techniques that you have learned throughout the workbook to help you answer the questions.

PRACTICE PASSAGE 1 (TIME: 4 MINUTES)

A hydraulics engineer is gathering data about fluid dynamics from a leaking water tower whose base is at a height of 15 meters above the ground. The engineer measures the speed of the water exiting at the center of the hole and the horizontal distance the water lands from the base as the water level in the tank decreases. The height of the water tank is 10 meters, and the diameter of the hole at the bottom of the tower is 1 meter.

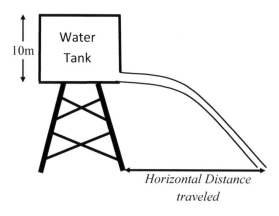

Note: Figure is not drawn to scale.

Figure 1

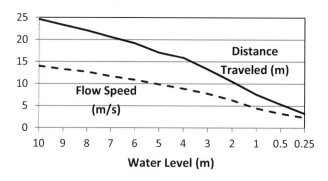

Figure 2

To determine whether lighter fluids would exert less pressure on the tank to increase its longevity, the engineer then compares the fluid pressure of water and gasoline at various fluid heights in the tank. The engineer measures the fluid pressure by inserting multiple pressure sensors inside the tank at different heights. Assume the height of the tower and tank remain unchanged from before, and that the tank remains filled to capacity during all the measurements. The engineer's data are plotted in Figure 3. Based on his results, he concludes that greater pressures from heavier liquids decrease tank longevity.

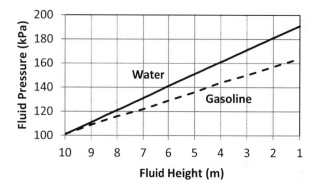

Figure 3

1. Based on the data presented in Figure 1, as the water level of the tank increases, its flow speed:

   (A) increases linearly.
   (B) decreases linearly.
   (C) increases less gradually when the water level is more than 2 m than it does when the water level is less than 2 m.
   (D) increases more gradually when the water level is more than 2 m than it does when the water level is less than 2 m.

2. The pressures of two new liquids, Liquid A and Liquid B, were measured to be 120 kPa and 180 kPa, respectively, at a height of 6 meters in a tank positioned 15 meters above the ground. Which of the following correctly lists the liquids in order of *decreasing* tank longevity?

    (A) Liquid B, water, gasoline, Liquid A
    (B) Liquid A, Liquid B, gasoline, water
    (C) Liquid B, Liquid A, water, gasoline
    (D) Liquid A, gasoline, water, Liquid B

3. Water traveling a distance of 30 meters from a tank identical to the one used in the passage could have a fluid pressure of:

    (A) 90 kPa.
    (B) 100 kPa.
    (C) 110 kPa.
    (D) It cannot be determined.

4. Using a new water tank identical to the one used in the passage, the engineer finds that the flow speed of the water increases if he raises the height of the tank from 10 meters to 15 meters above the ground. Given these findings, which of the following could be the flow speed of the water exiting the same water tank at a water level of 6 meters if the tank were lowered to a height of 5 meters above the ground?

    (A) 7 m/s
    (B) 11 m/s
    (C) 16 m/s
    (D) 20 m/s

5. The engineer sets up three new identical tanks with the same-sized holes at the bottom and fills the tanks with water, Liquid 1, and Liquid 2, respectively. If, in identical conditions to those used in the passage, Liquids 1 and 2 had traveled 20 meters and 10 meters, respectively, at fluid heights of 10 meters, which of the following correctly lists in *increasing* order the amount of time needed for the tanks to completely empty?

    (A) Water, Liquid 1, Liquid 2
    (B) Water, Liquid 2, Liquid 1
    (C) Liquid 2, water, Liquid 1
    (D) Liquid 1, water, Liquid 2

C2 education
be smarter

PRACTICE PASSAGE 2 (TIME: 5 MINUTES)

Most animals have the ability to actively control their sensory systems: e.g., through eye movements for vision or finger movements for touch. Bats and other animals use a sensory system known as *echolocation*, but the degree of control they exert over the signals they emit has not been studied in detail.

To sense their environment, Egyptian fruit bats emit signals using tongue clicks and listen for the echoes from nearby objects. The bats emit sonar clicks in pairs: one click directed to the left of the target, and one to the right. The angle between the pair of left-right clicks is called the *inter-click angle* (shown in Figure 1). The size of the inter-click angle determines the bats' acoustic field of view.

Figure 1

In the following experiments, scientists study how Egyptian fruit bats can actively adjust the inter-click angle and intensity of the sonar clicks they emit, depending on their proximity to the target and on the complexity of their surroundings.

Experiment 1

First, the scientists train the bats to approach and land on a sphere (about the size of the fruit eaten by the bats) in an empty room. Using an array of microphones distributed around the edges of the room, the scientists measure the inter-click angle of the click pairs of each bat as it approaches the target. At a certain point in its approach, the bat "locks" on to the target—the average direction between its click pairs coincides with the direction to the target. Figure 2 plots the inter-click angles of seven bats as a function of time relative to locking (where 0 is the moment the bat locks onto the target, negative times indicate the bat has not locked on, and positive times indicate the bat has locked on).

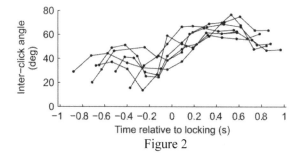

Figure 2

Experiment 2

Next, the scientists measure the sound intensity of the bats' sonar clicks as they approach the landing sphere. Figure 3 plots the intensity in decibels of six different bats as a function of time relative to locking. The solid gray line represents the average intensity.

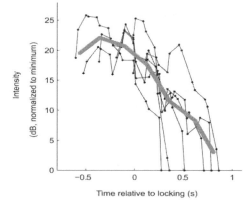

Figure 3

Experiment 3

The scientists study how changing the complexity of the environment affects both inter-click angle and intensity of the clicks. The environment of the single landing sphere used in Experiments 1 and 2 becomes the "one-object" case. The scientists measure intensity and the angle of each click relative to the center of the pair in a less complex "no-object" case, and in a more complex "multiple-object" case, which the scientists create by adding two nets around the landing sphere. The results are plotted in Figure 4. The pair of dashed lines that intersects all three graphs represents the bats' field of view.

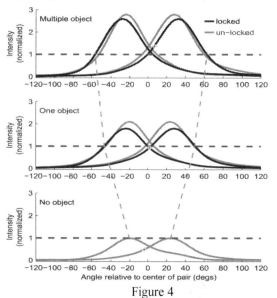

Figure 4

6. As the bat approaches its target, its:

    (A) inter-click angle decreases, and click intensity increases.
    (B) inter-click angle increases, and click intensity decreases.
    (C) inter-click angle, and click intensity both increase.
    (D) inter-click angle, and click intensity both decrease.

7. Which of the following is a reasonable estimation of the sound intensity of the bat's clicks 0.5 seconds after it locks onto its target?

    (A) 0 dB
    (B) 10 dB
    (C) 30 dB
    (D) 100 dB

8. In Experiments 1 and 2, at the moment of locking, a bat's inter-click angle and click intensity, respectively, would likely be in the ranges of:

    (A) 35 to 55 degrees and 18 to 23 dB.
    (B) 35 to 55 degrees and 8 to 13 dB.
    (C) 45 to 70 degrees and 18 to 23 dB.
    (D) 45 to 70 degrees and 8 to 13 dB.

9. In Figure 4, what is the most likely reason that the graph for each case contains two peaks?

    (A) The maximum click intensity of one of the bats is higher than the maximum click intensity of the other.
    (B) The click intensities of the two bats peak at two different times.
    (C) The two peaks represent two different possible maximum click intensities for the same bat.
    (D) The two peaks represent the directions of the pair of clicks that has the highest intensity.

10. In the multiple-object case, at which inter-click angle do the clicks have the highest intensity, whether locked or unlocked?

    (A) 0 degrees
    (B) 30 degrees
    (C) 60 degrees
    (D) 160 degrees

11. If in the multiple-object case, a bat's inter-click angle and click intensity are +50 degrees and 22 dB, respectively, at some point in its approach toward a target, then in the one-object case, the bat's inter-click angle and click intensity at the same point in its approach could be:

    (A) 46 degrees and 19 dB.
    (B) 59 degrees and 24 dB.
    (C) 40 degrees and 27 dB.
    (D) 55 degrees and 15 dB.

sP19B

Directions: The following two passages are similar to real ACT test passages. Read each passage and answer the questions that follow. Use the methods and techniques that you have learned throughout the workbook to help you answer the questions.

HOMEWORK PASSAGE 1 (TIME: 6 MINUTES)

Two physicists discuss the significance of the long-sought and elusive particle, the Higgs boson.

Scientist 1

The Higgs boson is the most significant scientific discovery in recent history. The Standard Model, a set of equations that encompasses physicists' current understanding of the physical laws of the universe, requires the existence of the Higgs boson. Most other predictions of the Standard Model are well supported by experiments conducted in past decades, but until recently, the Higgs boson was the most significant missing piece in the question of why matter has mass, and why different particles have different masses.

In the Standard Model explanation, mass is what keeps particles from being able to move at the speed of light (unlike photons, which have no mass and can only move at the speed of light). According to the theory, in the period immediately following the big bang, particles had no mass. The Higgs field, an invisible field generated by heavy Higgs boson particles that permeated the universe following the big bang, is what imbued these particles with mass. As particles moved through the field, some particles interacted with the Higgs field to a greater extent than others did, and, thus, ended up with more mass.

But both the Higgs field and the Higgs boson are so unstable that the Higgs field falls apart and the Higgs boson decays into other types of particles within moments. So the only way to demonstrate that the events in the Standard Model theory ever occurred would be to momentarily recreate the Higgs particle, with the use of a powerful particle accelerator, and then examine the properties of the daughter particles into which the Higgs particle decayed for clues about the Higgs particle.

Until recently, no particle accelerator had been powerful enough to produce a Higgs boson, so there was no empirical evidence of the Higgs field. The discovery of the Higgs boson is a major confirmation of an aspect of the Standard Model that has been in doubt for decades.

Scientist 2

Rather than neatly confirming the Standard Model, the discovery of the Higgs boson actually raises more questions than it answers.

The Standard Model predicts, among other things, what mass the Higgs boson should have, and with what frequencies it should decay into different kinds of particles. The Higgs boson that scientists have found does not follow these predictions exactly.

The mass of the Higgs boson is measured by measuring the energy of its daughter particles and working backwards to determine what mass would have produced that amount of energy. But measuring the energy of two different kinds of particles into which the Higgs boson can decay—Z bosons and photons—yields two slightly different Higgs boson masses: 123.5 GeV for the Z bosons and 126.6 GeV for the photons. The Standard Model provides no explanation for why the two modes of measurement should yield two different masses.

The Standard Model also predicts the frequency with which the Higgs boson should decay into its different types of daughter particles. For Z bosons, the data fits the predictions. But the Higgs particle appears to decay into photons much more frequently than predicted. This could be a statistical fluctuation, but if the effect remains consistent even with more data, the frequency difference would also require an explanation not currently provided by the Standard Model.

In addition to these discrepancies, many scientists believe the Standard Model is still incomplete, or that there are alternative theories. Many alternative theories propose multiple types of Higgs particles, one of which should resemble a Standard-Model-type Higgs. The other types of Higgs particles could be even more difficult to detect than the Standard Model type, which would explain why they have not been discovered yet. So the discovery of the Standard-Model-type Higgs boson still does not rule out alternatives to the Standard Model.

1. Scientist 1 would most likely *disagree* with which of the following?

   (A) The mass of the Higgs boson is measured by measuring the energy of its daughter particles.
   (B) The Standard Model predicts, among other things, what mass the Higgs boson should have, and with what frequencies it should decay into different kinds of particles.
   (C) So many other predictions of the Standard Model are well supported by experiments that there was no need to find the Higgs boson.
   (D) The fact that the Higgs boson exists is sufficient to confirm the Standard Model.

2. Both Scientists 1 and 2 would most likely agree that:

   (A) the Higgs boson that was discovered behaves exactly as predicted by the Standard Model.
   (B) discovering the Higgs boson means that scientists can study it directly rather than having to study its daughter particles.
   (C) the Higgs boson that was discovered does not behave as predicted by the Standard Model.
   (D) the discovery of the Higgs boson does not rule out the possibility that other Higgs-like particles exist.

3. Scientist 2's argument assumes that:

   (A) the discrepancies between the predictions of the Standard Model and the properties of the discovered Higgs boson disproves the Standard Model.
   (B) the fact that the Higgs boson is calculated to have two different masses is not a statistical fluctuation.
   (C) multiple types of Higgs particles exist.
   (D) the Standard Model does not require the existence of the Higgs boson.

4. Which of the following discoveries would most weaken Scientist 2's argument?

   (A) The observation that the Higgs decays into photons more frequently than expected remains consistent even with more data.
   (B) Another particle is discovered that is similar to the Higgs, but not predicted to exist by the Standard Model.
   (C) The observation that the Higgs decays into photons more frequently than expected becomes moot with the addition of more data.
   (D) The difference in measurements of the Higgs boson's mass remains consistent with the addition of more data.

5. More precise measurements show that the Higgs boson does not have the spin that the Standard Model predicts it should have. What effect would this discovery have on the two scientists' arguments?

   (A) It would support Scientist 1's argument and weaken Scientist 2's.
   (B) It would weaken Scientist 1's argument and support Scientist 2's.
   (C) It would support both scientists' arguments.
   (D) It would weaken both scientists' arguments.

6. The particle accelerator that measured the properties of the Higgs boson is found to have had technical issues. After it is repaired, it measures the Higgs boson to be exactly 125.0 GeV using either Z bosons or photons as daughter particles. Which scientist's argument would be weakened by this discovery?

   (A) Scientist 1, because the Standard Model predicts that the Higgs boson should have no mass.
   (B) Scientist 1, because without a discrepancy between measurements of the Higgs boson's mass, the particle does not create as many problems for the Standard Model.
   (C) Scientist 2, because the Standard Model predicts that the Higgs boson should have no mass.
   (D) Scientist 2, because without a discrepancy between measurements of the Higgs boson's mass, the particle does not create as many problems for the Standard Model.

7. Which of the following arguments would Scientist 1 *least* likely use in response to Scientist 2's argument?

   (A) Measuring photons and Z bosons is not a valid way of measuring properties of the Higgs boson.
   (B) The difference in mass measurements is a statistical fluke.
   (C) Until other types of Higgs particles are found, the Standard Model is the best explanation we have of observable phenomena.
   (D) The discovery of a particle similar to the predicted Higgs particle is significant, even if the properties of the discovered particle do not exactly match the predictions.

HOMEWORK PASSAGE 2 (TIME: 5 MINUTES)

Cooperative species are species whose individual organisms produce goods for common consumption. Cooperative species typically have greater fitness, or successful ability to produce viable offspring, at higher population densities. However, their fitness can be affected by "cheater" organisms, which take advantage of the common goods without producing any themselves, and, thus, grow at the expense of the cooperators.

In the following experiments, scientists study these population dynamics by examining the behavior of one social microbial species: budding yeast in sucrose. Each yeast cell that has SUC2, the cooperative gene, converts the surrounding sucrose to glucose, 99% of which diffuses away to be used by other cells in the population, while the remaining 1% is used by the cell that produced it. Cells that do not have the SUC2 gene are cheater cells, and only use glucose produced by other cells.

Experiment 1

In the first experiment, no cheater cells are introduced, and the SUC2 gene frequency is 100%, i.e., all cells are cooperators. The growth or collapse of the population depends solely on the starting population density: populations that start at too low a density are not able to convert enough sucrose into glucose to sustain their growth. Each line in Figure 1 represents the growth of one population of yeast cells.

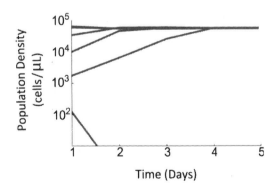

Figure 1

Experiment 2

Next, the scientists introduce some cheater cells, initiating populations at varying population densities and SUC2 gene frequencies. They plot the results on the graph in Figure 2.

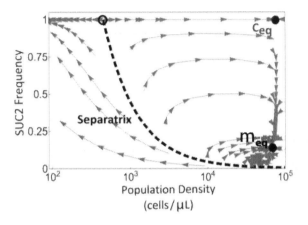

Figure 2

The scientists find that the populations either grow to an equilibrium point or go extinct, depending on both starting population density and SUC2 frequency. Each path in Figure 2 represents the growth or extinction of one population over a span of several days. The *separatrix* represents what were found to be the points of minimum population density and SUC2 frequency for a population to grow. Populations with greater density and/or SUC2 frequency than the minimum spiraled to the indicated equilibrium point, m_{eq}, while populations that started lower than the minimum went extinct. C_{eq} represents the equilibrium population density that all populations with SUC2 frequency of 100% reach and remain at.

8. Which of the following is true in a population with a SUC2 gene frequency of 50%:

(A) half the cells are cooperators, and half the cells can be either cooperators or cheaters.
(B) all cells have a 50% chance of converting from cooperators to cheaters and vice versa.
(C) half the cells are cooperators, and half the cells are cheaters.
(D) 25% of the cells are cooperators, 25% are cheaters, and 50% can be either cooperators or cheaters.

9. In a population with a SUC2 gene frequency of 100%, the minimum starting population density required for the population to continue to grow rather than becoming extinct is:

   (A) lower than 10^2 cells/μL.
   (B) between 10^2 and 10^3 cells/μL.
   (C) between 10^3 and 10^4 cells/μL.
   (D) higher than 10^4 cells/μL.

10. The scientists are surprised to find that, as shown in Figure 2, at the equilibrium point of mixed cooperator/cheater populations, the SUC2 frequency is about 12%, but the population density is only slightly lower than that of the pure cooperator equilibrium. This could mean that:

    (A) a low SUC2 frequency requires a low population density.
    (B) maintaining equilibrium population density requires only a small proportion of the population to be cooperators.
    (C) a high population density requires a low SUC2 frequency.
    (D) a small proportion of cheaters can prevent the entire population from reaching equilibrium.

11. A population that becomes extinct could have started at:

    (A) population density 10,000 cells/μL and SUC2 frequency 0.2.
    (B) population density 5000 cells/μL and SUC2 frequency 0.5.
    (C) population density 2500 cells/μL and SUC2 frequency 0.8.
    (D) population density 1000 cells/μL and SUC2 frequency 0.3.

12. In a population in Experiment 2 that started at a population density of 5000 cells/μL and a SUC2 frequency of 0.3, as its population density increased, the proportion of cooperators would:

    (A) increase only.
    (B) remain constant.
    (C) decrease, then increase.
    (D) increase, then decrease.

13. Which of the following conclusions *cannot* be drawn from the results of the experiments?

    (A) The presence of cheaters causes a cooperative population to go extinct.
    (B) There is a starting population density below which the population will go extinct regardless of SUC2 frequency.
    (C) Pure cooperator populations and mixed cooperator/cheater populations react differently to sudden changes in the environment.
    (D) In a given population, both population density and the ratio of cooperators to cheaters can change over time.

sP20A

Directions: The following two passages are similar to real ACT test passages. Read each passage and answer the questions that follow. Use the methods and techniques that you have learned throughout the workbook to help you answer the questions.

PRACTICE PASSAGE 1 (TIME: 4 MINUTES)

In electric circuits, the voltage (V) of a battery represents the electromotive force (emf) or push that electrons feel while moving through a wire. The current (I) moving through a wire represents the amount of charge passing per unit time. Resistance (R) is the measure of the degree to which an object opposes the electric current passing through it. Devices, such as computers or light bulbs, which are plugged into an electrical outlet represent a resistor and possess a specific resistance.

Series circuits are those in which the electrons in the wire have only one path to and from the battery. Thus, all of the current passes through all the resistors. Parallel circuits are those in which electrons may have multiple paths to and from the battery. In this case, resistors with greater resistance receive less current than do resistors with less resistance. Figure 1 shows simple constructions of series and parallel circuits. Current flows from the positive terminal of the battery to its negative terminal. The total resistance in a parallel circuit is inversely related to the sum of its individual resistances as shown in the equation below.

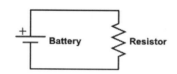

$$R_{Total} = R_1 + R_2 + R_3 + \cdots$$

Series

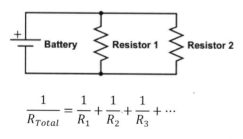

$$\frac{1}{R_{Total}} = \frac{1}{R_1} + \frac{1}{R_2} + \frac{1}{R_3} + \cdots$$

Parallel

Figure 1

In the following experiments, a student works with series and parallel circuits to study their voltages, currents, and resistances.

Experiment 1

The student first constructs three series circuits, each with a different number of 10-Ω resistors, and measures the currents passing through the circuits. Table 1 shows the voltage in the batteries, the number of resistors in each circuit, and current produced in each circuit.

Table 1

Circuit	Voltage (V)	Number of Resistors	Current (A)
I	80	2	4.0
II	160	4	4.0
III	160	8	2.0
IV	320	4	8.0

Experiment 2

The student then connects four light bulbs, each with equal resistance, to a battery in series and uses an ammeter to record the current passing through each bulb in Trial 1. Using the same battery, he then rearranges the same bulbs into parallel only and mixed series and parallel connections for three more trials and again records the current passing through each bulb. Table 2 shows his data.

Table 2

Trial	Bulb 1	Bulb 2	Bulb 3	Bulb 4
I	10 A	10 A	10 A	10 A
II	2.5 A	2.5 A	2.5 A	2.5 A
III	5 A	5 A	5 A	5 A
IV	7.5 A	7.5 A	7.5 A	7.5 A

1. Based on the data presented in the passage, which of the following relationships is NOT true?

   (A) Voltage is directly related to resistance.
   (B) Current is directly related to voltage.
   (C) Resistance is inversely related to current.
   (D) All of the above are true.

2. If all the resistors in each of the circuits in Experiment 1 were in parallel, which of the following would correctly list the total resistances (R_{Total}) of the circuits in *decreasing* order?

   (A) $R_I > R_{II} > R_{III}$
   (B) $R_{III} > R_{II} > R_I$
   (C) $R_I = R_{II} > R_{III}$
   (D) $R_{III} > R_{II} = R_I$

3. Based on the results of Experiment 1, a circuit with voltage of 160 V and 2 10-Ω resistors should be able to carry how much current?

   (A) 1 A
   (B) 2 A
   (C) 4 A
   (D) 8 A

4. Based on the data presented in Table 2 in Experiment 2, the four light bulbs in Trial 3 must be arranged in:

   (A) series only.
   (B) parallel only.
   (C) in a combination of series and parallel.
   (D) It cannot be determined.

5. Based on the information presented in the passage, what would happen to the total current of a circuit if all its resistors were changed from parallel to series, assuming the total voltage remains constant?

   (A) The total current would increase.
   (B) The total current would decrease.
   (C) The total current would remain constant.
   (D) It cannot be determined.

PRACTICE PASSAGE 2 (TIME: 5 MINUTES)

Pollinating bees, which forage for nutrients, typically develop *traplines*, or specific routes for visiting familiar foraging sites that minimize the distance they need to travel. In the following experiments, scientists use artificial flowers and radar tracking to study how bees learn to optimize their routes when introduced to a new foraging environment.

Experiment 1

The scientists arrange five artificial flowers in a regular pentagon with sides 50 m long. The bees' nest box is also 50 m from the nearest two flowers. The shortest possible distance of a single *foraging bout*, which begins at the nest box, includes all five flowers, and concludes back at the nest box, is 300 m.

The scientists then introduce seven bees to the environment and observe them for several hours. For each of 30 foraging bouts the scientists record the bees' combined average number of flowers visited, number of empty flowers revisited (indicating the bee is not yet familiar enough with its route to recognize a flower it has already visited), total distance traveled, and speed of the bees' flight.

The data are shown in Table 1, with the foraging bouts grouped in order—e.g., "Foraging bouts 1-5" indicates the data for the bees' first five bouts.

Table 1

Foraging bouts	Flowers visited	Empty flowers revisited	Distance traveled (m)	Flight speed (m/s)
1-5	2.28	2.80	1923	1.47
6-10	2.85	2.52	1524	1.99
11-15	3.44	2.27	1012	2.32
16-20	3.91	1.84	789	2.85
21-25	4.55	1.53	535	3.36
26-30	4.96	1.21	461	3.68

After a certain number of foraging bouts, each bee eventually developed a trapline: one specific route that it followed more frequently than any other route. For all bees, this trapline was indeed the shortest path through all five points: either clockwise around the pentagon, or counterclockwise. (This does not imply that any of the bees traveled the shortest possible distance, as they did not necessarily fly in perfectly straight lines.) For three of the bees (referred to as X, Y, and Z), Figure 1 plots each bee's cumulative usage

of its own trapline against its cumulative number of foraging bouts. (For any given bee, when its cumulative trapline usage goes up by 1, that indicates that it used the trapline for that particular foraging bout; when its number of foraging bouts goes up, but its trapline usage does not, that indicates that it used a different route.) When a bee starts to use its trapline reliably on every foraging bout, its trapline has stabilized.

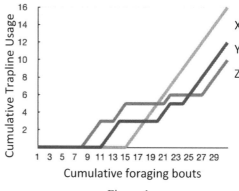

Figure 1

Experiment 2

The scientists change the arrangement of the artificial flowers, moving the one farthest from the nest box to one side of the previous arrangement.

When the scientists release the bees from Experiment 1 back into the environment, they notice a change in the bees' flight pattern: rather than flying only in fairly straight segments from flower to flower, the bees spend part of each foraging bout flying in straight nest-to-flower or flower-to-flower segments, and part of the bout flying in slower loops to explore the area. The scientists record the bees' flower visits and speed of both types of flight for 5 foraging bouts. The data is shown in Table 2.

Table 2

Foraging bouts	Flowers visited	Empty flowers revisited	Flight speed (straight) (m/s)	Flight speed (loops) (m/s)
1-5	3.08	2.45	3.57	1.49

6. In Experiment 1, as the bees gained more experience with the new environment:

   (A) The numbers of flowers visited and empty flowers revisited increased, while distance traveled and flight speed decreased.
   (B) The numbers of flowers visited and flight speed increased, while empty flowers revisited and distance traveled decreased.
   (C) Distance traveled and flight speed increased, while flowers visited and empty flowers revisited decreased.
   (D) Empty flowers revisited and distance traveled increased, while flowers visited and flight speed decreased.

7. On the 100th foraging bout, the bees' average number of flowers visited and distance traveled, respectively, would be expected to approach:

   (A) 5.00 and 300 m
   (B) 10.00 and 300 m
   (C) 15.00 and 25 m
   (D) It cannot be determined from the given information.

8. Assuming that all three bees' traplines are stabilized by the 30th bout, which of the following conclusions can be drawn from the data in Figure 1?

   (A) Bee X was the last to find its trapline, and the last to stabilize it.
   (B) Bee Z was the first to find its trapline, but the last to stabilize it.
   (C) Bee Z was the last to stabilize its trapline, but used its trapline on the highest number of bouts.
   (D) The three bees first found their traplines at different times, but stabilized them at the same time.

9. Based on the data in Tables 1 and 2, how did the bees react to one of the flowers being moved?

   (A) The bees were unfamiliar with the environment again, but more familiar than they were at the beginning of Experiment 1.
   (B) The bees were completely unfamiliar with the environment and foraged as they would in a new environment.
   (C) The bees were completely familiar with the environment and foraged as if it were the same environment as in Experiment 1.
   (D) It cannot be determined without recording data for more foraging bouts.

10. If the scientists in Experiment 2 continued to record the data for 30 foraging bouts, just as in Experiment 1, the data in the last row (bouts 26-30) for flowers visited, empty flowers revisited, flight speed (straight), and flight speed (loops), respectively, would be mostly likely to read:

    (A) 4.22, 0.63, n/a (no straight segments), 3.67
    (B) 4.97, 2.59, 3.95, n/a (no loops)
    (C) 5.80, 0.81, n/a (no straight segments), 5.24
    (D) 4.98, 0.52, 4.43, n/a (no loops)

11. Which of the following hypotheses would be most *weakened* by the results of Experiments 1 and 2?

    (A) Bees have the ability to recognize that some elements of a given environment are familiar to them while others are new.
    (B) Bees cannot adapt to new foraging environments unless they are trained to do so.
    (C) As bees become more familiar with the foraging sites in a given environment, their foraging bouts become more efficient.
    (D) Bees have the ability to recognize an optimal route soon after they discover it.

sP20B

Directions: The following two passages are similar to real ACT test passages. Read each passage and answer the questions that follow. Use the methods and techniques that you have learned throughout the workbook to help you answer the questions.

HOMEWORK PASSAGE 1 (TIME: 6 MINUTES)

Two chemists discuss their views on the usage of the term "atomic weight."

Chemist 1

There are those who would alter the term "atomic weight" to the so-called more up-to-date "atomic mass." Such a change is not only unnecessary, but one that will lead to needless confusion. Terminology needs to be consistent for precise scientific language to be easily communicated. Changing terms every time some new finding comes about would lead to chaos. The mean weight of an atomic sample has been called atomic weight since 1808, so there needs to be a substantial reason to make a change to something used in texts and experiments for centuries; there is no such reason.

For nearly as long as the term has been in use, atomic weights have been determined by weighing samples. Even today, for many samples this is the preferred method of obtaining information on the amount of substance at hand. Even if mass is the value sought, weight is the means to reach it. Just because we determine another means of ascertaining a quantity does not mean that the name of that quantity should change.

Calorimeters have been out of vogue for some time now, and yet food labels are rife with the term calorie. Other common scientific terms like electromotive force (which is not a force) and molar concentration (which is not a molar quantity) would all need changing under this paradigm. Would we then have to continually update these terms in the future as technology advances, and new ways of finding values are discovered?

Keep "atomic weight" as it is now. "Atomic mass" can be used to refer to the mass of a specific isotope. Weight, though, is and should continue to be used to refer to the weighted mean of a sample of a given substance. Change for change's sake is never good, and we need to preserve even seemingly archaic terminology, lest the students of tomorrow be incapable of reading the works published today.

Chemist 2

"Atomic weight" is a needlessly confusing term. There's nothing gravimeteric about these "weights." These values are constant anywhere in the universe, weightless or otherwise. Weight is a term that refers to the downward pull of gravity, and yet that is not at all what we measure when we seek the mass of a sample. We seek the amount of matter, nothing more and nothing less. "Relative atomic mass" makes much more sense.

Terminology is updated constantly. In relatively recent terms, the secularization of dated standards from A.D. to CE certainly impacted an immense deal of older reference materials, and yet no confused cries come out of the various history departments. Terminology can be easily updated so long as the update is uniformly applied.

Furthermore, chemistry is a science that relies on precision. SI units are related to precise values. In fact, older definitions of meter tied it to the length from the north pole of the Earth to the equator. It is now related to the distance light travels in a vacuum. We not only update the terminology but the precise definitions themselves. When the meter was fixed in terms of its definition to the speed of light itself, laser measurements lost a great deal of uncertainty due to the elimination of interferometer errors. Clearly each change reduces uncertainty and enhances precision. Science is defined by progress, and stagnation, even stagnation of terminology, is the antithesis of science.

1. Chemist 1 would probably cite which of the following facts as evidence to support his argument?

    (A) The medical community has embraced the substitution of the word "obese" for "overweight" to classify children in the 95th percentile of their BMI.
    (B) People still use the word "dial" when referring to making telephone calls, even though it was originally a term related to the rotary phone and has no connection to the process of using a modern telephone.
    (C) Atomic weight is primarily determined by the amount of protons and neutrons in an atom.
    (D) The academic community has substituted the term "Indian" with the more accurate term "Native American."

2. Both chemists would agree that the scientific community should:

    (A) Agree to use terminology that remains the same, regardless of new discoveries.
    (B) Constantly change terminology to reflect the latest trend of concepts and discoveries.
    (C) Use terminology that does not lead to unnecessary confusion.
    (D) Bring calorimeters back as the dominant device for measuring the heat of chemical reactions.

3. A group of high school students were given a survey, and the results indicated that they felt confused by their teachers' constant updating of terms and phrases in some of their classes. This information strengthens:

    (A) Chemist 1's argument.
    (B) Chemist 2's argument.
    (C) Both chemists' arguments.
    (D) Neither chemist's argument.

4. According to Chemist 2, new scientific terms can be used as long as they:

    (A) In some way reflect the terms of the past.
    (B) Are used for a fixed period of time.
    (C) Promote the fact that weight is not determined by gravimetric conditions.
    (D) Are used consistently.

5. What does Chemist 1 believe the result of changing scientific terminology would be?

    (A) The focus in the scientific community would rightfully be more centered on precision rather than adhering to archaic notions.
    (B) Students of the future would be less likely to understand the published work of today.
    (C) Use of the term "atomic weight" would become more prevalent than "atomic mass."
    (D) Chemists would no longer consider weight as a valid form of measurement.

6. Why does Chemist 2 believe that the term "atomic mass" is better than "atomic weight?"

    (A) "Atomic mass" refers to the downward pull of gravity.
    (B) The mean weight has been called "atomic mass" since 1808.
    (C) "Atomic mass" exclusively defines the amount of matter.
    (D) Students of the future will be able to understand the published works of today.

7. Isotopes are atoms of the same element with varying number of neutrons. Therefore, each isotope of an element has a different atomic weight. This information weakens:

    (A) Chemist 1's argument.
    (B) Chemist 2's argument.
    (C) Both chemists' argument.
    (D) Neither chemist's argument.

HOMEWORK PASSAGE 2 (TIME: 5 MINUTES)

The cells of many animals, including humans, do not divide indefinitely; after a certain number of divisions, they stop dividing and enter a dormant state known as cellular senescence. If an error occurs in the process of a cell's entering senescence, the cell may become cancerous.

One pathway that leads to the stopping of cell division and cellular senescence involves the *p53 tumor suppressor* protein, coded by the *p53* gene. In the following experiments, scientists examine mice with and without this gene, or with a *truncated*, or shortened, form of the gene, to study the link between cancer and aging.

Experiment 1

Each mouse has two *alleles*, or forms, of the p53 gene: one from each parent. p53$^+$ denotes the normal allele, p53$^-$ denotes no allele (one copy deleted), and p53^m denotes a truncated mutant of the allele. Scientists divide the mice into three groups: one with two normal alleles (p53$^{+/+}$), one with one normal allele and one copy deleted (p53$^{+/-}$), and one with one normal allele and one truncated mutant (p53$^{+/m}$). Each group has 50 mice.

Table 1 records the percentage of mice in each group that developed tumors, and the number of weeks until only 50% of the mice were still alive (as an indicator of average lifespan). Figure 1 plots the cumulative survival of each group as a function of time in weeks.

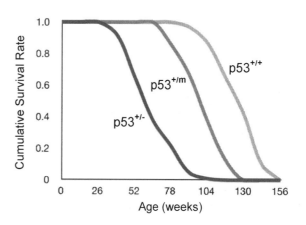

Figure 1

Experiment 2

Each group of mice in Experiment 1 had at least one normal allele of the p53 gene. To study the effect of the missing and truncated alleles in the absence of normal alleles, the scientists then repeated the experiment with two additional groups of 50 mice: one that was missing both copies of p53 (p53$^{-/-}$) and one that had one missing copy and one truncated copy (p53$^{-/m}$).

Table 2 records the percentage of mice in each group that developed tumors, and the number of weeks until only 50% of the mice were still alive. Figure 2 plots the cumulative survival of each group as a function of time in weeks.

Table 1

Genotype	Developed tumors	Weeks to 50% survival
p53$^{+/+}$	46%	112
p53$^{+/-}$	82%	71
p53$^{+/m}$	6%	98

Table 2

Genotype	Developed tumors	Weeks to 50% survival
p53$^{-/-}$	96%	16
p53$^{-/m}$	91%	27

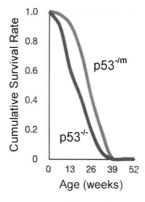

Figure 2

8. The genotype of two truncated p53 alleles would be denoted:

   (A) $p53^{-/-}$
   (B) $p53^{+/+}$
   (C) $p53^{-/+}$
   (D) $p53^{m/m}$

9. The results of Experiment 1 suggest that the average lifespan of normal mice could be about:

   (A) 70 weeks
   (B) 90 weeks
   (C) 110 weeks
   (D) 220 weeks

10. Which of the following conclusions can be drawn from the results of Experiment 1?

    (A) Having one missing p53 allele made mice more likely to develop tumors and shortened lifespan, while having one truncated p53 allele prevented tumors, but still shortened lifespan.
    (B) Having one missing p53 allele made mice more likely to develop tumors and shortened lifespan, while having one truncated p53 allele prevented tumors and lengthened lifespan.
    (C) Having one missing p53 allele made mice less likely to develop tumors and lengthened lifespan, while having one truncated p53 allele made mice more likely to have tumors and shortened lifespan.
    (D) Having one missing p53 allele made mice much more likely to develop tumors and significantly shortened lifespan, while having one truncated p53 allele made mice slightly more likely to develop tumors and slightly shortened lifespan.

11. For about how much longer were all the mice in Experiment 1 alive (i.e., time elapsed *before* the first mice started to die) than the mice in Experiment 2?

    (A) 0 weeks
    (B) 30 weeks
    (C) 80 weeks
    (D) 120 weeks

12. Which of the following lists the genotypes in order by how much their tumor rates differ (in either direction) from that of normal mice, from least to greatest difference?

    (A) $p53^{+/-}$, $p53^{+/m}$, $p53^{-/m}$, $p53^{-/-}$
    (B) $p53^{+/m}$, $p53^{+/-}$, $p53^{-/m}$, $p53^{-/-}$
    (C) $p53^{+/-}$, $p53^{-/m}$, $p53^{+/+}$, $p53^{-/-}$
    (D) $p53^{-/-}$, $p53^{-/m}$, $p53^{+/-}$, $p53^{+/m}$

13. What is the most significant difference between Experiments 1 and 2?

    (A) All mice in Experiment 1 had at least one missing copy of the p53 allele; all mice in Experiment 2 had at least one normal copy.
    (B) In Experiment 1, genotype was the independent variable, and tumor rate and lifespan were dependent variables, while in Experiment 2, genotype was the dependent variable, and tumor rate and lifespan were independent variables.
    (C) All mice in Experiment 1 had at least one normal copy of the p53 allele; all mice in Experiment 2 had at least one missing copy.
    (D) In Experiment 1, tumor rate was the independent variable and lifespan was the dependent variable, while in Experiment 2, tumor rate was the dependent variable, and lifespan was the independent variable.